Government, Markets and Vocational Qualifications

Government, Markets and Vocational Qualifications

An Anatomy of Policy

Peter Raggatt and Steve Williams

 Routledge
Taylor & Francis Group

LONDON AND NEW YORK

First published 1999 by Routledge
2 Park Square, Milton Park, Abingdon, Oxon, OX14 4RN

Simultaneously published in the USA and Canada
270 Madison Ave, New York NY 10016

Routledge is an imprint of the Taylor & Francis Group

Transferred to Digital Printing 2007

© 1999 Peter Raggatt and Steve Williams

Typeset in Times by
BC Typesetting, Bristol

British Library Cataloguing in Publication Data
A catalogue record for this book is available from the British Library

Library of Congress Cataloging in Publication Data
Raggatt, Peter C. M.
    Government, markets, and vocational qualifications: an anatomy of
policy/Peter Raggatt and Steve Williams.
        p.   cm.
    Includes bibliographical references.
    1. Vocational qualifications–Great Britain. 2. National
Vocational Qualifications (Great Britain) I. Williams, Steve,
1968– . II. Title.
    HF5381.6.R34 1999
    331.11′42′0041–dc21   99-28029
                                                                 CIP

ISBN 0–7507–0917–0 (hbk)
ISBN 0–7507–0916–2 (pbk)

Publisher's Note
The publisher has gone to great lengths to ensure the quality of this reprint
but points out that some imperfections in the original may be apparent

Contents

Tables

Abbreviations

AAT	Association of Accounting Technicians
AB	Awarding Body
ABCTG	Administration, Business and Commercial Training Group
AS level	Advanced Supplementary level
BCCCA	Biscuit, Cake, Chocolate and Confectionary Alliance
BEC	Business Education Council
BTEC	Business and Technician Education Council (Business and Technology Education Council from 1991 onwards)
CAPITB	Clothing and Allied Trades Industry Training Board
CBI	Confederation of British Industry
CIA	Chemical Industries Association
CISC	Construction Industry Standing Conference
CITB	Construction Industry Training Board
CPRS	Central Policy Review Staff
CPS	Crown Prosecution Service
CPVE	Certificate of Pre-Vocational Education
CSA	Child Support Agency
CVCP	Committee of Vice-Chancellors and Principals
DE	Department of Employment (sometimes referred to as the ED)
DES	Department of Education and Science
DfE	Department for Education
DfEE	Department for Education and Employment
DTI	Department of Trade and Industry
EGO	Extra-Governmental Organisation
EITB	Engineering Industry Training Board
EMTA	Engineering and Marine Training Authority
ENTRA	Engineering Training Authority
ERA	Education Reform Act
ESSC	Engineering Services Standing Conference
ET	Employment Training
FAS	Funding Agency for Schools
FE	Further Education

FEFC	Further Education Funding Council
FEU	Further Education Unit
GCSE	General Certificate of Secondary Education
GES	Guildford Education Services
GNVQ	General National Vocational Qualification
GSVQ	General Scottish Vocational Qualification
HE	Higher Education
HNC	Higher National Certificate
HND	Higher National Diploma
IMS	Institute for Manpower Studies
IPPR	Institute for Public Policy Research
ITA	Industrial Training Act
ITB	Industry Training Board
ITO	Industry Training Organisation
LCCI	London Chamber of Commerce Institute
LEA	Local Education Authority
LECs	Local Enterprise Companies
LMS	Local Management of Schools
MCI	Management Charter Initiative
META	Marine Engineering Training Authority
MSC	Manpower Services Commission
NAO	National Audit Office
NCC	National Curriculum Council
NCITO	National Council of Industry Training Organisations
NCVQ	National Council for Vocational Qualifications
NDPB	Non-Departmental Public Body
NEDC	National Economic Development Council
NHS	National Health Service
NSTO	Non-Statutory Training Organisation
NTI	New Training Initiative
NTO	National Training Organisation
NVQ	National Vocational Qualification
OECD	Organisation for Economic Co-operation and Development
OFSTED	Office for Standards in Education
ORT	Organisation for Rehabilitation through Training
OSC	Occupational Standards Council
OTF	Occupational Training Family
PAQ	Professional Accountancy Qualifications Group
QCA	Qualifications and Curriculum Authority
QNCA	Qualifications and National Curriculum Authority
QUANGO	Quasi Autonomous Non-Governmental Organisation
RSA	Royal Society of Arts Examination Board
RVQ	Review of Vocational Qualifications in England and Wales
SCAA	Schools Curriculum and Assessment Authority
SCEM	Standing Conference on Engineering Manufacture

SCEP	Standing Conference on Extracting and Processing
SCOTVEC	Scottish Vocational Education Council
SEAC	Schools Examinations and Assessment Council
SED	Scottish Education Department
SNP	Scottish National Party
SQA	Scottish Qualifications Authority
SVQ	Scottish Vocational Qualification
TA	Training Agency
TAG	Technical Advisory Group
TDLB	Training and Development Lead Body
TEC	Technician Education Council
TECs	Training and Enterprise Councils
TEED	Training, Enterprise and Employment Directorate
TTA	Teacher Training Agency
TUC	Trades Union Congress
UK	United Kingdom
UK-IPG	United Kingdom Inter-Professional Group
UVP	Unified Vocational Preparation
VET	Vocational Education and Training
VQ	Vocational Qualification
YCB	Youth Certification Board
YOP	Youth Opportunities Programme
YT	Youth Training
YTS	Youth Training Scheme

Acknowledgments

Although we have not identified them, our foremost thanks must nonetheless go to the individuals who gave up their time to talk to us about the reform of vocational qualifications. We would also like to thank Pat Ainley, Alan Brown, Roy Canning, Mark Corney, Marion Dunlop, Richard Edwards, Irena Grugalis, Ewart Keep, Peter Senker, Thomas Spielhofer, Geoff Stanton, Andrew Thomson and Christine Ward either for discussions which helped to point us in the right direction during the research process or for providing useful information, and the staff of the Open University library in Milton Keynes and the DfEE library in Sheffield for their assistance. Funding for the research was supplied by the Open University's Centre for Educational Policy and Management and the Economic and Social Research Council. Finally, at the Open University the administrative support of Di Coats, Anne Missing, Jo Nixon and Hazel Sampson was much appreciated.

Introduction

It [the NVQ policy] looked and, if you'll allow me to say so, was credible. Any government of the day, indeed all of us, might have adopted that. We might have tinkered a bit at the edges, but it's the implementation of it afterwards that's led to . . . difficulties.

(senior Manpower Services Commission official)

There has been a considerable amount of interest in recent years in the extent to which the economic performance of nation states can be improved by enhancing the skills of their workforces. Increasingly, the quality of their stock of human resources has been identified as a critical source of improved competitiveness (see Porter, 1990; Reich, 1991), particularly as economic and technological changes are perceived to reduce demand for workers without formal qualifications. The view of a previous United Kingdom (UK) government illustrates a common perception:

Unlocking the potential of individual people by giving them the chance to acquire skills and qualifications will be of greatest importance in the years ahead. It will not only determine success and self-fulfilment for individuals themselves. It will also be essential to sustain a successful national economy in an increasingly competitive world.

(DE, 1992, p. 23)

One of the major ways in which it has sought to boost skills has been through the elaboration of a national system of vocational qualifications comprising National and Scottish Vocational Qualifications (NVQs and SVQs)[1] and General National Vocational Qualifications (GNVQs). Perhaps the most striking aspect of the new system of vocational qualifications is the way in which their assessment has been founded upon, or related to, the concept of occupational competence, in contrast to traditional approaches in which an examination of knowledge or time served was the main basis of certification. The competence-based approach, which appears to have originated in the United States (Tuxworth, 1989), is characterized by: a focus on measurable learning outcomes, not inputs; the separation of learning from assessment; no time-serving requirements or any other artificial barriers to assessment; and an emphasis on performance in the workplace, or a close simulation of it, as the most desirable source of evidence about whether an individual is competent or not. The use of such an approach is supposedly advantageous for employers, in that it provides them with individuals who are certified as capable of undertaking defined job roles, and for individuals themselves, since both previous, unaccredited learning and tacit skills are capable of being acknowledged, and not just those associated with the successful passing of examinations.

Given the scale of the changes to which the UK's system of vocational qualifications has been subjected, and the increasing amount of attention which the model has attracted internationally,[2] it is surprising that no attempt has hitherto been made to document and explain them. For the most part, studies of N/SVQs and GNVQs fall into one of three categories. They are either prescriptive (e.g. Jessup, 1991); evaluative (e.g. Robinson, 1996a; Wolf, 1997); or else focus on the concept of competence that underpins N/SVQs (e.g. Bates, 1995; Wolf, 1995), something which has frequently been the target of sustained criticism (e.g. Hyland, 1994; Smithers, 1993). However, we lack any substantial understanding of how and why the reforms were formulated and progressed in the way that they were.[3] In aiming to address this lacuna our book has three main purposes. First, it offers an in-depth chronicle of how the reforms to the vocational qualifications system were advanced and implemented from about the early 1980s to 1997. Second, it identifies the causes of some of the much-attested weaknesses of the new qualifications and also the factors that have contributed to their resilience. Third, it provides a case study of several important aspects of vocational education and training policy, some of which, arguably, are common to the recent formulation of public policy in general in the UK.

The account we offer here is based on a considerable amount of research involving the analysis of substantial amounts of documentary evidence and data derived from nearly a hundred interviews with key informants in the policy process. A more detailed discussion of the methodology employed is given in an appendix. In Chapter 1 we examine the evolution of the UK's system of vocational qualifications, prior to the reforms of the 1980s and 1990s. The principal concern of Chapter 2 is to trace the way in which policy-makers increasingly became attracted to a somewhat ill-defined concept of competence as a way of organizing vocational education and training. A radical overhaul of the vocational qualifications system was set in train by the 1985–86 *Review of Vocational Qualifications in England and Wales*. Chapter 3 describes the immediate origins, the progress and the recommendations of this review, one of the main proposals of which was the development of a more coherent, national framework of vocational awards to be based more explicitly on the assessment of competence. The initial implementation of the competence-based NVQ policy is described in Chapter 4. Given the increasing amount of critical attention that the new qualifications were attracting, and the slow pace of reform, policy-makers needed to expend a considerable amount of effort to sustain the initiative and embed NVQs in the UK's system of vocational education and training, something that included the establishment of SVQs. In this respect we trace the maturation of NVQ policy in Chapter 5. In Chapter 6 we account for, and describe, the origins and development of GNVQs – awards that, while they are related to the N/SVQ concept, are not competence-based and are designed to be delivered in schools and colleges rather than workplaces. In response to widespread external and internal criticism, between 1994 and 1997 both N/SVQs and GNVQs were subjected to considerable revision. We examine the imperatives for, and the character of, these changes in Chapter 7.

The study of education policy has been a fertile ground for theoretical innovation in recent years (see Ranson, 1995). The elaboration of sophisticated theory, however, has frequently come at the expense of explanation and coherence. Our purpose here is not to add to this already over-inflated theoretical literature, but rather it is to elucidate, by means of an in-depth case study approach, the direction of vocational qualifications policy during the 1980s and 1990s. In Chapter 8, however, we adopt a more analytical approach, drawing out a number of overarching issues that shaped the way in which the reforms progressed. We examine, for example, the powerful commitment given to the primacy of voluntarism; the institutional mechanisms within which vocational qualifications policy was formulated and delivered; and the relative power of politicians and officials in shaping and advancing policy initiatives. Finally, in the conclusion we will consider, among other things, the relationship between the strong support accorded to voluntarism, the operation of market forces in vocational education and training, and the nature of government intervention.

Notes

1 In the remainder of this book we use the term 'N/SVQs' when discussing matters pertaining to both NVQs and SVQs; in other cases we refer to NVQs and SVQs separately.
2 For example, in the late 1980s and the 1990s the newly established Australian National Training Board and the New Zealand Qualifications Authority drew heavily on advice and support from UK bodies in developing new systems. By 1997 a mounting volume of enquiries led the UK government to set up British Training International to advise other countries on the technical and infrastructural aspects of vocational qualifications' reforms.
3 We should note that there have been two exceptions to this. Sharp (1998) has provided an analysis of what he calls the 'beginnings' of GNVQs. Although his main empirical findings are consonant with the account of the origins and development of GNVQ policy which we present in Chapter 6, the article is problematic in two

significant respects. First, it relies too heavily on a very limited range of sources; and second, it fails to locate the emergence of GNVQs within a broader political and institutional context, something which is probably an expression of the author's concern to ascribe policy innovation to the actions of key individuals. Gokulsing et al. (1996) examine both GNVQ and NVQ policy developments. However, although their book has been held up as 'a detailed account of the development of NVQs and GNVQs and the political influences that shaped their present form' (Gokulsing et al., 1997, p. 26), given its brevity it is clearly nothing of the kind.

1 Vocational Qualifications Past and Present

Introduction

It is necessary to do two things before we begin our investigation into how the recent reforms to the UK's system of vocational qualifications progressed: we must situate the changes within a broad historical context, and we also need to give an initial indication of their scale and scope. In the first half of this chapter, then, a brief examination of the way in which the vocational qualifications system developed during the nineteenth and twentieth centuries will be provided. Like vocational education and training in general, it evolved in a piecemeal, fragmented manner, for the most part without any interventions by the state. We will then focus on the increasing degree of governmental intervention that characterized vocational education and training during the 1960s and 1970s, and, more specifically, the extent to which the vocational qualifications system was the object of reform. Yet the attempt by the UK government from the mid-1980s onwards to create a single, coherent national framework of competence-based, or related, vocational qualifications – comprising NVQs, SVQs and GNVQs – is indicative of a degree of intervention of a qualitatively different kind. We will therefore provide a a brief introductory analysis of the extent and nature of the reforms and highlight some of the key criticisms that they have attracted.

The Evolution of the Vocational Qualifications System in the UK

Attention has frequently been drawn to the historical weakness of technical and vocational education in the UK, particularly as it has been cited as a cause of relative economic decline in the twentieth century (see for example, Coates, 1994, pp. 46–8). As Keep and Mayhew (1988) have reminded us, concerns about the poor state of technical education and training, and its potentially deleterious impact on economic performance, can be identified as far back as the 1850s. The Samuelson Royal Commission on Technical Instruction, for example, was established in the 1880s 'to investigate the link between economic performance and the functioning of the education system, and to draw comparisons between Britain and her major competitors' (Perry, 1976, p. 30). Perhaps the most well-known explanation for the historic low status of technical and vocational education in the UK is that which has been provided by Martin Wiener. Briefly, Wiener (1981) argued that the nineteenth century witnessed the continuing cultural dominance of aristocratic, anti-industrial values in the UK and that the evolving education system, within which traditional academic topics predominated, reflected an unfulfilled bourgeois advance (for a related argument see also Barnett, 1986).

More convincingly, however, Andy Green (1990) has ascribed the weakness of technical and vocational education to the fusion of economic and political factors. The process of industrialization in the UK corresponded with the predominance of a *laissez-faire* political climate, and the absence of state intervention militated against the development of a coordinated national system of education in the UK in general in the nineteenth century. The primacy of voluntarism meant that technical and vocational education in particular evolved in a loose, incoherent and fragmented way, with the major locus of responsibility falling on the work-based, and exclusive, apprenticeship system – the principal method of skill formation in industry (More, 1980). Apprenticeships, however, were particular to certain industries, dominated by males, based largely on time served rather than the quality of the learning process or the outcomes of training, and restricted to young workers. In addition to apprenticeships, a network of local technical colleges emerged towards the end of the nineteenth century. This constituted a second major feature of the UK's system of technical and vocational education. Yet, given their localized focus and the absence of any duty upon local authorities to provide a service, it has been observed that 'technical colleges lacked both resources and prestige' (Pile, 1979, p. 137). Moreover, Green concluded that, 'developed in a fragmented and improvised manner; initially of low status, conservatively rooted in workshop and hostile to theoretical knowledge, publicly funded technical education became normatively part-time and institutionally marooned between the workplace and mainstream education. A century later it would still be seen as the Cinderella of the educational system' (1990, p. 299).

The large extent to which, historically, the UK's system of technical education was characterized by *laissez-faire*, or the 'play of market forces', has frequently been noted by commentators (Stringer and Richardson, 1982, p. 23; see also Perry, 1976; Senker, 1992), a greater degree of interventionism during both world wars notwithstanding. The vocational qualifications system, moreover, developed, like technical education in general, in a similarly localized, fragmented and voluntaristic manner. There was no state intervention and an absence of coordination, resulting in the emergence of a diverse pattern of unconnected awards (GES, 1986). The first prominent providers of examinations in technical subjects were the local Mechanics'

Institutes that increasingly became established during the first half of the nineteenth century (Perry, 1976). In 1856 the Royal Society of Arts (RSA) brought many of these Institutes together and, while the intention was to coordinate their efforts, many stayed outside. Dissatisfaction with the state of existing provision among City of London livery companies prompted them to establish a separate organization – City and Guilds of London Institute – in 1878, which took over the RSA's craft and technical examinations. Thenceforth, the RSA concentrated on providing awards in business and commercial areas. From the 1880s until the 1970s, these two bodies – both of which were private organizations dependent upon examination fees for their income – were the two major national providers of examinations in craft, commercial and technical subjects. Those Mechanics' Institutes that had kept control of their products in the 1850s gradually came together in six regional examining bodies over the course of the twentieth century, for example the Welsh Joint Education Committee. Apart from the development, from the 1920s onwards, of a series of National Certificates in certain occupations, frequently sponsored by relevant professional bodies, by the 1960s the system of vocational qualifications was substantially the same as that which had been in place at the beginning of the twentieth century. Like vocational education and training in general, there was no proper national system. Moreover, the major national providers were private organizations and their awards either overlapped, or had no connection at all, with the examinations provided by the multiplicity of professional and local awarding bodies.

During the 1960s, however, there was to be a considerable shift in the direction of vocational education and training policy. Apart from support for the unemployed through Government Training Centres and a number of wartime measures, the state had consistently followed a policy of non-intervention in industrial training. Some 70 industries or sections of industry did have nationally agreed training schemes in the post-war period but their activities were not well known, even within their own industries, and had little impact (Sheldrake and Vickerstaff, 1987, p. 27). Concern over the employment prospects of a greater number of young workers entering the labour market led to the establishment of the Carr Committee in 1958. It restricted itself, however, largely to an investigation of the apprenticeship system. The Committee concluded that 'the responsibility for industrial training of apprentices should rest firmly with industry' (quoted in Sheldrake and Vickerstaff, 1987, p. 30; c.f. Senker, 1992; Stringer and Richardson, 1982), a view that was endorsed by the then Conservative government. Yet the 1962 White Paper – *Industrial Training: Government Proposals* – and the subsequent Industrial Training Act (ITA) of 1964 signalled the arrival of a new consensus behind a more interventionist approach to training policy.

The principal outcome of the 1964 ITA was the establishment of a series of Industrial Training Boards (ITBs) during the mid to late 1960s. By the end of that decade, 27 such bodies had come into existence, of which the

Engineering Industry Training Board (EITB) was the most prominent and the Construction Industry Training Board (CITB) among the most long-lasting. They were empowered to raise levies from firms in their sectors and were expected to use the income that accrued to promote and enhance skills training so that an adequate supply of skilled labour was guaranteed. Not only were employers represented on the newly established ITBs, but trade unions and educational representatives were also entitled to be members. Two connected factors explain the shift from a voluntaristic ethos to a more interventionist approach in training policy. First, by the beginning of the 1960s there was an increasing realization that measures were necessary to combat the UK's relatively slow economic growth (Senker, 1992). Indeed, this period was characterized by the emergence of more coordinated arrangements and institutions for the management of economic policy in general, the establishment of the National Economic Development Council (NEDC) for example (Middlemas, 1979). Second, policy-makers recognized that '*laissez-faire* attitudes on the part of governments had failed to secure a supply of skilled labour which was adequate for industrial expansion' (Anderson and Fairley, 1983, pp. 193–4). Some ITBs did make considerable progress in reforming training methods in their sectors. The EITB, for example, attempted to mitigate time-serving arrangements and pioneered a modular approach in its apprenticeship system. It also produced written standards of performance that were used for testing individual trainees. These developments helped to change the apprenticeship system from being a 'device restricting the supply of labour to a more purely training device' (Anderson and Fairley, 1983, p. 195; c.f. Perry, 1976). In general, however, the power of ITBs to influence the scale, and particularly the quality, of training was severely constrained because responsibility for it was largely devolved to individual firms (Senker, 1992). Although they were statutorily empowered to impose a training levy on companies in their respective sectors, the ITBs had no power over key decisions, such as the length of apprenticeships or entry requirements, nor could they control the content, structure, organization and assessment of training. As indus-try-based training boards, moreover, they 'perpetuated a concentration on industry specific skills instead of fostering awareness of the value of cross-sector transferable skills and thus did little to pave the way for greater flexibility in the labour market' (Sheldrake and Vickerstaff, 1987, p. 40).

Increasing criticism of the ITB system, particularly from small employers who were hostile to the levy-grant arrangement, induced the incoming Conservative government of 1970 to promise to review its operation. The subsequent Employment and Training Act of 1973 introduced an exemption to the levy-grant mechanism and reduced some of the bureaucracy associated with the working of the ITB network. Much more significantly, however, though it is doubtful that this was realized at the time, the Act provided for the establishment of a national training agency which would not only coordinate the work of the ITBs and run public employment services, but would also help to forecast and strategically provide for skill changes. The Manpower Services Commission (MSC) was set up as a body independent of government to coordinate the work of the Training Services Division and Employment Services Division of the Department of Employment (DE), although they were soon to become integrated within the organization itself, and its operations were overseen by commissioners from the Trades Union Congress (TUC), the Confederation of British Industry (CBI) and the local authorities. As later chapters will show, before its demise in 1987 the MSC played a strong, interventionist role in promoting vocational education and training in general, and the reform of vocational qualifications in particular.

However, before the MSC turned its attention to this area during the 1960s and 1970s, some measures were taken to improve the system of vocational qualifications in the UK. In 1961, for example, the government issued a White Paper – *Better Opportunities in Technical Education* – which among other things prompted the introduction of craft and technician courses, leading to National Certificates and Diplomas for the latter, to run alongside the already existing National Certificates (GES, 1986; GES, 1990). The Haslegrave Committee, moreover, met between 1967 and 1969, under the auspices of the Department of Education and Science (DES), to consider ways of further improving the provision of business and technical awards. There appear to have been a number of imperatives for these attempts at reform. In the first place, the 1959 Crowther Report had identified a need for a broader curriculum at age 15 and above, given its recommendation that the school leaving age be increased (Perry, 1976). Second, the complexity and incoherence of the system of awards, the organic way in which National Certificates had developed in particular, militated against progression and understanding. Courses leading to National Certificates, moreover, were characterized by high drop-out and failure rates (GES, 1986). Third, the growing significance of the tertiary sector led to an increased awareness of the importance of suitable training in business and commercial subjects where employment opportunities were growing. There was a 'multiplicity of examinations and qualifications' in these areas, however (Perry, 1976, p. 228). The final factor was the establishment of the ITBs. These encouraged a more formal approach to training in many sectors and, while this led to increased demand for appropriate qualifications, which some ITBs developed themselves (Gospel, 1995), it not only made the system more complicated, but it also directed attention to the 'haphazard and generally unsatisfactory' arrangements for individuals in sectors not covered by them (GES, 1990, p. 5).

Following the recommendations of the Haslegrave Committee, in 1973 the government set up a Technician Education Council (TEC) and a Business Education Council (BEC) a year later. The principal remit of these bodies, which were later to come together as the Business and Technician Education Council (BTEC) in 1983, was to coordinate and enhance the provision of higher-level vocational awards within a single, standard framework. To this end, TEC, for example, became responsible for endorsing the National Certificates and Diplomas that had hitherto been the sole responsibility of a multiplicity of awarding bodies. According to the official history of BTEC, the 'Government's remit for TEC was to establish a unified system for technical education which did away with the plethora of previous technician level qualifications. Alignment to a standard framework rather than adhering to standardization was the watchword' (BTEC, 1994, p. 1). Although City and Guilds initially provided BEC and TEC with administrative and organizational support, under contract from the DES, it lost responsibility for much of its higher level provision to the latter body, leading it to concentrate increasingly on craft level awards. This separation of responsibilities is one indication that the rationalization of the vocational qualifications system envisaged by Haslegrave never really progressed very far. More seriously perhaps, rather than improving the coordination of existing provision, TEC appears to have set about developing a 'pattern involving new levels of qualifications based on the validation of college-devised curricula, syllabuses and examinations within its own new framework' (Stevens, 1993, p. 141; c.f. BTEC, 1994).

While the DES, then, had attempted to introduce a greater degree of coherence into the system of vocational qualifications, progress was limited due to the tension that existed between City and Guilds and TEC (BTEC).[1] A prominent example of this occurred during the early 1980s. In an attempt to boost the quality of vocational preparation, as well as to try to fend off increasing intervention by the MSC in this area, the DES initiated a new award, the Certificate of Pre-Vocational Education (CPVE), to be overseen by a joint board comprising BTEC, City and Guilds and the RSA, although the RSA's involvement was short-lived. It was launched in September 1985 and was 'intended to provide a broad programme of vocationally related education for 16- to 17-year-olds, to develop skills which will be of relevance in employment, and also to give students an understanding of the world of work' (GES, 1990, p. 26). Although City and Guilds withdrew some of its foundation courses to accommodate the CPVE, BTEC launched a new competing qualification, the 'First', in three subjects a year later, a development that caused a considerable amount of dismay amongst its partners (BTEC, 1994). Eventually BTEC compromised by agreeing to restrict its First awards to students aged 17 and over. Nevertheless, this example shows the difficulty the DES faced in trying to promote a coherent system of vocational awards, given the mass of competing interest groups that operated in this field. Further to this, we must not forget the existence of six Regional Examining Bodies which, after 'years of unsatisfactory relationships', reached agreement with City and Guilds over the development of a 'unified system' of craft technician awards only in 1979 (GES, 1986, p. 21), or the prominent role played by other substantial providers of vocational qualifications, for example the RSA. Scotland, moreover, was left outside the scope of the Haslegrave review. Here two organizations – SCOTEC and SCOTBEC (later to be merged as SCOTVEC – the Scottish Vocational Education Council) were established as examining bodies – TEC and BEC only validated courses (GES, 1990).

By the mid-1980s, then, notwithstanding some limited intervention by the DES to promote coherence, the system of vocational qualifications in the UK continued to be characterized by a voluntaristic ethos in which the principle of competition was upheld. Major national providers, such as City and Guilds and the RSA, were private bodies dependent upon certification fees for their income. BTEC, moreover, while it was nominally under the suzerainty of the DES, was keen to establish an independent role for itself. Such a state of affairs appeared readily defensible. The examining and validating bodies could not only point to high and rising levels of take-up for their respective offerings – in 1983–84 BTEC had over 180,000 registrations (GES, 1986) – but also to the large extent to which their products met the needs of individual students and employers. For example, advisory committees comprising representatives from both education and industry were responsible for monitoring the content of City and Guilds awards (Bush, 1993).

The Reformed System of Vocational Qualifications

The move towards a reformed system of vocational qualifications was initiated by the MSC during the early to mid-1980s. The origins, development and implementation of this policy will be the subject of in-depth analysis in the chapters that follow. It is important, however, briefly to highlight the following: the principal features of the reformed system; the extent of the progress that was made in implementing the new qualifications; and some of the major critical interventions directed at them. In 1985 the UK government established a Working Group, sponsored by the MSC and the DES, to examine, and make recommendations for, the improvement of the system of vocational qualifications in England and Wales. The *Review of Vocational Qualifications in England and Wales* (RVQ) proposed that a new National Council for Vocational Qualifications (NCVQ) be established, which would be charged with the responsibility of developing and overseeing a framework of National Vocational Qualifications (NVQs). Furthermore, it was recommended that an NVQ should be 'a statement of competence, clearly relevant to work and intended to facilitate entry into, and progression in, employment, further education and training, issued by a recognised body to an individual' (MSC/DES, 1986, p. 17). Following the report of the Working Group the government issued a White Paper – *Working Together: Education and Training* (DE/DES, 1986) – which broadly accepted its recommendations. The NCVQ itself was instituted in the autumn of 1986, and it was given the 'vital' task of reforming 'the present heterogeneous pattern of vocational qualifications' in England and Wales (DE/DES,

Table 1.1: Total NVQ certificates awarded in each framework area and level as at 30 June 1997

Framework area	Level 1	Level 2	Levels 3	Levels 4 and 5	Total	% of all awards
Tending animals, plants and land	18,262	23,995	2,310	26	44,593	2.8
Extracting and providing natural resources	322	9,156	133	–	9,611	0.6
Constructing	22,915	69,286	35,311	43	127,555	7.9
Engineering	16,883	96,116	50,554	3,330	166,883	10.3
Manufacturing	11,948	33,448	1,251	4	46,651	2.9
Transporting	1,560	17,809	1,252	–	20,621	1.3
Providing goods and services	104,898	313,798	24,518	146	443,360	27.3
Providing health, social care and protective services	48,454	70,695	14,526	17	133,842	8.3
Providing business services	135,251	333,126	99,126	52,343	619,846	38.2
Communicating	–	166	118	422	706	–
Developing and extending knowledge and skill	–	95	6,261	1,539	7,895	0.5
Total	360,493	967,690	235,360	58,020	**1,621,563**	

Source: QCA, 1997a, pp. 12–13.

1986, p. 16). The NCVQ was assigned the job of 'rationalising' the existing structure and was directed to 'design', 'monitor' and 'adapt as necessary' a new framework of qualifications – NVQs – to simplify the 'qualifications jungle . . . within a single, coherent system' (DE/DES, 1986, p. 19). The government further accepted the recommendations of the *Review of Vocational Qualifications* that the new system of NVQs should be 'clear, coherent, comprehensive and cost effective' and centred on 'the assessment of competence directly relevant to the needs of employment and the needs of the individual' (DE/DES, 1986, p. 17).

From 1987 onwards, sectoral 'lead bodies' were given, with the assistance of the MSC, the responsibility for designing the occupational standards of competence upon which the NVQs would be based. About 160 of these employer-led organizations were eventually formed. Once the standards of occupational competence had been drawn up, responsibility for the production of the qualifications based on the standards was given to awarding bodies, of which BTEC, City and Guilds and the RSA were to become the most prominent. They would actually offer the qualifications, submitting the provisional NVQs to the NCVQ for accreditation and, if successful, inclusion in the national framework at one of four levels. Level one, for example, was designed to accommodate basic entry-level occupations and it was anticipated that supervisory and some managerial occupations would be encompassed by level four NVQs. Attainment at level three was later deemed to be the vocational equivalent of gaining an A level. The first awards to be accredited as NVQs by the NCVQ appeared in summer 1987. Later, in 1989, the government gave the NCVQ the go-ahead to include a fifth level so that awards offered by professional bodies could be incorporated within the system. Also in 1989, the government charged SCOTVEC with developing a system of Scottish Vocational Qualifications (SVQs) to run alongside NVQs in England and Wales, and the first of these awards became available in 1990.

According to official figures, between 1987, when the first NVQs became available, and July 1997 over 1.6 million of the qualifications were awarded.[2] As we have already noted, the NVQ framework is founded upon five levels. It is also based on eleven 'framework areas'. Table 1.1 shows the number of NVQ certificates awarded by level and framework area as at 30 June 1997.

These data are immensely revealing.[3] First, it is apparent that the majority of NVQs – some 82 per cent – have been awarded at levels one and two. The predominance of awards at level two in particular can be ascribed to the way in which they have been utilized as outcome measures for the government's publicly funded training programmes (see below). Second, following on from this, the dearth of awards at levels four and five is also especially striking – just 3.6 per cent of the overall figure. By the end of September 1996 just 3,281 level five awards had been attained, all of them in just one NVQ: Management (NCVQ, 1997b). Third, two framework areas – 'Providing Goods and Services' and 'Providing Business Services' – make up most of the market for NVQs, with over 65 per cent of awards having been made in them. NVQs in retailing and hairdressing dominate in the former, whereas the latter largely comprises NVQs in various aspects of business administration. It is interesting to note that one award, the level two NVQ in Hairdressing, accounts for about 5 per cent of all the NVQs that have ever been awarded (NCVQ, 1997b). As Peter Robinson (1996a) has also pointed out, on the basis of earlier data, there has been significant delivery of NVQs in only three of the other nine framework areas: 'Constructing'; 'Engineering'; and 'Providing Health, Social Care and Protective Services'. However, that the provision and attainment of NVQs has been generally restricted to certain occupations and sectors, and at the lower levels of the framework, can be interpreted as a sign of the success of the qualifications. Proponents of the competence-based approach to assessment that underpins NVQs have claimed that the measurement of successful performance in the workplace, or a simulated environment, which this involves, allows key attributes and skills held by individuals, that might previously have gone unrecognized, to be recorded and accredited. Mature women employed in retailing, for example, would have had limited opportunities to gain a qualification before the appearance of NVQs. Felstead et al. (1995) have shown the large extent to which the attainment of vocational qualifications has generally been dominated by men. There is some evidence that the arrival of NVQs has altered the traditional pattern because they appear to have a higher take-up rate among women than among men. According to official data, in 1995–96, 41 per cent of N/SVQs were awarded to men and 59 per cent to women. For other vocational awards the position was almost reversed, in that men attained 57 per cent of them and women 43 per cent (DfEE, 1998a). The argument that, because the take-up of the new qualifications is higher among women, they must represent a qualitative improvement on the more traditional awards has been criticized by Peter Robinson. He noted that, insofar as NVQs tended to predominate in certain areas, which were typified by high levels of women's employment – retailing, clerical and personal service occupations in particular – 'the gender pattern in the holding of NVQs is a reflection of the occupational pattern in the distribution of NVQs.' Robinson concluded that,

> one might be tempted to advance the argument that NVQs are helping to reverse the traditional under-representation of women in the holding of vocational qualifications. But if most of these women who hold NVQs have them at levels 1 and 2 in areas such as hairdressing, care, retailing and clerical and secretarial work, it is unclear how far this can really be said to be a blow for equal opportunities.
>
> (1996a, p. 16)

The decision to proceed with a new, broader 'general NVQ' was announced in the government's May 1991 White Paper *Education and Training for the*

21st Century (DES/DE, 1991). The NCVQ was charged with developing the new qualifications in conjunction with the major, national vocational awarding bodies – BTEC, the RSA and City and Guilds. Between June 1991 and September 1992 these bodies worked to develop the new general NVQs, and the NCVQ consulted widely on the matter. The GNVQ, as the new qualification formally became known, was piloted in five subject areas – Art and Design, Business, Health and Social Care, Information Technology, and Leisure and Tourism – in a limited number of schools and colleges during the 1992–93 academic year. These GNVQs were then launched on a nationwide basis in September 1993. Subsequently GNVQs have become available in a further 10 areas. Between 1993 and 1996 GNVQs were piloted and introduced in Construction, Engineering, Hospitality and Catering, Science, Retail and Distribution, Media Communication and Production, Management and Manufacturing. Finally, GNVQs in Land and Environment and the Performing Arts and Entertainment Industries were piloted during 1996–97. The total number of overall GNVQ registrations in 1996–97 was 188,739. See Table 1.2 for data regarding the attainment of GNVQ full awards.[4]

GNVQs were made generally available at three levels: one, two and three, later to be retitled 'Foundation', 'Intermediate' and 'Advanced'. The Advanced level GNVQ has been held to be the vocational equivalent of two A levels, while the Intermediate and Foundation awards are supposed

Table 1.2: GNVQs and full awards by area 1996–7

GNVQ	Year nationally available	Full awards 1996/7
Art and Design	1993/4	9,259
Business	1993/4	29,031
Health and Social Care	1993/4	19,179
Manufacturing	1993/4	629
Leisure and Tourism	1993/4	16,147
Construction and the Built Environment	1994/5	1,858
Science	1994/5	2,892
Hospitality and Catering	1994/5	2,107
Engineering	1995/6	2,979
Information Technology	1995/6	4,846
Management	1995/6	60 [5]
Media Communication and Production	1995/6	1,221
Retail and Distribution	1995/6	130
Land and Environment	(pilot)	27
Performing Arts and Entertainment	(pilot)	111
Total		**90,476**

Source: QCA figures.

Table 1.3: GNVQ registrations by level 1993/4–1996/7

	Foundation	Intermediate	Advanced
1993/4	4,786	44,875	38,125
1994/5	14,475	78,251	74,461
1995/6	19,317	87,284	79,458
1996/7	18,934	85,820	83,985

Source: NCVQ, 1997a.

to be broadly equivalent to four GCSEs. Table 1.3 shows the number of GNVQ registrations by level since 1993–94.

As we will see later, since 1995 parts of the Foundation and Intermediate level awards have been piloted in some schools for 14- to 16-year-olds, although attempts to establish GNVQs at 'higher levels', thus establishing equivalence with provision in higher education, have been shelved for the time being. Reflecting the extent to which they were related to the competence-based approach of N/SVQs, GNVQs were launched as unit-based qualifications in a broad vocational area (12 units for the advanced GNVQ), and there were three mandatory 'core skills' (later renamed 'key skills') units: application of number, communication and information technology. Each unit contained a number (usually between three and five) of outcome-based elements, and it was necessary for students to show that they had achieved the performance criteria for each element, collecting their 'evidence' of this in a portfolio, which was assessed internally by a tutor. In order to attain a GNVQ unit students were also required to pass an externally set multiple-choice examination. However, the final grade of the GNVQ – pass, merit or distinction – was not based on these straight pass–fail tests. Rather, it depended upon the internal assessor (usually the student's tutor) making a judgment, following guidance laid down by the NCVQ, about the presence of certain criteria (eight in the case of the Advanced GNVQ) grouped in four themes – 'planning', 'information seeking and handling', 'evaluation' and 'quality of outcomes' – in one third or more of the student's portfolio. Following their launch in September 1992, GNVQs quickly became an established part of the 16 to 19 curriculum in schools and colleges in England and Wales. Surveys showed that GNVQs achieved a great deal of popularity among both colleges and students (e.g. OFSTED, 1993; Jackson, 1995), and they appear to have had some success in providing an alternative (non-A level) route into higher education (FEFC, 1995).[6]

Despite the progress of the N/SVQ and GNVQ policies, they have nonetheless been the focus of considerable criticism. Studies have revealed the limited extent to which employers have taken up N/SVQs, or are even aware of them (Callender, 1992; Spilsbury, et al., 1995). Robinson (1996a), moreover, has pointed to the high number of available NVQs that have never been awarded. The early qualifications attracted a considerable amount of criticism on account of their task-based character and the way in which theoretical and knowledge-based skills were held to have been marginalized within the competence-based approach to assessment that was adopted (Smithers, 1993; Hyland, 1994; Senker, 1996). Prais questioned whether level one NVQs should be deemed vocational qualifications at all because no other European country awards qualifications 'with so narrow a scope' (1989, p. 53). As we shall see later, although the establishment of a coherent system of vocational awards had been a major aim of policy-makers, the provision of N/SVQs appears to have actually had the opposite effect. Peter Robinson discovered that in 1994–95 NVQs constituted just 35 per cent of all vocational qualifications awarded. He observed that 'individuals and employers now face a wider array of qualifications than was the case before the introduction of NVQs' (Robinson, 1996a, p. 34; c.f. DfEE, 1998). Finally, the implementation of GNVQs in England and Wales has also been a somewhat difficult affair. The speed with which they were introduced resulted in many schools and colleges being unprepared to deliver them (OFSTED, 1993); studies have revealed that the assessment and grading requirements of the GNVQs have been difficult to manage on the ground (OFSTED, 1994; Dearing, 1996); the reliability of the assessment and grading has also been shown to be problematic and difficult to apply consistently (FEFC, 1995; OFSTED, 1996); GNVQs have been shown to have suffered from relatively poor completion rates (Robinson, 1996a); and the advanced award appears to have been employed as an analogue to A levels for the purpose of entry into higher education, rather than as a way of preparing people for employment (Wolf, 1997).

Conclusion

The purpose of this book is not to add to the ever-increasing prescriptive, evaluative and critical literature that the N/SVQ and GNVQ initiatives have attracted. Its principal aim is to present an account of how the reforms to vocational qualifications were originated, developed and implemented, primarily between 1981 and 1997. Our analysis of how vocational qualifications policy progressed during this period will not only highlight and account for the emergence of some of the main tensions, but it will also identify the key ways in which policy-makers have attempted to manage them. Given the scale of the reforms that have taken place, it is perhaps unsurprising that considerable difficulties have arisen as they have become established. This is especially so given the limited headway made by previous DES-sponsored efforts to promote a more coherent vocational qualifications system. To a large degree this lack of progress was a function of the voluntaristic heritage that characterized vocational education and training in the UK. While an increasing degree of state intervention occurred from the 1960s onwards, the providers of vocational qualifications – the examining and validating bodies – were, in the main, private bodies reliant for their survival on income from certification fees. Not only could they point to the appeal of their products to employers and individuals, but their markets were expanding. Given such a state of affairs, it would require a considerable amount of effort to bring in a single, national system of vocational qualifications.[7] The following chapters will show how the government, on the initiative of the MSC to begin with, strove – and arguably failed – to do so.

Notes

1 It is also important to note the increasing divergence between the curriculum approaches adopted by (B)TEC and City and Guilds. The former, which concentrated on validating higher level technical awards delivered largely in further and higher education, came to place a great deal of emphasis on the establishment of suitable course inputs. 'While recognising that students should be assessed on what they could do at the end of their programmes, it had been shown through the experience of BTEC and its predecessors that it was not possible to separate this assessment from the quality of learning' (BTEC, 1994, p. 17). The awards of City and Guilds, however, were increasingly directed towards the 'attainment by the student of the necessary competencies, rather than with the means by which these competencies are obtained' (GES, 1986, p. 28).

2 This is not the same as saying that 1.6 million people hold NVQs; individuals may have obtained NVQs at different levels (see Robinson, 1996a).

3 For a more thorough analysis of NVQ take-up, albeit based on earlier data, see Robinson (1996a).

4 In Scotland, General Scottish Vocational Qualifications (GSVQs) were also launched, although they have so far made little impact upon the distinctive Scottish system of post-compulsory education.

5 The GNVQ in Management Studies was piloted at advanced level only, but it has now been discontinued.

6 Although this has been seen as a criticism – see p. 17.

7 A prominent advocate of reform commented that a 'free market has operated in vocational qualifications and several independent national systems have grown up', but there 'is no agreement between them on the form, size, shape or status of qualifications, or the terms used to describe them or the processes involved in their award' (Jessup, 1991, p. 9).

2 Towards a Competence-based System: Contextualizing the Reform of Vocational Qualifications

Introduction

One of the most notable features of the reformed system of vocational qualifications has been the way in which it has been founded upon or, in the case of the GNVQ, related to the notion of occupational competence. The principal aim of this chapter, then, will be to trace and account for the increasing prominence of the concept of competence, as a way of organizing vocational education and training, particularly in the context of the MSC's New Training Initiative (NTI) of 1981. Although the need for changes to vocational qualifications was not made explicit by the NTI, it recommended that training should increasingly be based on the attainment of competence by an individual, and it also led the way for the massive Youth Training Scheme (YTS), in the context of which much of the initial research and development work into the characteristics of a competence-based approach was undertaken. We will begin, however, by examining the broader, contextual factors pertaining to the emergence of competence as a way of organizing vocational education and training: the imperative to replace initial skill-formation arrangements based on time served with training to standards in some sectors; the need to make education more vocationally relevant; and the development of vocational curricula for use in training schemes for the increasing numbers of young unemployed in the 1970s. The conception and implementation of the NTI was, as we shall see, not only an outcome of concern among senior MSC officials that the UK's system of vocational education and training was in need of drastic improvement, but also of the short-term political pressure to manage rapidly rising youth unemployment. Following a discussion of the policy and institutional implications of the NTI proposals, the remainder of the chapter is devoted to an exploration of the emergence of the competence-based approach, particularly in the context of the YTS; progress in improving sectoral and adult arrangements was much more patchy.

Restrictive Practices in Skill Formation

Perhaps the first prominent expression of the desirability of basing training on standards came in the Report of the *Royal Commission on Trade Unions and Employers' Associations*, popularly known as the Donovan Commission (Royal Commission, 1968). The Donovan Commission was established in 1965 because of a growing concern that powerful trade unionism, excessive strike activity and restrictive practices were having detrimental effects on the performance of the economy. The Commission observed that training was 'an area in which restrictive traditions have especially deep roots in British industry and where the pressure of technological advance makes the need for a radical change in outlook particularly urgent' (p. 85). Specifically, the predominance of the apprenticeship system in initial skill formation came in for a substantial amount of criticism: the way in which it limited access to training on the basis of age and gender; the often narrow content; the dependence on time-serving arrangements as the means of certifying craft status rather than the quality of the training or objective measures of the ability to do the job; and the part it played in perpetuating outdated craft restrictions and demarcations between trades. However, it was also argued that economic change would increasingly require workers to move between different occupations. Given this context, 'there would be neither social justice nor economic sense in denying them training simply because the jobs for which they had originally been trained had disappeared and they were now past the age of apprenticeship' (p. 88). The Commission observed that there was 'no doubt that an urgent need exists to secure the rapid and general adoption of systems of training which accord with the social and economic needs of a modern industrial society', and called for 'objective standards to be laid down by which qualifications may be judged' (pp. 92–3).

While the Donovan proposals had some impact on the reform of industrial relations in the ensuing decade, in respect of training policy its recommendations had little immediate effect. Nevertheless, the EITB did oversee the development of modular and standards-based training in its sector, in part to mitigate restrictive practices (Senker, 1992), and there was an increase in the amount of off-the-job training leading to formal qualifications more generally (Gospel, 1995). This limited progress notwithstanding, policymakers in the MSC maintained an interest in the establishment of training to standards during the 1970s. For example, in its *Training for Skills* policy document, the MSC called for training to 'agreed standards in appropriate skills' (MSC, 1977a, p. 20; see also MSC, 1980). A senior MSC figure reflected on the importance given to this issue in the late 1970s:

> the move towards, and I'm going on to quality of training now, the move
> towards standards, training based on standards achieved and not time
> spent, seemed to be a crucial element in the development of a training

policy in the future . . . We would have a strong view in favour of training to standards. This view would be held with the commissioners as individuals, they would be held by officials and there was a unanimous wish to move in that direction . . . This was one of the areas in which the MSC was active and seeking ways forward.

The 'pre-supposition that labour practices were a central cause of lower levels of labour productivity', and were therefore having an adverse impact on the performance of the economy continued to be widely acknowledged (Cutler, 1992, p. 167).[1] Perhaps unsurprisingly, then, the desirability of training to standards was increasingly articulated in the context of the need to counter restrictive practices; for example in the proposals of the Centre for Policy Studies, a right-wing think-tank (Senker, 1992). More prominently, the Central Policy Review Staff (CPRS) undertook an analysis of vocational education and training in the UK. Among other things its report – *Education, Training and Industrial Performance* – condemned the system as 'rigid, conservative and slow to respond to new industrial requirements', and responsible for the continuation of 'restrictive labour practices' (CPRS, 1980, p. 17). Apprenticeships were restricted to a limited number of sectors, and there were too few opportunities for adults to upgrade their skills. The CPRS report reasserted and endorsed the principles set out by the Donovan Commission over ten years before. It called for: 'objective standards to be laid down by which qualifications may be judged; a person who has attained such standards to be universally accepted as qualified and eligible to do the work in question; the content and duration of training courses to be determined by what is required to enable trainees to reach set standards; and the removal of all artificially restrictive barriers affecting access to training or re-training, for example on grounds of age, sex, colour, etc.' (CPRS, 1980, p. 22). In more detail it argued for 'a modular system in which skills and knowledge would be broken up into self-contained units . . . Where possible each would be assessed by reference to objective standards such as the satisfactory completion of a task or demonstration in an examination that an area of knowledge was mastered' (p. 22). Given subsequent developments, it is interesting to note that in a later section of the report there is criticism of the 'jungle of qualifications and examination bodies' (p. 27).

The similarities between the policy proposals made by the CPRS and the thinking of the MSC leadership did not simply arise from a common view among policy-makers about the problems of training and appropriate solutions; nor was it a matter of coincidence. Senior MSC figures took considerable trouble to ensure that both they and officials in the CPRS came up with similar analyses and proposals. According to one MSC official:

When doing [their report] the CPRS people spent a great deal of time talking with us and we spent a great deal of time, because of the politics of it and where CPRS was [in the Cabinet Office], trying to get them and us pointing in the same direction. I think they picked up an emerging idea in terms of productivity and performance.

Therefore, the New Training Initiative of 1981, and the emphasis on instituting training to recognized standards of competence contained within it, was in part an outcome of a long-term concern among policy-makers that existing methods of skill formation, the apprenticeship system in particular, were riddled with restrictive practices and should be the subject of considerable reform.

> The notion of standards was somehow there in the [New] Training Initiative. I think that was mainly as a result of trying to get away from time-serving. [Training] was being used as a form of restrictive practice really, for trade unions to restrict entry and therefore raise skill shortages – [to] raise wages by creating skill shortages.
>
> (MSC official)

> In some industries, printing being the prime and most notorious example, the trade unions were using restrictive practices to limit numbers entering . . . The whole thing [apprenticeship] from an employer's point of view was getting less and less worth the candle.
>
> (MSC official)

The Pressure for Vocational Relevance

By the mid-1970s there was a considerable amount of dissatisfaction with the ability of the education system in the UK to deliver opportunities for all young people. In the post-World War II period, with politicians and administrators preoccupied with access and structural issues, the content of the curriculum, particularly that for low achievers who were not working towards external examinations, largely became the domain of teachers. Although the priorities of young people and their parents were focused on the attainment of knowledge and skills that would provide access to the best jobs and careers, the achievement of vocational success was not a major objective of education. Teachers chose instead to place the emphasis on the development of the characters, personalities, ethical values and social relationships of young people (Schools Council, 1968).[2] The mismatch between the different priorities became more apparent when the economy moved into recession and unemployment rose from the mid-1970s. School leavers were particularly badly affected, as the number of apprenticeships declined and the labour market for unskilled young people contracted. Between 1974 and 1977 the proportion of young people among the total unemployed rose from 5 per cent to 30 per cent (Ainley and Corney, 1990).

The lack of basic skills among many of the young unemployed focused attention on the effectiveness, or rather the lack of effectiveness, of schools and on the poor preparation of young people for working life. Teachers were criticized for being too concerned with the personal and social development of young people and insufficiently aware of their future economic and vocational roles (Ranson, 1984), and there were increasing appeals for education to become more vocationally relevant. In the mid-1970s employers were vocal critics of the state of education. They argued that schools were failing the economy on two counts. First, the inadequacy of the basic skills possessed by young people when they left school made them 'unemployable' (e.g. Methven, 1976). Second, teachers were deemed to be 'anti-industrial' and conveyed this attitude to young people (Weinstock, 1976).[3] Thus on the one hand teachers were criticized for ineffective teaching (of basic skills), and on the other hand for teaching anti-industrial values too effectively. The views of employers were given added weight by the then Prime Minister, James Callaghan, in a 1976 speech at Ruskin College.

> I am concerned on my journeys to find complaints from industry that new recruits from the schools sometimes do not have the basic skills to do the job that is required. I have been concerned to find that many of our best trained students who have completed the higher levels of education at university or polytechnic have no desire or intention of joining industry. Their preferences are to stay in academic life (very pleasant, I know) or to find their way into the civil service. There seems to be a need for a more technological bias in science teaching that will lead towards practical application in industry rather than towards academic study.
>
> (*Times Educational Supplement*, 22 October 1976, p. 72)

Callaghan called for a national debate on education in which employers and other 'non-educationalists' would be involved, and bluntly told teachers that they 'must satisfy the parents and industry that what you are doing meets their requirements and the needs of their children'. Apart from endorsing the 'new vocationalism', the speech signalled that the content of the curriculum and teaching methods were now matters of political interest. The conclusions of this debate were summarized in a Green Paper. It confirmed, unsurprisingly, that Callaghan's observations were well-founded; stressed the importance of effective vocational preparation; and asserted that it was 'vital to Britain's recovery and standard of living that the performance of manufacturing industry was improved and that the whole range of government policies, including education, contribute as much as possible to improving industrial performance' (DES, 1977, para 1.16).

By the late 1970s, the direction of policy was unambiguous and widely held within the government: education was increasingly seen as an arm of economic policy, insofar as it should prepare young people for their future economic and vocational roles (Ranson, 1984). The notion that education is an important engine of economic regeneration and that there should, therefore, be strong functional links between education and the economy established the policy framework for the 1980s and 1990s. However, while it would be easy to attribute the emergence of a 'new vocationalism' as part of a right-wing trend towards the greater penetration of education by economic imperatives, its origins and support were much more complex, including a radical critique from the left and a slide in confidence on the part of many committed educationalists in the ability of the education system to deliver opportunities for more disadvantaged young people. According to a former DES official:

> [The] new vocationalism was not so simple a concept. You'd often get so-called left wing and so-called right wing positions meeting up in the middle. In the early 1980s there was a coming together of a more humane and socially aware approach to the education of the disadvantaged on the one hand, and, on the other a greater sense of vocational relevance.

Many of the educationalists who became active in developing vocational curricula during the late 1970s and early 1980s were influenced by the radical critique of the formal education system in liberal democracies that had been developed by Illich (1971), Reimer (1971) and Freire (1972), among others. In these studies the education system was depicted as serving Western capitalism through the propagation of practices that reproduced economic and labour market inequalities. Schools, then, perpetuate inequality by defining merit in accordance with the structure of the society served by the schools (Reimer, 1971, p. 43).[4] Added to growing concern about the consistent failure of the educational system to mitigate inequality, with the most evident example of this being the large number of low achievers, this prompted educationalists on the left to become disillusioned with the performance of schools and colleges.

> There was certainly a feeling around that education had not done a very good job. It was not serving the needs of employment. . . . A lot of the key [MSC] project workers were FE [further education] based, but radicals who recognised the problems FE was having.
>
> (Consultant)

One consequence of this dissatisfaction with existing methods of educational provision, particularly further education, was that curriculum innovators attached to the MSC and its associated agencies became increasingly interested in the notions of work-based and experiential learning accompanied by the assessment of learning outcomes rather than teaching and course inputs.[5] It was hoped that the individual learner would come to replace bureaucratic and ineffective educational establishments as the dominant focus in the education system. Such novel and distinctive approaches to learning, and the consequent production of qualifications, seemed potentially more effective in delivering opportunities for young people. The combined effects of these critiques, presenting an image of an under-performing system dominated by producer interest and sustaining privilege and inequality, diminished and displaced the authority of the 'educational establishment' and its ideas. Not only did this come from the right of the political spectrum, where there was a concern, among other things, to make education more vocationally relevant and suited to the requirements of employers, but it was also a feature of progressive and radical perspectives on educational reform. Any attempt to contextualize the origins of competence-based vocational qualifications, which are based on the assessment of performance in the workplace or a similar environment, must therefore acknowledge the extent of the distrust of the established education system during the late 1970s and early 1980s, an attitude which was shared by many educationalists and led to their willingness to participate in youth training programmes.

Youth Unemployment and the Vocational Curriculum

While the hopes that schools would deliver opportunities for 'low achievers' were largely not borne out, the MSC increasingly sought to provide an alternative with its emphasis on vocational preparation for young people. Although the MSC had been established to provide a strategic skills planning role, it quickly became caught up in 'managing' unemployment, particularly the politically sensitive issue of youth unemployment (Ainley and Corney, 1990). By the mid-1970s the scale of the problem was considerable. From 1973 to 1976 the overall unemployment rate increased from about 2½ per cent to over 6 per cent. In the same period the unemployment rate for young people under 20 rose from 12½ per cent to over 27 per cent. By 1976 over 800,000 young people were out of work and youth unemployment was rising three times as fast as among the working-age population as a whole. Moreover, the average duration for which young people were unemployed had increased sharply, as had the proportion of young people among the long-term unemployed. There is little doubt that the scale of youth unemployment and the speed with which it developed took the MSC (and most others) by surprise nor, therefore, that its early responses were – admittedly – somewhat *ad hoc*[6] and temporary.[7] One of the leading policymakers in the MSC recalled that:

> The MSC could never get the programmes running as well as it would have liked to have done because as fast as it developed a new programme here, [there was] more unemployment there. It was stimulating us I must say, but it was a big distraction. It meant that all the time we were pushed

to invent short-term measures, much needed particularly for the long term unemployed and the youth unemployment . . . We were pushed always to react to short term crisis. It turned out to be a permanent one, of course . . .

Thus the MSC experienced some difficulties in sustaining its long-term strategy of enhancing Britain's skills base, given the short-term political imperative to manage the effects of rising unemployment. In its *Towards a Comprehensive Manpower Policy* document of 1976, the MSC found it necessary to restate the strategic importance of transforming the training culture in the UK. It noted that manpower 'is a key resource, perhaps the country's most valuable asset, and it should be in the forefront of government, industry and company strategy and not a residual factor as so often happens at present' (MSC, 1976, p. 6). Nevertheless, although it was held that manpower policy should not be 'regarded as a fire-fighting activity to deal with short-term problems', there was still a need for the MSC to adopt a 'problem solving role' (p. 6). In the mid- to late 1970s, though, it was the latter which dominated the work of the MSC, principally because the problem of unemployment controlled the organization's agenda. The emphasis on its short-term fire-fighting role notwithstanding, the MSC nonetheless attempted to use measures to counteract youth unemployment as vehicles to pursue its more strategic objectives.

Towards a Comprehensive Manpower Policy was followed by a report from a Working Party set up to 'study the feasibility of ensuring that all those in the age bracket 16–18 who have left school and are not engaged in full-time education and are unable to get a job should have the opportunity of training or of participating in programmes such as the job creation programme and work experience' (MSC, 1977b, p. 6). This report – *Young People and Work* – shifted the ground of the policy debate. Although the notion that technological advances and structural changes were now permanent features of the economic landscape, and that counter-cyclical measures were thus an insufficient response to increasing unemployment, had already been strongly argued (see MSC, 1975), *Young People and Work* was, according to one senior MSC official:

the first hard graph thing which suggested that we were into something structural and not just cyclical . . . The graphs for youth unemployment showed year after year higher totals at the same point each year as in the preceding year. The fact that it wasn't going to go away, it most certainly did frighten the Labour government of that time.

Noting the deteriorating unemployment situation for young people, the report recommended a major expansion of youth training provision. The government endorsed the proposal but, worried about the growth in the number of young unemployed, insisted that it cover all school leavers, even though the MSC was not yet prepared to take the further step of committing to a permanent programme of education or training for all 16- to 18-year-olds. Responsibility for developing and delivering the programme was vested in the newly created Special Programmes Division of the MSC and the Youth Opportunities Programme (YOP) was launched in September 1978.

YOP grew rapidly. In its first year it encompassed one in eight school leavers (162,000 places), but by 1982 it was providing for one in two (553,000 places); and in 1983 there were more school leavers on YOP than were in normal jobs (Finn, 1984). The aim of YOP had been to provide an 'effective bridge to permanent employment' for young people (MSC, 1977b, p. 7), but with mounting unemployment it never got near that and its credibility diminished. As unemployment rose, and the programme expanded, 'more and more trainees were placed with private employers, many in small, low-paying, non-unionised workplaces'. It 'became impossible to monitor and "police" the scheme; vetting was perfunctory, and fewer on-site inspections were carried out' (Youthaid, 1981; quoted in Finn, 1984, p. 149; c.f. Keep, 1986). Substitution of trainees for workers was commonplace and the provision of off-the-job education or training was unsatisfactory. Yet for all the weaknesses and the criticisms, YOP demonstrated that the MSC could deliver a very large-scale programme very quickly. With youth unemployment set to remain at high levels, as the *Young People and Work* report had forecast, senior officals at the MSC saw an opportunity to use the very weaknesses of YOP to promote its longer-term strategic goal of a youth training scheme that would, the MSC suggested, provide a permanent bridge between school and work.

While the principal short-term imperative was to manage youth unemployment, there was also a growing realization among policy-makers that, as measures to alleviate the problem took on an increasingly permanent character, a new type of vocationally oriented curriculum was needed. Thus the MSC and the newly established Further Education Unit (FEU) of the DES took steps to develop and implement work-related curricula suitable for young people on training schemes. Perhaps the most notable development was the establishment of the Unified Vocational Preparation (UVP) programme in 1976 (Wray et al., 1982). Its objective was to provide 'a limited programme of experimental schemes of vocational preparation for those young people who left school and entered jobs where hitherto they received little or no systematic education and training' (Farley, 1985, p. 77). One of the most significant features of attempts to design a work-related curriculum for the young unemployed was the recognition that 'traditional' college-based models of further education were unsuited to the needs of these people, to whom the prospect of spending more time attending college would be inimical. Thus it is in this context that one can identify an imperative, albeit a somewhat implicit one, to move away from the traditional 'input' paradigm towards a model of vocational education and training in which the outcomes that individuals achieve are given recognition (see, for example, the FEU's 1979 document *A Basis For Choice*). Shortly before the 1979 general election, moreover, the government produced a consultative paper that proposed a comprehensive system of traineeships for all 16- to 18-year-olds. These 'Traineeships' would be: directed at young people who entered jobs with no further education or training; work-based; and last between three and twelve months. Trainees would be provided with induction to the job, to the industry and to working life, and be taught both job skills and social skills in an integrated programme of education and training that would take place both on and off the job (Finn, 1987). However, these proposals were not picked up by the incoming Conservative government.

The 1981 New Training Initiative

By the beginning of the 1980s, then, the direction of vocational and education policy in the UK was shaped by three factors: the increasing attention given to establishing objective standards of attainment; the need to develop schemes of vocational preparation for school leavers unable to find conventional jobs; and the greater importance attached to the way in which education could assist the economy in general. Moreover, the part played by the MSC in instituting policy in this area was growing in importance. The issue of training, however, was low on the agenda of the new Conservative government. Its election manifesto had signalled an intention to review the role and structure of the ITBs, but there were no other commitments. Training was regarded as a matter to be arranged between employers and individuals, and not an issue for the state. The role of the MSC as a national training agency with responsibility for skills planning did not fit with this position, and its future appeared bleak. Rapidly deteriorating economic conditions in 1980–81, however, and the sharp rise in unemployment – especially among young people – in particular, led to the MSC being retained and indeed strengthened (Evans, 1992). This was politically uncomfortable, but there were mounting concerns within the government about the potential for social disorder that high youth unemployment might engender (Keep, 1986). The economic recession, moreover, had further debilitated the apprenticeship system and, following its manifesto commitment, the government was in the process of abolishing 17 of the 23 statutory ITBs.[8] Not only was the position of the MSC enhanced, because of the way in which it already demonstrated its capacity to respond creatively to the pressures generated by rising unemployment, but it was also given an opportunity to put forward proposals for a radical overhaul in the UK's vocational education and training arrangements.

The ability of the MSC to formulate its New Training Initiative in 1981 was, then, a function both of a political imperative to ensure that the social problems caused by youth unemployment were effectively contained and the need to fill the vacuum in the system of vocational education and training that had resulted from a dramatic decline in apprenticeships (see Gospel, 1995), and the dismantling of much of the ITB network. Existing policies and provision were reviewed by the MSC in *A New Training Initiative: A Consultative Document* (MSC, 1981a) in the spring of 1981. It concluded that the UK lacked 'a reliable system or clear framework for providing either the key skills the new technologies demand or the wide range of skills at many different levels which all firms increasingly need' (MSC, 1981a, p. 3). Radical changes in the UK's training arrangements were proposed:

1 We must develop skill training including apprenticeship in such a way as to enable young people entering at different ages and with different educational qualifications to acquire agreed standards of skill appropriate to the jobs available and to provide them with a basis for progress to further learning;

2 We must move towards a position where all young people under the age of 18 have the opportunity either of continuing in full-time education or of entering a full-time education or of entering training or a period of planned work experience combined with work-related training and education;

3 We must open widespread opportunities for adults, whether employed, unemployed or returning to work, to acquire, increase or update their skills and knowledge during the course of their working lives.

(MSC, 1981a, p. 4)

Further objectives of a reformed system of vocational education and training included: the better recognition of experience and skills which adults already have (i.e. the accreditation of prior achievements) and the importance of breadth, flexibility and skills transfer. Employers 'know that an individual is much more valuable and is much more able to adapt to change if he or she has acquired some competence in a range of related jobs or skills rather than being limited to the ability to perform one task in one context' (MSC, 1981a, p. 5). These points reflect the perception held by policymakers in the MSC that fundamental changes were occurring in the nature of work – in particular the increasing utilization of new technology was transforming the way in which it was designed and organized – which affected the skills mix required of individual employees. Thus, in developing the case for 'agreed standards of skills', senior MSC officials were influenced by some of the tenets of post-industrial thinking (see Bell, 1973). Not only was there a recognition of the increasing importance of the service sector, and of the dearth of adequate arrangements for skills training therein, but there was also an appreciation that economic change would increase demand for diagnostic, higher level and knowledge-based skills.

At about that time the great debate was raging about the tragedy of the death of manufacturing employment and the growth of the service sector and how appalling it was etc, etc. Anybody who'd thought about it for a moment would realise that employment was bound to decline in manufacturing because of international competitiveness, wage levels, technology and so forth. Part of the skills of a new kind was skills which up to then had been somehow . . . thought of in the traditional world of training as second rate. That's to say the service sector, the professions, the personal service area, the care area and so on. So part of it was that there was a whole dimension of skill, competence . . . over a much wider spectrum of occupations and that the country would not simply be all right if you just get manufacturing apprenticeships back.

(MSC official)

The new markets and technologies require a more highly skilled, better educated and more mobile workforce in which a much larger number of professional and technical staff are supported by a range of more or less highly trained workers who perform a range of tasks and who are involved in a process rather than a repetitive assembly or manufacture of a part of a specific product.

(MSC, 1981b, p. 3)

The MSC became concerned, therefore, with formulating a new model of skill formation: one which was suitable for the growing service sector; was not contaminated by being associated with restrictive practices in the way the apprenticeship system was; and was capable of capturing the broad-based skills and flexibility seen to be increasingly required in employment.[9]

During 1981 the MSC consulted on the NTI both externally and within the government. In December of that year it published its *A New Training Initiative: An Agenda for Action* on the same day as the government produced a similarly titled White Paper – *A New Training Initiative: A Programme for Action* (MSC, 1981b; DE, 1981). The government endorsed the MSC's proposals, which closely followed those set out in the earlier consultation document, and which framed subsequent policies and arrangements for vocational education and training. Clearly the most prominent new feature was the announcement of a new £1 billion Youth Training Scheme (YTS). It would guarantee a year's foundation training for all those leaving school at the minimum age without a job, provide vocational preparation for young people with 'modest examination achievements', and was expected to be in place by 1983. Significantly, it was envisaged that the new YTS would be designed to ensure that young people were equipped 'not merely to do the immediate task required by the job, but with a basic competence and flexibility which they can build on as they change jobs' (DE, 1981, p. 6). The White Paper, moreover, confirmed that 'the concerns of training and education policy [were], increasingly, closely linked' and endorsed the

MSC's target of '1985 as the date by which relevant standards of competence . . . should be available for all significant skilled occupations' (DE, 1981, p. 11).

Two aspects of the NTI deserve further analysis. First, the government's support for the MSC's proposals is somewhat striking, given the lack of interest it had exhibited in this area hitherto, and the readiness to intervene needs to be explained. The need to manage the effects of high youth unemployment clearly dominated the agenda of the Conservative government:

> We were a very useful body around in times of unemployment, putting it in political terms, and I didn't kid myself when the government did eventually bless things like the New Training Initiative that they weren't going into it for, let's say, quite the width of objectives that the MSC had in mind. Without a shadow of a doubt response to unemployment was the thing that unlocked the key to resources in the first instance.
>
> (MSC official)

While a major thrust, then, of the government's policy in matters of training during the early 1980s was the restoration of market forces and the principle of voluntarism, with the abolition of most of the ITBs being the most concrete example of this (Keep, 1986), the social consequences of unemployment nonetheless provoked substantial intervention in the area of youth training (Goldstein, 1984; Ryan, 1984). The government, moreover:

> were also aware that they'd been busy destroying things and where on earth were we going? The NTI document, you notice, was nonthreatening to government as well – and not accidentally. The 10 year time horizon, of course, takes you beyond at least one and probably two general elections . . . I think they were ready to receive this at that moment in time, not least because it coincided with Mrs Thatcher becoming extremely anxious about the state of the education system.
>
> (MSC, official)

Second, as the last informant observed, the MSC benefited from the weak position of the established education service. In Chapter 1 we observed that the DES had been seeking to change vocational education and training, although its interventions had been somewhat tentative. For example, it had shared the responsibility with the MSC for the UVP scheme during the late 1970s, and it had also sponsored the development of the CPVE in the early 1980s. This involvement notwithstanding, the commitment of the DES to the matter of vocational education had come in for substantial criticism. In 1974 the Organisation for Economic Co-operation and Development (OECD) had accused the DES of being characterized by 'passivity', 'inertia' and 'obsessive secrecy'. Further, the Department exhibited a 'lack of a balanced analysis of persisting and new trends in society, in technological development or the role of the state, and of the place of education and science in the process of production' (OECD, 1975, p. 74), charges which were subsequently endorsed by a House of Commons Select Committee (see Ainley and Corney, 1990). According to one commentator, then, 'unfettered by the political and financial constraints on the education sector, and more ideologically in tune with the government's industrial strategy, the MSC was able to win control over this whole area of institutional exapansion' (Finn, 1987, p. 113).

The DES experienced organizational, political and ideological difficulties in pressing its case for changes in vocational education and training. First, it lacked power, typically having to work through discussion and negotiation with local authorities and teachers' organizations. Although, the DES did endeavour to reconstruct the educational service and improve vocational preparation for young people (Ranson, 1984), it had little control over the content of curricula or examinations, nor could it direct how central government funding was used by local councils. Second, the election of a Conservative government in 1979 further weakened the influence of the DES and, as a corollary, gave the MSC a boost when the need came to reform the system of vocational education and training.

> I have to say that seen from where I was there was never any doubt [about which agency would be responsible for implementing the reform agenda]. There was never any doubt partly for a good reason and partly for a prejudiced reason. One forgets . . . the dominance, drive and charisma of Mrs Thatcher in her heyday and she was in her heyday then. She had a prejudice against the DES as such and a prejudice against educationalists as such. So she was prejudiced in the MSC direction to begin with. But, secondly . . . she realised that something had to be delivered in the field and it was the lack of a delivery mechanism which was a reliable delivery mechanism . . . we had by then, remember through YOP and the other special programmes, we'd invented this kind of central government contract with deliverers through a network of area offices and so on. We had . . . built up a track record of reliably delivering things by certain dates. Over at the DES was this outfit she could remember all too familiarly, which she regarded as being in the pockets of the LEAs (Local Education Authorities) on the one hand and the teacher unions on the other.
>
> (MSC official)

Third, Mrs Thatcher may have had her prejudices, but the DES also suffered from a more profound difficulty in providing policy leadership in the area of vocational education. Despite the policy initiatives we have described, both in this chapter and the previous one, vocational education historically had not been accorded much importance in the DES. Externally and internally there were criticisms of its attitude towards vocational and further education:

The majority, I think, of the MSC people were totally behind us, absolutely behind it. Almost without exception the Department of Education side were against it. They were against it on two of the worst possible grounds, one turf and that's awful . . . secondly, ideological. They actually were not in favour of technical and vocational education.

(Employment Minister)

[In the DES] FE was regarded as a bit of a backwater, nobody understood it very much.

(DES official)

The DES, then, had little influence on the way in which vocational education and training policy developed in this period. As the introduction of the Technical and Vocational Education Initiative from 1982 onwards and its appropriation of a quarter of the budget for work-related non-advanced further education in 1984 show, the MSC increasingly came to dominate policy innovation in this area and, according to its critics, furthered its attempts to remake the working class by instilling greater 'labour discipline' (Ainley, 1988, p. 96; Finn, 1987).

Towards a Competence-based System: The Implementation of the New Training Initiative 1982–1984

The principal way in which the MSC progressed vocational preparation was increasingly through the new YTS, which became operational in 1983. For our purposes the most notable aspect of the development and early implementation of the YTS was the effort that went into providing suitable work-related curricula and certification arrangements for the many young people involved, not least because it was recognized that criticisms of the poor quality of the MSC's existing programmes were well-directed. A leading educationalist who was close to the MSC leadership at that time noted the 'appalling quality of YOP and the first stages of YTS', and ascribed it to their being 'more about solving, temporarily anyway, the unemployment problem . . . rather than producing a proper training scheme'. Clearly, the most obvious way of demonstrating, or ensuring, that the YTS programmes were not just ways of keeping young people off the streets was to establish suitable certification and qualification arrangements.[10] According to a former MSC official:

A big effort had to be put in, first of all, to get YTS off the ground in terms of numbers, over 350,000 at the time; but also to make it a credible scheme. And the qualifications dimension was an important part of developing a credible training scheme.

The demands of the YTS, however, meant that existing awards were largely unsuitable; not least because they were directed either towards college students on full-time courses or apprentices on day release in a limited number of areas. Thus the MSC, through its Youth Development Branch, sponsored a number of research and development projects that were charged with producing appropriate curricula and certification arrangements aimed at the YTS in particular. Three imperatives guided this work. First, given the way in which individual YTS programmes were, ideally, expected to be delivered on employers' premises, there was a demand that the vocational preparation involved should be largely work-based. It was felt, moreover, that such an approach would be attractive to individual participants, many of whom were entering YTS programmes because they had not benefited from established educational methods. Second, given the perception held by policy-makers in the MSC that changes in the labour market would demand more flexibility from individuals, there was a keen interest in the notion of transferable skills. A key concern was with promoting:

> Generally, those skills that could be transferable, were transferable. Skills that did build upon mathematical skills and communication skills, building in quite good understanding of new technology, specifically in relation to whatever the specific area of interest, technician area, was. Particularly seeking to develop adaptability, and also seeking to develop a willingness to face up to the whole concept of change, much of which was technology led, or which was coming to be technology led.
>
> (MSC official)

Third, with this emphasis on flexibility and transfer across jobs and occupations the concept of 'skill', insofar as a linkage with specific jobs or occupations was implied by it, came under strain and was increasingly overshadowed by the notion of broadly based competences that could be applied in a variety of contexts. An influential consultant for the MSC recalled that:

> Our starting point was to say, stop looking at skill and start looking at the outcomes people will need to achieve. [The] issue is not about training people to be an operative, it's about how they are going to interact, resolve problems [and] plan the work they are going to do.

Two major areas of work sponsored by the MSC during the early 1980s in which these ingredients emerged and were then articulated can be identified. The first of these was the development of the concept of Occupational Training Families (OTFs), interest in which had been stimulated by a report on Canadian research (Melling, 1978). The MSC commissioned the Institute of Manpower Studies (IMS) to identify:

learning objectives across a wide range of occupational sectors for 16–18 year olds; to provide information on how to assess these learning objectives; [and] to consider the relationship between the learning objectives within a framework consisting of specific and broadly related work skills, the world of non-employment, personal effectiveness, and the ownership of skills – the capacity to transfer skills when moving to new and unfamiliar work.

(Hayes et al., 1983, p. 9)

Two important features of this work by the IMS need to be highlighted. First, it provided a blueprint for the YTS. The FEU noted that the 'YTS approach is based on the idea that there are identified core areas which are common to Occupational Training Families, which can be learned in any one of these families and which transfer to another' (cited in FEU, 1983, p. 27). In respect of YTS, five core areas were identified: number and its application; communication; problem solving and planning; manual dexterity; and computer literacy/information technology. Skills developed within these core areas were defined as generic transferable skills and were capable of application to other areas. The IMS report proposed a scheme based on a grouping of jobs into 11 occupational families; a statement of the Key Purpose for each OTF; a system of learning objectives for each family which represent the 'quintessential key competencies' associated with work in that family (these were identified empirically in discussions with supervisors and managers in 100 companies and provided the base on which functional analysis was developed); and a set of 'transfer learning objectives' for each family that would enable young people to become effective in new or unfamiliar jobs within that family. Second, the remit of the IMS work required that the 'project be concerned with outcomes, not with the processes by which they are to be achieved' (Hayes et al., 1983, p. 9). Thus assessment should be based on 'recording trainee's performances on-job whilst occupied on real tasks'. This, it was held, was 'consistent with the aspirations of YTS and recognises the key role that employers will be called to play as the main element in delivering occupationally relevant training'. Hence assessment of competencies and performance of tasks was work-based, not work-related. After giving consideration to the suitability of a wide range of assessment methods, the IMS report rejected the use of a mixture of methods, which might have improved validity, and instead recommended the use of just one: observation. Hence a supervisor, for example, could decide whether or not a trainee was 'competent' by observing their performance in the workplace; relevant knowledge and understanding could, it was claimed, also be inferred from this.

Despite some unease about the OTF approach (e.g. FEU, 1983), the work of the IMS was significant as a major contribution to the design of YTS. It was expected that trainees would be given training in at least one of the OTFs (Finn, 1987). The articulation of process skills, rather than outcomes, was an important part of the second major piece of developmental work overseen by the MSC at this time: the Core Skills Project.[11] In the context of the NTI, the project was established to investigate the design of a work-based learning model suitable for use in YTS, and to provide a range of tools and policy instruments which could aid policy-makers, training providers and administrators in bringing about the innovation and change in vocational education and training sought by the government (Levy, 1987, p. 3). The project team initially undertook a detailed interrogation and analysis of government policy statements and documents. Hence the scope of the project offers a confident view of policy intentions at that time: the development of a technically competent, flexible and versatile workforce; an employer-led, work-based programme providing access to learning; new standards relating to the conduct of a job with performance-based criteria; new certification and progression arrangements; and the importance of skill transfer (Levy, 1995). Core skills were defined as 'those skills which are common in a wide range of tasks and which are essential for competence in those tasks' (Levy, 1987, p. 7). They were regarded as underpinning the concept of skill transfer and were associated with how number, communication, problem solving and practical skills were deployed in the workplace. Perhaps the most notable intervention made by the project team at this time, though, was its identification of how policy-makers had paid little heed to the highly technical nature of assessment in an outcome-based system of vocational education and training (Levy, 1995, p. 233).[12] While much effort went into the development of generic, transferable skills, other concepts and procedures received less attention. As in the IMS work noted above, little attention was given to knowledge *per se*. As one member of the development team, reflecting on the early work, recalled:

> We were very naive on knowledge at the start. We thought that if you demonstrated something – if you could cook in a restaurant (for example) that's all you needed. You could obviously cook and do it anywhere. We hadn't addressed the real issue of understanding the principles, transferring thinking [to other settings] . . . We were dealing with a low level of qualifications of course and of competence. We hadn't seriously addressed the assessment of knowledge at all and no one did for a year or two.

Yet the delivery of these curriculum initiatives ran into more substantial obstacles even before this. Although the character of the OTF and core skills work reflected the stated belief of MSC policy-makers that the YTS should provide young people with transferable skills (Silver, 1990), other research carried out for the MSC itself questioned the assumptions about skills transfer and flexibility contained within the OTF approach, and there was little evidence of this kind of broad-based vocational preparation on the ground (Ainley, 1988). According to Finn (1986), there was 'a yawning gap between the stated objectives of the MSC's schemes and the practical everyday experience of trainees' (p. 53), given the well-documented attachment of employers to training for specific jobs.

The significance of these MSC-sponsored development projects notwithstanding, perhaps the most substantial reform of curricula and assessment systems in vocational education and training occurred in Scotland. Far from coming under the auspices of the MSC, moreover, the Scottish Action Plan (SED, 1983) was developed, in part, as a means of rebutting its advances in the education sector in Scotland. The 'Action Plan', which came to be implemented in Scotland from 1984 onwards under the oversight of the SCOTVEC, proposed the establishment of a system of modular-based National Certificates, founded upon the assessment of the 'learning outcomes' attained by an individual, which would replace existing non-advanced vocational provision. In contrast to the approach being pioneered by the MSC, however, National Certificate modules were designed to be deliverable in both further education colleges and the workplace.[13] This, and the emphasis on 'learning outcomes' rather than competence, not only meant that the reform of vocational provision in Scotland had a more educational bias, but also that the specification of knowledge components was better articulated. While the National Certificate initiative was not designed to be a competitor with the YTS, being primarily aimed at improving opportunities in further education, it nonetheless stemmed from a realization that education needed to be made more relevant to work, and it also made a strong impression on MSC officials.

Much of the progress in developing competence or outcome-based approaches in vocational education and training in the aftermath of the publication of the NTI, then, occurred in the context of vocational preparation. Despite the call for appropriate standards of competence to be in place for all significant occupations by 1985, beyond one or two prominent sectors there was little real progress. In engineering, for example, where the EITB had already pioneered a module-based approach among other things during the 1960s and 1970s, a group of influential employers were prominent in bringing about the ending of all vestiges of time-serving from the apprenticeship system (Senker, 1992); there were also moves towards the institution of standards-based training in printing (Stuart, 1996), another sector where training arrangements were held to be characterized by restrictive practices. Perhaps the most notable development at this time, however, took place in the chemicals sector. The significance of one of the strategic aims of the 1981 NTI – that training arrangements should become increasingly founded upon standards of competence – was picked up by the Chemical Industries Association (CIA), a leading NSTO. It got together with City and Guilds in 1984 to assess the extent to which such an approach was capable of being delivered in its sector. Given the reportedly positive response from the sites that were visited (see *City and Guilds Broadsheet*, February 1985), a development project was initiated with the financial support of the MSC. The resulting standards of competence were produced in the autumn of 1985. They attested to, 'the technical performance expected on the completion of training; the precise criteria by which attainment of performance can be assessed; [and] the conditions under which the performance must be carried out' (*City and Guilds Broadsheet*, February 1986, p. 13). The significance of the CIA's initiative was twofold. First, as we have already observed, the advancement of training based on standards of competence, the blueprint of the MSC notwithstanding, was a very limited affair elsewhere. This can be ascribed to the weakness of many of the new NSTOs and the emergence of a rather fragmented and incoherent infrastructure of industrial training following the abolition of the majority of the ITBs in 1981 (See Marquand, 1989). Second, the CIA's work was progressed in a sector where the matter of restrictive practices in training arrangements was not directly a concern of employers.

An additional, notable aspect of this initiative was the participation of City and Guilds. Since the 1960s it had been operating skills testing services for industry, principally as a way of providing examination arrangements for those vocational courses which had been devised by some of the newly established ITBs. This work, and the influence of the US literature (see Tuxworth, 1989), directed City and Guilds increasingly towards the measurement of performance as the basis of its awards. According to Harry Knutton, then its Director-General, City and Guilds' awards were becoming increasingly founded upon the notion of competence, defined as: 'the skills, knowledge and attitude to complete a given task or series of tasks' (*City and Guilds Broadsheet*, May 1984, p. 2). One of its officials recalled that, '[by] the 1980s it was felt that we had to move the Institute from what was essentially a knowledge-based assessment system towards a competency-based assessment system . . . We took a policy decision to do that'.

The reform of sectoral training arrangements was not the only aspect of the 1981 NTI to have been characterized by little progress in the immediate period following its publication. The third prong of the policy stressed the need for adults to enhance their skills. Despite this aim, apart from a minor extension of funding for the Training Opportunities Scheme and the development of an Open Tech initiative, little immediate progress was made. Rather, the traditional belief that adult training was primarily a matter for employers appeared to be upheld. The political capital, moreover, was attached to improving the quality of youth training. An MSC official recalled that the 'New Training Initiative in effect said that young people are the most important thing. Adults are important too, but we don't quite know what to say about them yet'. After a couple of years the MSC produced its Adult Training Strategy in November 1983, a move that was endorsed by a subsequent government White Paper (DE, 1984). In respect of the Adult Training Strategy, the MSC's role was largely seen to be that of a facilitator seeking to bring about more positive attitudes towards training. Specifically, it would: mount a promotional drive to raise awareness of the importance of training; improve the operation of the market for training; and enhance its direct training programmes for the adult unemployed. Although this initiative, according to the MSC official quoted directly above, 'didn't get very far . . . because it didn't have a very clear focus', it did generate two studies of skill levels and the state of training in the UK, which proved to be very influential. In *Competence and Competition* (Hayes et al., 1984) it was shown that the UK had substantially fewer skilled workers than the USA, Germany and Japan at all levels, and also spent much less on vocational education and training. This had resulted in a relatively poor level of productivity. The second report, *A Challenge to Complacency*, commissioned from Coopers and Lybrand, revealed that there existed 'a widespread ignorance among top management of how their company's performance in training compared with that of their competitors', among other things (Coopers and Lybrand, 1985, p. 4). The findings imparted by these reports were picked up in the MSC. One official confessed that 'overall our national training performance was awful and probably deteriorating compared with our competitors', while another noted that by '1984 there was definitely an increasing awareness of our relative underperformance in the skills area'. By the mid-1980s, then, there was an increasing realization within the MSC that urgent action was needed to raise the competence of the workforce of the UK as a whole.

Conclusion

In this chapter we have explored the rise to prominence of competence-based vocational education and training, particularly through an examination of the origins, components and implications of the MSC's 1981 New Training Initiative. At this stage in its gestation the concept of competence was not precisely defined, but, understood in a general sense as a combination of key skills, technical skills, knowledge and attributes, it had a number of positive elements that appealed to different groups. It could be seen as: directly work-related and oriented to the needs of employers; part of a revival of managerial prerogative; focused on outcomes and the progress of the individual learner, and therefore attractive to progressive educationalists who were critical of existing forms of vocational education provision; consonant with wider economic changes, especially the shift from manufacturing to services and the perceived elaboration of an economy characterized by employment flexibility; and, insofar as it was oriented to the workplace, it could be utilized as the basis for YTS curricula. Policy makers in the MSC played a major part in propagating the establishment of competence as a device for organizing vocational education and training provision. While this was clearly an expression of their desire to bring about improvements in the skill levels of the UK's workforce, the development of the

YTS dominated their agenda from 1982 onwards. Given the limited progress made in reforming adult and sectoral training arrangements, then, the elaboration of the concept of competence rapidly became associated with measures to improve the quality of youth training; principally the imperative for suitable certification. In the next chapter we will look at the way in which the tension between the more strategic ambitions of the MSC and the need to enhance the way in which YTS programmes were delivered was played out in the decision to set in train a reformation of the system of vocational qualifications in England and Wales.

Notes

1 See for example Pratten (1976) and Caves (1980). For a substantial critique of this body of work see Nichols (1986).
2 See for example the critique of the right-wing 'Black Papers' (Cox and Dyson, 1971).
3 See Wiener (1981) and Barnett (1986) for the argument that Britain's longstanding economic decline is related to a deep-seated cultural disdain for industry and commerce.
4 Each insisted that most good learning is achieved by doing. Building on this, Illich and Reimer put forward the notion of networks of skill models who are prepared to share their skills with learners; Freire, working in the field of adult literacy in north-east Brazil, sought to raise the political consciousness and, through that, the literacy skills of peasants.
5 It is interesting to note the increasing extent to which the MSC, rather than the DES, dominated policy innovation in this area (see p. 32).
6 According to the *Young People and Work* report schemes 'have been introduced piecemeal, and opportunities are somewhat erratically related to the needs of any locality. Different agencies administer different schemes. Different programmes are in danger of competing with each other for provision of facilities or premises, for example, in employers' establishments' (MSC, 1977b, p. 29).
7 The Job Creation Programme, for example, provided temporary jobs that covered the costs of labour intensive projects; the Work Experience Scheme for unemployed young people; Community Industry; and the Temporary Employment Subsidy.
8 To be replaced by a network of Non-Statutory Training Organisations (NSTOs) (see Rainbird and Grant, 1985; Keep and Mayhew, 1994), later to become known as Industry Training Organisations (ITOs).
9 The beliefs of MSC policy-makers notwithstanding, the extent to which supposed post-industrial change was generating a greater demand for more broadly based and transferable skills in the workplace is highly questionable. To take one example from the period, in a study of clerical work in a bank, an insurance company and a local authority, Crompton and Jones (1984) discovered that the introduction of new technology, far from leading to an upskilling of work, had had a largely deleterious effect upon it. More fundamentally, Kumar (1986) has raised a number of questions about the appropriateness of the concept of 'post-industrialism', especially the novelty of the supposed shift from a manufacturing to a service-based economy.
10 It is important to distinguish between the MSC, which was keen to establish a proper training scheme, and the Conservative government, which was generally

more concerned with managing the short-term effects of high youth unemployment (Keep, 1986).

11 The project was funded from 1982–85 by the European Social Fund, and from 1986-90 by the MSC and the Training Agency (TA).

12 An interesting, implicit feature of Levy's account of the Core Skills project is the recurring theme of a shift in the locus of power from policy-makers to technical experts as policy moves from adoption to implementation.

13 See Raffe (1988) for an in-depth analysis of the origins and structure of the National Certificate system.

3 'Motherhood and Apple Pie': The Review of Vocational Qualifications in England and Wales 1985–1986

Introduction

In Chapter 2 we examined the way in which the MSC's New Training Initiative of 1981 aimed to provide a blueprint for the long-term reconfiguration of vocational education and training in the UK. With the exception of the institution of the YTS, however, behind which there were important political imperatives, in the immediate period following its publication progress was patchy. By 1984, though, the MSC had recognized this lacuna and, through its Adult Training Strategy, for example, it had begun to explore ways in which vocational education and training in general could be modernized. Moreover, largely from a desire to mitigate time-serving arrangements, a number of industry training organizations had also begun to reform – tentatively – their occupational training arrangements, so that they were more explictly founded upon 'standards', in line with the New Training Initiative's recommendations. Thus there were limited moves in the direction of basing training on standards of occupational competence within industry and in the delivery of the MSC's programmes, although beyond some general suppositions there was little specific understanding among policy-makers of what was meant by the concept of 'competence'.

What needs to be explained in this chapter, then, is not only how a version of 'competence' was defined and articulated, but also the way in which it came to underpin the reform of vocational qualifications and the establishment of NVQs. To begin with we will identify, and assess the significance of, two broadly related imperatives for the reform of the vocational qualifications system: first, the perceived weaknesses of the existing arrangements; and second, the needs of the YTS. Following on from this, the establishment, direction and proposals of the *Review of Vocational Qualifications in England and Wales* will be subjected to detailed analysis. The Working Group recommended, among other things, that a new National Council be set up to oversee the development of a national framework of vocational qualifications – NVQs – within which there would be greater regard to the exhibition of competence in employment.

The Immediate Imperatives for Reform

There appear to have been two major factors leading to the establishment of the *Review of Vocational Qualifications in England and Wales* (RVQ) in April 1985. The first of these reflects the broad view held at that time by senior officials of the MSC, and by some individuals within the government, that substantial reform of the vocational qualifications system was desirable as part of a general aim to promote greater vocationalism in education. Second, policy-makers were under considerable pressure to enhance quality within the YTS, particularly because it was soon to become a two-year programme, and the provision of proper, nationally recognized qualifications was seen to be one of the key elements of this. We have already seen that senior MSC officials had increasingly become attracted to the way in which an admittedly ill-defined concept of competence could be used to underpin industrial training. In its July 1984 statement on the *Modernisation of Occupational Training*, for example, the MSC reiterated that training must become more closely founded upon standards of competence, but it also recognized that the design of appropriate testing and assessment regimes needed to be developed in order to measure them (MSC, 1984).

There thus arose a concern about the quality of the existing provision of vocational qualifications, particularly as the MSC had recently published its Adult Training Strategy. An MSC official recalled that:

> We needed to focus on something practical and one of the things . . . was this absolute tangle of vocational qualifications, and that the vocational qualifications weren't based on the skills needed to do the job, but on really what the then lecturers and education trainers knew how to teach . . . the qualifications clearly weren't representing the skills of the adult workforce.

The vocational qualifications system was deemed to be unsatisfactory by the MSC in a number of other respects. Many awards, particularly in craft areas, contained an element of time serving. There were large areas of the economy where no recognized qualifications were available, or where their take-up was poor. In 1983 the Hotel and Catering ITB surveyed 500 establishments in its sector and discovered that fewer than 15 per cent of employees held a formal qualification (*Educa*, June 1984). Where vocational qualifications were available, however, they were often perceived – by MSC officials – to be insufficiently related to the needs of employment, relying too heavily on the assessment of knowledge rather than on practical skills. Furthermore, not only were there many overlapping awards in existence, but there was also no way of judging how they related to each other or provided for progression. The following comments about the system of vocational qualifications as it existed prior to the establishment of the NVQ framework come from former MSC officials:

> There were so many inadequacies which would have been generally admitted, but not in public. The examinations really bore very little relationship to what was being required of craftsmen, technicians or what have you . . . Those deficiencies were increasingly obvious, and those deficiencies in terms of the examinations not being an adequate test of skills that were necessary, those difficulties were compounded by the sheer complexity of the vocational examinations system, the lack of progression, the lack of relationship with academic qualifications.

> There was no common standard. Some of them were quite warmly regarded, but they were warmly regarded on a stand alone basis, for example BTEC HNDs [Higher National Diplomas] and so on, or certain aspects of City and Guilds. So it isn't that we were denigrating all of the vocational qualifications, but they lacked a common standard . . . And also some of them were rather Mickey Mouse, they were not underpinned by adequate knowledge and understanding, they didn't have a valid vocational content. A lot of them were dreamt up by people without direct contact with . . . employers.

> There was a maze of competing examining and qualifications bodies, [and] no way of relating qualifications to each other in terms of what level they implied.

> [B]efore 1987 . . . it was the awarding bodies that invented their own qualifications. Some people look back with idealism on that time, but it was dreadful; it really was quite dreadful. There was no relationship between any qualifications, no framework, none of them were based on any standards, employers didn't come within a mile of most of them and they were very patchily used and unpopular.

While it was not put explicitly in these terms at the time,[1] there was a feeling, then, that the 'jungle' of vocational qualifications needed to be sorted out if the competences that individuals were acquiring in employment were to be properly assessed and recognized. Unsuprisingly, the major national providers of existing qualifications did not share this analysis. Their officials maintained that their products were closely related to the needs of employment and that there were longstanding mechanisms in place to ensure that this was upheld. Moreover, while a 'jungle' of vocational qualifications might have existed, this was not necessarily something that was considered objectionable. Officials from both BTEC and City and Guilds remarked on how efficiently 'jungles' worked in practice, in that people who reside within them not only have a sophisticated understanding of their own individual position, and of how it relates to those of other inhabitants, but they are also able to navigate effectively their own routes. According to an official from City and Guilds, anybody taking one of their awards in the early 1980s 'was totally clear about what they were doing'. This may have been so, but it echoes the point made by one of the MSC officials, quoted above, in as much as it was not the integrity of individual awards or awarding bodies that concerned the MSC, but rather the lack of clarity, coherence and transparency in the system as a whole. While City and Guilds awards may have been entirely suitable for their respective purposes, there was no understanding of how they related to the products of other awarding bodies, and of how provision could be improved where take-up of awards was low. It would be wrong to suggest that the major awarding bodies saw no ways of improving the vocational qualifications system. According to an official from the RSA, for example, the complexity of the pattern of awards and the lack of standing of many of them in the eyes of employers was a function of the existence of a large number of relatively small providers:

> There were lots of, I'd call them minor awarding bodies offering similarly titled certificates, but not to the same standard. And to the uninitiated employer these read as if they should mean something, and then they got the person in and they found they weren't up to the sort of standard that they'd expected. That gave the whole system a bad name.

Furthermore, it was not particular awarding bodies or their products that were frequently held in low esteem by the government, but rather the way in which many awards were delivered by further education colleges. Lord Young, who prior to becoming a peer and entering the Cabinet as Minister Without Portfolio (with special responsibility for employment measures) in September 1984 was Chairman of the MSC, provided the crucial political impetus behind the proposed reform of the vocational qualifications system. In his later memoirs he wrote that he 'had long worried about the great number of vocational qualifications, over 750 of them. They simply did not relate to one another . . . How would any employer be able to value the qualification earned by an employee?' (Young, 1990, p. 134). Young had developed a considerable interest in, and knowledge of, vocational training in his erstwhile capacity as head of the Organisation for Rehabilitation through Training (ORT). However, he held a poor view of much of the existing education system, particularly the further education sector, and was characterized by one member of the RVQ as being 'anti-college'. At this time Young oversaw the transfer of a quarter of the budget for 'non-advanced further education' in colleges from the control of the local authorities to the MSC (Evans, 1992). The proposed reform of the vocational qualifications system, then, can be placed within the broader attempt by the

MSC to wrest for itself a greater degree of power over the delivery of education, with the particular aim of making it more relevant to the needs of employment (Ainley, 1988; Goldstein, 1984). In his ministerial capacity, Lord Young was closely involved, along with the MSC's leadership, in the decision to launch the RVQ in 1985. Indeed, without his political support it is unlikely that the RVQ would have been the major initiative it was, because the then Secretary of State for Employment, Tom King, showed very little interest in developing policy in this area. One MSC official recalled that, in respect of the RVQ, 'David Young was the key man politically', and that he 'more than anyone else . . . made sure the political channels were kept open'.

The 1985–86 RVQ was in part, then, an outcome of the concern among the MSC's senior officials, and within some parts of the government, that the reform of the UK's system of vocational qualifications, insofar as they were made more relevant to the needs of employment, was essential for the improvement of training provision. However, it would be misplaced to lay too much emphasis on the capacity of the MSC to translate strategic aims into tangible policy initiatives, because the imperative to have in place appropriate awards for the high profile YTS was equally important, and more so politically, as an imperative for change. From its inception in 1982, and its launch the following year, the YTS had been the subject of a considerable amount of critical comment, particularly to the effect that many of the individual programmes were doing little more than providing unscrupulous employers with cheap labour (see Finn, 1984; Lee et al., 1990). MSC officials were aware that the development and provision of appropriate certification for the YTS was an important way in which they could enhance its quality and thereby fulfill their aim of instituting a 'permanent bridge between school and work' (Ainley and Corney, 1990). As an MSC official noted:

> There was an increasing feeling that youth training should be more about forming part of young people's transition into the labour market and not just be about stop gap programmes aimed at keeping people off the streets. The corollary of that was that you had to have a good leaving certificate.

While the then Conservative government's principal political aim in respect of YTS was to use it as a way of massaging unprecedented post-war levels of youth unemployment, within the MSC there was a concern to make it a proper training scheme, and not just a palliative. The YTS leaving certificate, however, was widely regarded as a failure (Finn, 1986; c.f. MSC, 1985), even by some MSC officials themselves, largely because of the ambiguity that existed over what it represented; and the attainment of qualifications in general was low (Deakin, 1996). We have already seen in Chapter 2 that the MSC had initiated and managed a large amount of research into the appropriate components of a work-based YTS curriculum, the 'OTF' and 'core skills' projects for example. Yet this work was of an inherently long-term character. Indeed, the MSC did not publish its list of 103 core skills for use in YTS until January 1985. When the MSC did attempt to insert these concepts into the YTS programmes, moreover, their effect was only to help to conceal the low levels of skill that typified most YTS programmes in reality. They tended to be 'resisted by employers and young people alike. Employers preferred to train young people in skills which could be used immediately' (Finn, 1987, p. 180; c.f. *Educa*, February 1985).

Although widely forecast beforehand, the announcement in April 1985 that the YTS was to be extended from a one-year programme to two years, beginning in 1986, stimulated greater efforts by policy-makers to develop a suitable certification framework for it. In *Education and Training for Young People* (DE/DES, 1985), the White Paper that also announced the establishment of the RVQ, it was proposed that the 'new scheme will differ from the existing YTS in that its objective will be that all trainees should have the opportunity to seek recognized vocational qualifications' (p. 7). The MSC immediately set up a development group, under the chairmanship of Peter Reay, who was then Personnel Director at Cadbury-Schweppes, to work on the design framework for the two-year YTS.

Thus the need for the availability of recognized vocational qualifications became even more apparent as policy-makers began to consider the principles of a two-year YTS programme (Ainley and Corney, 1990). There was, then, further pressure for a review of the state of the existing provision of qualifications. Recalling the origins of the RVQ, an MSC official noted that: 'I think that by the time we got to devising, in 1985, with the promise of more government money, a two-year YTS, that's when this really took off in fact.' Another erstwhile MSC official emphasized the priority that was given to finding appropriate methods of certifying achievement in various occupations, but confessed that 'it soon became apparent there weren't many about' (c.f. Finn, 1987). The launch of the RVQ and the development of the two-year YTS progamme, within which the opportunity for participants to acquire vocational qualifications was given a high priority, were clearly closely related matters.

> I suppose what was going on at that time was that, yes, we should review qualifications, and Lord Young the minister at the time wanted that, but we were doing it in such a way that we knew that our particular imperative was that government programmes should have a new type of qualification . . . The need for good qualifications for YTS was a driving force in the RVQ.
>
> (MSC official)

> The dominant political motivation (for the RVQ) had to do with the fact that there were all these bloody schemes. YTS was just the latest and there were no qualifications which appeared to be appropriate. Ministers

were shit scared – you can quote me on that – that there were all these kids going through these schemes with bugger all to show at the end.

(DES official)

Thus the RVQ was launched, in April 1985, with a specific remit to produce an interim report within six months. The 'review is expected to concentrate initially on improving the structure of qualifications to meet the needs of the extended Youth Training Scheme' (DE/DES, 1985, p. 9). It might appear, then, that the RVQ was established principally from a concern to improve the quality of the YTS, especially as it was planned to become a two-year affair, and thus appease the short-term political objectives of a government, which was largely concerned with making sure that youths were kept 'off the streets'. MSC officials were adamant, however, that the decision to have the RVQ also stemmed from the more strategic motives we identified earlier in this chapter. One of them recalled that:

It certainly wasn't set up with just youth training in mind. Without a shadow of a doubt there'd been a growing feeling, I think on the educa-tion side even . . . that the whole thing was getting a bit of a mess . . . I think people reckoned it was time for a very fundamental look at the whole of the system in fact.

We must bear in mind that senior figures in the MSC did not see the youth unemployment issue simply in 'fire-fighting' terms, but rather identified an opportunity to establish a 'permanent bridge from school to work' (Ainley and Corney, 1990), and thus build an increasingly skilled workforce. Never-theless, without the pressure provided by the government's political need to be seen to be mitigating the effects of high levels of unemployment, it is unlikely that the RVQ would ever have been such a major undertaking, the MSC's strategic aims notwithstanding. While the interest of Lord Young in the reform of vocational qualifications ensured that it had political sup-port, such a significant reform would still have been unlikely to have taken place without the urgency provided by the unemployment issue. As one senior figure, who was closely associated with the decision to have the RVQ, recalled, 'you had to show a reason for NVQs.'

The Establishment of the Review of Vocational Qualifications in England and Wales

The *Review of Vocational Qualifications in England and Wales* (RVQ) was established by the White Paper *Education and Training for Young People* (DE/DES, 1985). The Working Group was expected to produce an interim report in respect of YTS certification within six months; but it was envisaged that its more substantial proposals for the reform of the system of vocational qualifications in general would take a year to emerge. Scottish provision was largely excluded from the RVQ's remit on account of the implementation of the 'Action Plan' (see Chapter 2). The Working Group was given a number of terms of reference. It was asked 'to recommend a structure of vocational qualifications in England and Wales', and to 'design a timetabled programme to achieve this which has the support of employers, examining and validating bodies and others concerned', which:

- is relevant to the needs of people with a wide range of abilities
- is comprehensible to users
- is easy of access
- recognizes competence and capability in the application of knowledge and skill
- provides opportunities for progression to higher education and professional qualifications
- allows for the certification of education and training and work experience within an integrated programme.

(MSC/DES, 1986)

The RVQ Working Group was chaired by Oscar De Ville, an industrialist, and its Chief Officer was George Tolley, head of the MSC's Quality Branch. It was nonetheless formally a joint effort by the MSC and the DES. Thus the latter provided an official to act as an adviser. That the DES and MSC were ostensibly collaborating in developing education and training policy is worthy of comment itself, because, in the words of one MSC official, the relationship between the two organizations at that time was a bit like that which existed between 'North and South Korea' (see Ainley and Corney, 1990). The influence of the DES should not be overstated, however, its joint sponsorship of the RVQ notwithstanding. Formally, it had to have an important part in the review because so many policy areas which nominally fell into its sphere of influence were obviously implicated, including further education, access to higher education, the relationship between vocational and academic awards and the structure and policies of the existing examining and validating bodies. Nevertheless, the DES's shared leading role was, in effect, a formal one only, because the MSC provided the main drive for reform, for example through the preparation of the draft discussion papers. One member of the RVQ recalled that 'the DES lost out. On the RVQ, no doubt about it, it was outgunned by the MSC.' Even at a political level, Lord Young, who succeeded Tom King to become Secretary of State for Employment in September 1985, took a much closer interest in developments than did his counterpart in the DES, Sir Keith Joseph.

The membership of the RVQ Working Group was drawn from industry, the vocational examining and validating bodies, trade unions, and professional bodies, among others. It met on a monthly basis when the usual procedure was for MSC officials, and George Tolley in particular, to introduce papers pertaining to various aspects of the vocational qualifications system for discussion. According to one member of the Working Group, Tolley tended to 'give you four alternatives which ranged from the eminently sensible to the loony'. He went on to recall that 'you'd guess which one he was going to push for. But he drove us pretty strongly step by step, very cogently, very coherently.' The Working Group, through the MSC, also commissioned a number of pieces of research to inform its deliberations (e.g. GES, 1986). Evidently, the MSC and its officials, George Tolley in particular, largely shaped and directed the discussions of the Working Group, through the presentation of papers and options for reform. The role of the individuals in the group was, in the words of one of them, to 'be reactive'. While there were a large number of educational bodies and interest groups represented on the Working Group, then, their influence did not reflect their numerical dominance, although they were somewhat vocal and occasionally successful in asserting their wishes, as in the articulation of the concept of NVQ 'levels' for example (see p. 55). Although the course of the Working Group's deliberations was given little attention in the DES, Lord Young kept in touch with developments through meetings with Oscar De Ville and George Tolley. He was keen for progress to be rapid – pressure that occasionally had to be resisted.

Before the Working Group produced its interim report, in July 1985 Peter Reay's group produced, under considerable pressure of time, its recommendations in respect of a design framework for the two-year YTS. The report stated that the 'overall objective of the new Scheme should be to provide a foundation of education and training and planned work experience which gives all trainees the opportunity to seek a vocational qualification related strongly to competence in the workplace'. Competence was defined 'so as to include all aspects of carrying out tasks at work in a satisfactory manner. Thus it should read to include practical skill, knowledge, understanding and attitudes' (MSC, 1985, p. 4). In building on the experience of the delivery of the one-year YTS programme, Reay's group recommended that the extended scheme should also comprise a mixture of off-the-job training and work-based learning. Yet successful trainees should also be able to demonstrate four outcomes on completing their programmes: 'competence in a job/and or range of occupations'; 'competence in a range of core skills'; the 'ability to transfer skills and knowledge in new situations'; and 'personal effectiveness' (MSC, 1985, p. 6).

While the importance of having in place a 'credible and respected YTS Certificate' was affirmed, it was acknowledged that the existing product was unsatisfactory. Although this was being resolved, it was nonetheless considered that 'all trainees should be given the opportunity to seek a relevant vocational qualification demonstrating occupational competence, or to obtain credit towards such a qualification' (p. 6). Despite having been impressed by the modular approach which was being developed in Scotland under the 'Action Plan', particularly the emphasis on flexibility, access and modularity, Reay's group recognized that little progress had been made in properly assessing work-based learning, although it was hoped that the various standards development programmes that the MSC had recently initiated would eventually bear fruit (see p. 53). Nevertheless, the establishment of 'a comprehensive and systematic programme of consultation, review and assistance, whereby industry bodies, in conjunction with appropriate examining and validating bodies, are encouraged and assisted to develop a modular structure based upon standards of competence' (p. 11) was considered to be an essential way forward, and that the forthcoming proposals expected from the RVQ Working Group would be helpful in that respect.

The RVQ Working Group produced its Interim Report two months later, in September 1985. It specified five factors that should underpin a proper system of vocational qualifications: comprehensibility; relevance, including the importance of awards being based on standards of competence encompassing applied knowledge, skills and understanding; credibility; accessibility; and cost-effectiveness (MSC/DES, 1985, p. 4). The importance of a 'single, coherent framework' was attested and different ways of bringing it into being, varying in the degree of change that each embodied, were presented for consideration, as was the question of what kind of body should be responsible for overseeing and progressing reform (pp. 5–6). Interestingly, in the light of later developments, there was a concern that, in trying to bring about reform, a reliance on the 'voluntary agreement of each and every examining and validating body' would be 'fraught with difficulties because of the many interests involved' (p. 6).

The principal objective of the Working Group's Interim Report, however, was to recommend appropriate ways of providing certification for the anticipated two-year YTS programmes. It restated the proposals of Reay's design group that all trainees should have an opportunity to gain a vocational qualification, or part qualification, which was based upon standards of competence as defined by industry bodies, and that individuals should be assessed on them in the workplace wherever possible. Yet the Working Group also recommended that government officials should nominate a small number of bodies to be responsible for setting standards of competence, in association with industry bodies, and for providing YTS certification. As a short-term measure, until its wider recommendations for the reform of the vocational qualifications system in general were published and implemented, the setting up of 'a consortium of designated bodies' to regulate and oversee activity in this area was proposed (p. 7). The principal outcome was the establishment of the Youth Certification Board (YCB) in March 1986. Comprising representatives from employers, BTEC, City and Guilds, the RSA and SCOTVEC, and under the chairmanship of Peter Reay, its job was to select appropriate qualifications for use in the two-year YTS until such time as whatever institutional arrangements were to be recommended by the RVQ Working Group made its job superfluous. Given that the MSC's development work on occupational standards of competence was in its infancy, the YCB began by endorsing qualifications that were largely combinations of examinations of knowledge and industry-derived skills tests.[2]

Why was so much attention given to the need for 'competence-based' awards? For a start, it has to be remembered that in many of the sectors where there was a high proportion of YTS trainees, in retail distribution for example, few qualifications of any kind were available. That having been said, the emphasis placed on work-based learning and assessment in the YTS was, first, a reflection of the widely held assumption among senior MSC officials that vocational qualifications delivered through the further education sector were insufficiently related to the needs of employment. According to one of them:

> it's one thing to cook a meal in a college kitchen when it's the only thing that you're actually doing and you haven't got the head chef bellowing at you . . . and waiters running in and out. It's not real that situation, and the fact that you can prepare the meal under one set of circumstances, [that] you know technically how to do it, it doesn't mean you can transfer that to the working environment.

Second, it was also recognized that many of the young people at whom the YTS was directed were low achievers at school. This further motivated MSC officials to explore ways of instituting certification processes that excluded formal educational provision. Added to which, the MSC was faced by two (potentially) conflicting priorities. Its officials were expected to maintain and enhance quality within YTS programmes. Yet they were also under pressure to ensure the efficient use of resources. Thus the large scale of the YTS operation nationwide ruled out the use of traditional methods of assessing and certifying the vocational capabilities of individuals. Measures to ensure that all providers of YTS programmes were offering participants proper training inputs would have been prohibitively expensive. This impelled the MSC to focus attention on the measurable outcomes that YTS participants could display for the purposes of certification.

Although the MSC had initiated a considerable amount of research work into the development of work-based curricula for use in YTS programmes, the imperative for improved certification arrangements, especially given the desire to move to a two-year scheme, directed its attention towards matters of assessment and accreditation. Given the scepticism that concepts such as the 'OTFs' and 'core skills' met on the ground (Finn, 1986), there was also a concern to found them more explicitly upon job roles. Thus a concept of 'competence' became formally articulated during 1984, when the MSC's Quality Branch, in conjunction with a body known as the 'Oxford Group',[3] took the lead in developing assessable standards suitable for use in YTS programmes. They came up with a concept of competence based on 'standard tasks'. Each of these 'standard tasks' would comprise a 'title'; a precise definition of the task, including, as appropriate, objectives, conditions, equipment available etc; [and] a precise statement of the criteria for the successful performance of the task' (Jessup, 1991, p. 32).

Following this groundwork, during 1984 MSC officials experimented with the development of standards of competence in a number of areas which had a high throughput of YTS trainees – in retail and business administration for example. Although the Clothing and Allied Products ITB (CAPITB) and the Institute of Meat were funded by the MSC in 1985 to formulate a structure of qualifications based on the assessment of competence in the workplace for their respective sectors, perhaps the most notable initiative at this time was the Caterbase scheme. In May 1985 the MSC charged the Hotel and Catering ITB with elaborating a system of work-based assessment to underpin vocational qualifications in its sector. One of the development officers recalled that 'it was very much tied up to providing a system of assessment for qualifications based on standards which should be used to provide qualifications at the end of, or through, YTS.' As with the CAPITB scheme, qualifications were designed on a modular basis. Each module contained specific performance criteria, the exhibition of which attested to an individual's competence, and assessment was carried out by the candidate's own supervisor in the workplace. The final certificate was awarded on the completion by the candidate of a City and Guilds 'knowledge test' (MSC, 1988a). Several key imperatives of YTS policy thus led MSC policymakers to explore ways in which the competences of trainees in the work environment could be assessed. At the time of the RVQ in 1985–86, and the subsequent setting up of the NCVQ in late 1986, with its imperative to advance a framework of vocational qualifications founded on competence in employment (see p. 53), practically the only relevant pre-existing developmental work in this area had been carried out in the context of the delivery of YTS, and only then since 1984.

The Recommendations of the Review of Vocational Qualifications in England and Wales

The RVQ Working Group's main recommendations for the overall reform of the vocational qualifications system in England and Wales were enshrined in its report of April 1986 – the *Review of Vocational Qualifications in England and Wales* (MSC/DES, 1986). It noted that there were certain strengths attached to the existing vocational qualifications system. There was, among other things, 'a stability in organisations which engenders respect and trust'; a set of 'established bodies' which 'have credibility with employers'; 'diversity of provision'; the 'international standing' of many qualifications; and 'a well developed partnership between the further education system and many of the bodies awarding qualifications' (p. 15). Nevertheless, a number of shortcomings were identified, including the absence of a 'clear, readily understandable pattern of provision'; the existence of 'gaps in provision'; ill-defined or impractical 'arrangements for progression and transfer'; 'barriers to access', such as 'attendance and entry requirements for courses', for example; the bias 'towards testing either of knowledge or of skill rather than of competence'; and the 'very limited take-up of vocational qualifications in some important occupational areas, for example, in the distribution industry' (p. 16). It was acknowledged that, while the diversity of the vocational qualifications system reflected the differing demands of users, and that to enforce 'uniformity' would therefore be undesirable, there was nonetheless 'scope for rationalisation' and 'greater coherence'; and that 'it cannot be said that there is an effective national system for vocational qualifications' in existence (p. 16). Before it enunciated its specific proposals for the improvement of the vocational qualifications system in England and Wales, the Working Group found it worthwhile to offer its definition of a proper award:

> A vocational qualification is a statement of competence clearly relevant to work and intended to facilitate entry into, or progression in, employment, further education and training, issued by a recognized body to an individual. This statement of competence should incorporate the assessment of:
> - skills to specified standards;
> - relevant knowledge and understanding;
> - the ability to use skills and to apply knowledge and understanding to the performance of relevant tasks.
>
> (p. 17)

It was recognized that many existing qualifications would not meet these specifications, so some change would clearly be necessary. Moreover, the report recommended that the reformed (where necessary) awards should become 'part of a proper national system of vocational qualifications' (p. 17), and thus be comprehensive, relevant, credible, accessible and cost-effective (pp. 17–18). In order to bring about this objective, the Working Group recommended that existing vocational qualifications 'be brought within the national framework – to be called the National Vocational Qualification (NVQ)' (p. 25). According to one member of the Working Group, it had been 'agreed' that the vocational qualifications system was a 'jungle'. Therefore it was reasonable to propose that existing awards, albeit modified and improved if necessary in order to bring them into line with the definition of a 'vocational qualification' that the Working Group had agreed, would form the basis of the new national framework. Importantly, while it was accepted that the reform process would involve more than an 'orderly classification of existing qualifications', presumably because this would not have stimulated efforts to reduce the gaps in provision that had been identified, it was not envisaged that the proposed change would be 'to design a completely new structure to replace existing qualifications' (p. 25). A senior figure associated with the Working Group emphasized that:

We deliberately went for a structure that would absorb what was already there rather than try to push through an entirely new system. This was because, in my view anyway, there was a lot of good stuff going on in British industry and some of these people, like the awarding bodies, were doing a thoroughly good job. [The job was] to lay down principles rather than a straightjacket.[4]

Fairly late on in the deliberations of the Working Group the structure of the proposed system of NVQs was given greater specification, largely through the emergence of the framework of five levels, from entry level to professional occupations.[5] It was envisaged, then, that existing qualifications would, after being modified if necessary, be inserted into the new framework, and hallmarked as an NVQ at a particular level. Given the emphasis on progression that the proponents of the system of levels stressed, this was the principal area in which the representatives of educational interests and bodies on the Working Group succeeded in establishing their aims. Employers' representatives were less well disposed to the concept of levels because they feared its possible impact upon work structures and industrial relations arrangements.

The terms of reference for the Working Group had specified that it should consider how to bring into being a system of vocational qualifications within which 'competence and capability in the application of knowledge and skill' were given greater recognition. As we have just observed, moreover, in defining a 'vocational qualification', the Working Group recommended that it should be a 'statement of competence'. It found that too few awards were based on standards of competence. Therefore a key, early task of the proposed new National Council (see p. 56) would be to 'establish a clear focus for national action to secure the specification of standards of competence', and that 'arrangements should be made to ensure specification of standards by effective and appropriate industry bodies for the comprehensive coverage of industry and occupational groupings' (p. 31). Importantly, it was envisaged that only a small number of these bodies would need to be established. Although there were some 85 joint industry councils and 120 ITOs and ITBs in existence, which could have been entrusted with the task of drawing up occupational standards of competence, the Working Group considered that 'proposals be formulated for a more limited number of standards-setting bodies which, where appropriate, would bring together common and contiguous interests across a number of occupational groupings and which would be capable between them of providing a comprehensive coverage across all occupations' (pp. 31–2). It was anticipated that such an arrangement would serve to maximize the scope for ensuring flexibility, transferability and recognition. One member of the Working Group recalled that it was anticipated:

that there would be a very limited number of standard-setting bodies. It would have been horrified, that group, at the suggestion that you should have 150, 200 lead bodies. That was not remotely envisaged.

Despite the emerging developmental work which was being undertaken by the MSC in the context of YTS, there was only a very broad understanding within the Working Group about what was meant by 'occupational competence'. One influential member recalled that 'there was a general appreciation of the need to move in the direction of competence-based assessment, without having at that time a tremendously clear idea of what that meant.' Clearly, it was envisaged that, by being founded on 'standards of occupational competence', vocational qualifications would be more suited to the requirements of employment and oriented towards work-based learning. Yet there are two important, related points that need to be made here, given the way in which the NCVQ later came to implement NVQ policy. First, the Working Group proposed that the system of vocational qualifications should not be 'geared solely to the testing of knowledge and skills of immediate use to an employer', although this was valuable in itself, since it would take 'too little account of the longer term needs of employers, of the economy and – most importantly in our view – of the learning, personal development and career development needs of the individual' (p. 9). Second, although it called for an expansion of skills testing facilities in industry and recognized, largely from a concern to improve accessibility, that people should increasingly be able to have their competence attested at work, the Working Group made no recommendation that the workplace was the sole location where the occupational competence of an individual could be properly ascertained.

There is, it would appear, a degree of inconsistency between two of the principal recommendations of the Working Group that we have discussed. While it was envisaged that the proposed national framework of vocational qualifications would be largely predicated on existing awards, it was also asserted that these products were unsatisfactory because they insufficiently attested to the attainment of competence. Existing qualifications might therefore need to be modified and improved in order to be hallmarked as NVQs. However, there seems to have been no appreciation of the scale of the reform that would be necessary if such a process were to be undertaken. This ambiguity in the Working Group's proposals did not go unnoticed at the time. It was, however, seen to be a matter for the newly established National Council to resolve as it embarked on the implementation of NVQ policy.

The Working Group concluded that if the reform of the vocational qualifications system was to be properly carried out, then it would be necessary to establish a new body capable of providing the 'essential' 'focus for national action' (p. 20). Thus the establishment of a National Council for Vocational Qualifications (NCVQ) was proposed, a body whose remit should be 'to implement, or to secure action to implement, a system of vocational qualifications that will achieve the objectives of comprehensibility, relevance, credibility, accessibility and cost-effectiveness' (p. 20). More specifically, it was envisaged that the new National Council would, among other things: take the lead in securing the 'specification of standards of occupational competence'; build and develop a national framework of vocational qualifications; obtain the 'comprehensive provision of vocational qualifications by the certifying bodies; and put in place quality assurance arrangements' (pp. 20–21). In effect, the Working Group was proposing that a new quango (quasi-autonomous non governmental organization) should be established that would oversee and encourage the development of the national system of vocational qualifications in England and Wales.

Given the then Conservative government's ostensible antipathy towards quangos, this appears a somewhat odd arrangement. After all, on coming into office in 1979 the Conservatives had initiated a review of existing non-departmental public bodies (as quangos are formally known) with a view to reducing their number, although it was to have little impact (Pliatzky, 1992). Yet the establishment of a new quango to take forward the other recommendations of the Working Group was determined largely by the absence of other alternatives. Another option would have been to charge the existing major national providers of vocational awards – BTEC, City and Guilds and the RSA – with leading the reform process. It was felt, however, that the necessary cooperation would have been difficult to establish. According to an MSC official, these bodies 'had a wonderful opportunity in those days if they could have got together to sort of design qualifications for the future; but they always squabbled amongst themselves so they never did.' There had been an early feeling within the MSC that it should take on the responsibility for bringing the reformed vocational qualifications system into being. Its officials had, after all, been the principal advocates of policy innovation in this area. This did not happen for three reasons. First, while the MSC was at the height of its powers as a quango at this time (see Ainley and Vickerstaff, 1993; Evans, 1992; King, 1993), albeit of a rather special kind, there was no desire within government to increase its powers. Second, although the DES had evinced little concrete interest in advancing vocational qualifications policy, it would nonetheless have acted to protect its turf from further MSC incursions. As a former MSC official observed, it would have been 'politically impossible' for the MSC to have entirely taken over responsibility for this area of policy 'because it would have sent the DfE [sic] wild. They would never have worn it. It had to be set up as something that sat between the two departments.' Third, within the Working Group itself there was a view that, if the proposed new body was established within an existing department or quango, then it would fail to achieve sufficient independence and be more susceptible to government interference.

The Working Group considered that it was 'not necessary to seek legislation to establish the National Council' (p. 20) because this might mitigate the cooperation and 'goodwill' of other bodies and interested parties. Rather, it was anticipated that the success of the National Council would be brought about 'not so much by the vigour with which it seeks to apply sanctions, but by the relevance and validity of its policies' (p. 22). In effect its powers in reforming the vocational qualifications system would be limited to exhorting and encouraging other relevant parties, such as the providers of existing awards and employers, to cooperate. It was also speculated that other existing government policy instruments, the YTS programmes in particular, could be used to promote reform, although it was acknowledged that the National Council would have no influence in how they were used. The reluctance, despite some discussion, of the Working Group to recommend that the proposed National Council have statutory powers to enforce change reflects its appreciation of the well-attested preference of the then Conservative government for the establishment of voluntary arrangements wherever possible in matters that affected employment (MacInnes, 1987).[6] A member of the Working Group pointed out that the:

> RVQ, if you read it carefully, is couched in a voluntary mode. There was a lot of discussion in the group as to whether it should be statutory or voluntary . . . [but] you've got to be realistic . . . We had to push through something that was acceptable to the government.

Nevertheless, the Working Group proposed that, if voluntary arrangements were not to succeed, then it had 'no reservations in recommending that the Government should enact appropriate legislation' (p. 20). It also suggested that the National Council would need an annual budget of approximately £3 million, which would fund a substantial amount of research and development work as well as cover administrative costs. For the first five years of the National Council's existence, after which the NVQ framework should be in place at levels one to four, the Working Group anticipated that it would require pump-priming by the government. The Working Group also considered the longer-term funding options for the National Council: that it might rely entirely on government grant, although it was acknowledged that this would necessitate legislation; that it meet its costs wholly from the levy it would make on certifying bodies whose awards would be accredited as NVQs; or that it meet its needs through a combination of grant and levy income. Given the extent to which both the country and the individual certifying bodies would benefit from having a reformed system of vocational qualifications in place, the Working Group recommended that 'in due course, the National Council should be funded through a mixture of government grants and a levy of certifying bodies for the use of the NCVQ seal of approval' (p. 24). Such an arrangement was seen, moreover, not only to give the National Council a measure of independence from government, but also to ensure that a degree of accountability was maintained.

Although some members of the Working Group pressed for this, Oscar De Ville excluded the question of A level reform from its deliberations at an early stage. On the matter of the awards of professional bodies, however, there was a good deal more debate. The Working Group proposed that the National Council should 'seek the full co-operation and commitment of professional bodies', principally to get their agreement to the inclusion of 'all appropriate professional qualifications and part qualifications into levels I to IV of the National Vocational Qualification framework' by 1991 (p. 39). Opposition from within the Working Group itself, however, resulted in the absence of any recommendation that 'higher level' awards issued by professional bodies be initially inserted into the framework. Finally, while the situation of Scotland was excluded from the remit of the Working Group's inquiry, the establishment of 'an integrated UK system of vocational qualifications' was deemed desirable: 'in due course, and after appropriate consultations, there should be full Scottish participation in the National Council' (p. 40). The Working Group also recommended that its proposals should apply to Northern Ireland.

Given the diversity of parties represented on the Working Group, De Ville did well to ensure that a report was produced within a year. The unanimity of the final report, moreover, was an even more impressive achievement (see Cross, 1991). This came at a price, however, as the relationship between academic and vocational qualifications was hardly referred to at all, and the professional bodies were able to disentangle most of their awards from the scope of the review. More importantly, there was ambiguity about whether the national framework of vocational qualifications was to include existing offerings, modified where necessary, or new style awards based on the assessment of competence. In the main, employers' representatives favoured the more radical change. Yet the commitment of the providers of existing vocational qualifications and other educational bodies to reform also had to be achieved. Therefore, the proposals of the Working Group were framed in such a way that, while they forecast significant changes, they did not appear to damage, and indeed might even enhance, the interests of the major national examining and validating bodies. Clearly, there was no appreciation of the scale of the reforms to be undertaken later by the NCVQ; in fact many saw it simply as a much-needed tidying up job in an area where there was a considerable degree of incoherence.

Among some members of the Working Group there was even a feeling that little would change as a result of its recommendations. At that time the MSC had developed a reputation for developing and launching numerous short-term initiatives without adequate evaluation; a prominent member of the Working Group found it 'inclined to passing enthusiasms'. Nevertheless, the ambiguities we have identified in the RVQ report mean that we can reject the notion that the Working Group's findings were largely determined in advance by the MSC. Undoubtedly MSC officials did favour the development of a coherent vocational qualifications system within which individual awards were more closely related to occupational competence in employment, and this is reflected in the Working Group's terms of reference to a certain extent, but the notion of 'competence' remained ill-defined, and there was evidently no comprehension then of how competence-based vocational qualifications policy would later become operationalized by the NCVQ. Members of the Working Group, moreover, were able to influence the direction of the proposed reforms in quite significant ways. The best example of this was the introduction of the concept of 'levels' during its deliberations. Nevertheless, the MSC did have very deliberate objectives and, given the way in which its officials controlled the Working Group's agenda, the final report can be considered to be a good reflection of its aims in this area of policy.

The Establishment of NVQ Policy in England and Wales

Most of the Working Group's principal recommendations were encapsulated in the July 1986 White Paper, *Working Together – Education and Training* (DE/DES, 1986, pp. 16–24). In particular it was accepted that:

- – vocational qualifications in England and Wales should be brought within a new national framework to be called the National Vocational Qualification (NVQ)
- – a new National Council for Vocational Qualifications (NCVQ) should be set up to secure necessary changes, to develop the NVQ framework and to ensure standards of competence are set.

(p. 17)

The new National Council was given nine specific duties,[7] and while it would have no statutory powers to compel education and industrial bodies to cooperate in the reform process, it was stated that 'the Government will not hesitate to act should it appear that legislation is necessary to make the new NVQ framework effective' (p. 23). We can, however, identify some important differences between the recommendations of the Working Group and the proposals contained within the 1986 White Paper. First, in the RVQ report it had been proposed that, after an initial period of five years pump-priming by the government, the NCVQ should be funded by a combination of government grants and levies from awarding bodies. In the White Paper, however, the government directed that the NCVQ should aim to become self sufficient, that is to be entirely dependent on income derived from levies, by the beginning of 1990-91, by which time the full NVQ framework at levels one to four should be in existence.

Second, in the RVQ report it had been anticipated that the proposed NCVQ would take responsibility for 'securing the standards of occupational competence' (MSC/DES, 1986, p. 21). The White Paper, however, asked only that the NCVQ 'establish a clear focus for national action to secure the specification of standards by competence by effective and appropriate industry bodies' (DE/DES, 1986, p. 21). Because it was recognized that without a considerable amount of assistance such a task would be beyond the capacity of many of the existing ITOs, the MSC was asked to initiate matters on a sectoral basis by encouraging the development of 'individual action plans' (p. 22).

Third, we have already noted that the Working Group proposed the establishment of a five-level framework of vocational qualifications, which would include the awards offered by professional bodies, although it drew back from directly recommending that the fifth level be specified immediately. Following considerable lobbying by some professional bodies even this proposal was watered down in the ensuing White Paper as the NCVQ was given a remit to develop a four-level framework only. Although it was expected that professional bodies would cooperate with the NCVQ wherever necessary in advancing the NVQ framework at levels one to four, the option of extending the framework beyond this was rejected. For the time being it was expected that the new NCVQ would merely 'consult the appropriate professional and other bodies on how higher levels of professional qualifications can best be articulated within the proposed NVQ framework and to report back to Government' (DE/DES, 1986, p. 18). Finally, there is an assumption that the proposed framework of vocational qualifications would encompass existing awards. The White Paper states that the 'framework should be designed to incorporate and embrace existing vocational qualifications' (p. 17).[8] There was also an anticipation, moreover, that the NCVQ would build up a close working relationship with Scottish bodies, and it was proposed that the situation be reviewed after a period of two or three years (p. 17).

During the Summer of 1986 the MSC mounted a promotional campaign about the NCVQ and NVQ policy, particularly among employers. MSC officials found it difficult, however, to stimulate interest on a sectoral basis. Moreover, when employers' representatives did meet to consider and discuss the NVQ proposals, doubts were raised about whether they would take root within industry. Three potential obstacles were identified. First, there was some bewilderment at the scale of the envisaged reforms. Remember also that at this time the policy imperative was that existing qualifications would be modified and placed within the NVQ framework. Second, the increased emphasis on the assessment of occupational competence as the basis of vocational qualifications gave rise to concerns that employers would often not be able to deliver the facilities necessary for this. Third, employers expressed worries that the framework of levels would have deleterious industrial relations consequences for them, the possibility of inflated pay demands in particular (see *CBI Education and Training Bulletin*, December 1986).

The NCVQ formally came into existence as an independent company limited by guarantee on 1 October 1986. Two weeks later its council met for the first time at the Charing Cross Hotel in London. The former London headquarters of the National Union of Mineworkers in Euston Road had been earmarked for the use of the NCVQ, but the building was not yet ready. For a brief period of time, therefore, the NCVQ operated out of the DE's offices. While the NCVQ was established as a non-departmental public body (NDPB or a 'quango') under the joint sponsorship of the Employment, Education, Wales and Northern Ireland departments, it was formally responsible to the DE which acted as its 'host' department. Thus the Secretary of State for Employment, at that time Lord Young, was responsible for securing the appointment of a part-time Chairman and other council members. Oscar De Ville was invited to chair the NCVQ council, initially for a year, although he was eventually to stay on as Chairman until October 1990. The other council members – 13 in total – were appointed during the Summer of 1986 and were asked to participate on the basis of their personal abilities and expertise. Indeed, at the first meeting of the NCVQ council De Ville stressed that members had been appointed 'not as representatives of particular sectoral interests, but for the broad individual experience and knowledge that they could bring to the work of the council'. Initially, the council met for a morning once every six weeks or so, although meetings became more infrequent under the later chairmanship of Bryan Nicholson.

In September 1986 Professor Peter Thompson, Deputy Principal of the City of London Polytechnic, was appointed to the post of NCVQ Chief Executive by the Secretary of State for Employment. Because Thompson could not take up the post until December of that year, George Tolley, who had been the RVQ's chief officer, and was regarded by many as providing the major intellectual thrust behind the proposed reforms, stepped in to become the NCVQ's acting Chief Executive in the interim. Initially, the NCVQ began with two directorates, one for quality assurance and one for accreditation, which were headed by Ray Marks and Michael Ridley respectively. Later, during 1987, a third directorate was added to the NCVQ's internal structure when Gilbert Jessup was recruited from the MSC to become Director of Research and Development. The NCVQ was given an annual budget of approximately £3 million and, in line with the expectation of the 1986 White Paper, it was anticipated that by the start of the 1990-91 financial year it would become self-financing through income raised from the charge made on awards accredited as NVQs. The objective of financial self-sufficiency was perceived to be crucial by the leadership of the new NCVQ because it was hoped that this would, when it came, give the organization a strong degree of independence from government intervention and any future Treasury strictures.[9]

One of the first actions of the new NCVQ was the preparation and publication of a document that highlighted its 'purposes and aims' in early 1987

(NCVQ, 1987a). It restated the nature and importance of the tasks that had been given to the NCVQ by the White Paper, and it identified two principal 'thrusts' to the new organization's work: to 'design and implement a new national framework for vocational qualifications' and to 'get agreed national standards of occupational competence' (p. 5). It was emphasized that the NCVQ would not be responsible for awarding qualifications, but would 'work with established examining and awarding bodies to reform the existing vocational qualifications framework and introduce new simplified arrangements' (p. 5). At the outset of the NCVQ's work, then, it was envisaged that it would 'hallmark' existing vocational awards, and place them at the appropriate level in the national framework it had been charged with developing, once they had been amended and based more explicitly on agreed national standards of competence. The document noted that:

> The name and style National Vocational Qualification (NVQ) will be accorded to qualifications accredited by the NCVQ and awarded by bodies it has approved. A national framework for vocational qualifications will be introduced which will incorporate these qualifications, modified and updated to meet national standards of occupational competence, within a simple structure of levels.
>
> (NCVQ, 1987a, p. 6)

The remit of the NCVQ, then, was to develop a framework of vocational qualifications within which existing awards could be posted, once they had been reformed along competence-based lines. It was on this reading of the NCVQ's remit that its resources and business plan had been calculated. The prospect of a financially self-sufficient NCVQ was therefore seen to be feasible, since policy-makers assumed that it would work closely with the existing providers of vocational qualifications to create the new framework, and thus begin to raise income at an early stage.

Conclusion

In this chapter we have examined the way in which pressures for the reform of the vocational qualifications system and the imperative for proper YTS certification led to the inception of NVQ policy and the establishment of the NCVQ in late 1986, following the recommendations made by the *Review of Vocational Qualifications in England and Wales* Working Group and the provisions of the subsequent White Paper, *Working Together* (MSC/DES, 1986; DE/DES, 1986). While the 1981 New Training Initiative had provided a blueprint for policy innovation in this area, the needs of the YTS provided the short-term, and necessary, impetus for reform. There can be little doubt, however, that both the RVQ Working Group's members and MSC officials were desirous of change that would be of more general significance. Thus the Working Group recommended the establishment of a national framework of vocational qualifications, based on competence in employment, within which existing awards, suitably modified if appropriate, could be inserted by a new National Council. Implicitly, the NCVQ was conceptualized as a regulatory body, albeit with few powers to regulate, in that it was charged with establishing a framework of vocational qualifications and with ensuring that awards placed within that framework met certain designated criteria in respect of quality. Such a policy aim would seem to be largely uncontroversial. Indeed, more than one member of the Working Group with whom we spoke referred to the RVQ proposals as being like 'motherhood and apple pie'. The recommendations potentially appealed to the providers of existing awards, because it was assumed that the new national framework would embrace their products and presumably give them value-added status. Employers' representatives could support the thrust of the proposed reforms as well, given that it was suggested that vocational qualifications would become founded to a greater degree on the occupational competence of their employees.

Nevertheless, while the RVQ's officials and Chairman did a good job in getting the representatives of a diverse range of interest groups to agree to the production of a unanimous report, the Working Group's recommendations can be read in different ways. One interpretation of the proposals suggests a limited degree of change, with the establishment of a new framework centred around existing vocational qualifications, gradually modified to become based on competence. This is what most policy-makers envisaged. However, the Working Group's report can also be read as implying more radical change. That awards would not be accredited as NVQs unless they were explicitly competence-based. This ambiguity was left for the new NCVQ to work through during the initial implementation of NVQ policy.

Notes

1 Although see CPRS (1980).
2 For example, the National Craftsman's Certificate in the motor vehicle and repair industry, which had been jointly developed by the Road Transport ITB and City and Guilds.
3 This was a group of consultants under contract to the MSC. They had previously worked on the development of standards in the meat industry for use in YTS and this experience was used to advise on standards development in other industry sectors.
4 The importance of a coherent framework of vocational qualifications that embraced existing awards was also articulated by the RVQ Working Group's Chief Officer, George Tolley, in a talk given to the Royal Society of Arts in April 1986. Tolley envisaged that qualifications 'of existing bodies will be fitted within this framework through the process of accreditation' (Tolley, 1986, p. 714). Moreover, John Barnes of City and Guilds wrote of the Working Group's preference for 'an evolutionary rather than a revolutionary solution to the problem' (*City and Guilds Broadsheet* February 1986, p. 2).

5 The Working Group proposed that a five-level framework be established in order to provide 'a classification and hallmarking system for vocational qualifications that will secure standards against national criteria and simplify routes of progression to higher levels of achievement' (MSC/DES, 1986, pp. 26–7). The proposed levels were:

Level I   Occupational competence in performing a range of tasks under supervision.

Level II   Occupational competence in performing a wider range of more demanding tasks with limited supervision.

Level III   Occupational competence required for satisfactory, responsible performance in a defined occupation or range of jobs.

Level IV   Competence to design and specify designed tasks, products or processes and to accept responsibility for the work of others.

Level V should reflect competence at professional level, with mastery of a range of relevant knowledge and the ability to apply it at a higher level than IV (MSC/DES, 1986, p. 26).

It was anticipated that levels one to four of the framework would be in place by 1991.

6 It is interesting to note that the Working Group's Interim Report (MSC/DES, 1986) was quite cool about the value of voluntary arrangements. In the words of one of its members, in the end 'the creation and implementation of the NVQ framework was seen as sufficient to reduce confusion' itself (Cross, 1991, p. 171).

7 These were to:

- identify and bring about the changes necessary to achieve the specification and implementation of standards of occupational competence to meet the needs of the full range of employment, including the needs of the self-employed;
- design, monitor and adapt as necessary the new NVQ framework;
- secure the implementation of that framework by accrediting the provision of approved certifying bodies;
- secure arrangements for quality assurance;
- maintain effective liaison with those bodies having responsibilities for qualifications which give entry to, and progression within and from, the system of vocational qualifications into higher education and the higher levels of professional qualifications;
- collect, analyse and make available information on vocational qualifications and secure the operation of an effective, comprehensive and dependable data base;
- undertake or arrange to be undertaken research and development where necessary to discharge these functions;
- promote the interests of vocational education and training and, in particular, of vocational qualifications, and to disseminate good practice.

(DE/DES, 1986, p. 19)

8 The then Paymaster-General, Kenneth Clarke, reportedly announced in the House of Commons that the NCVQ 'will set up a framework into which all the qualifications from the certifying bodies can be fitted so that they can be accredited by the Council and people can relate exactly how one relates to another' (quoted in *City and Guilds Broadsheet*, October 1986, p. 3).

9 See House of Lords (1990) for a statement on the importance of self-sufficiency to the NCVQ by De Ville.

4 Ambiguity Resolved: The Implementation of NVQ Policy 1987–1989

Introduction

In this chapter we will examine how the NCVQ interpreted its remit and acted to implement NVQ policy between 1987 and 1989. It had been charged with establishing a new national framework of vocational qualifications within which existing awards could be slotted, and accredited as 'NVQs', once they had been modified to become more competence-based. Indeed, this is what the NCVQ initially understood its role to be (NCVQ, 1987a). Three factors affected the NCVQ's capacity to effect its remit, however. First, at the time the NCVQ was set up in October 1986, no satisfactory method of assessing occupational competence existed. What development work there had been was based entirely on the requirements of YTS certification and had only been running for a short period of time. Second, despite some misgivings, the RVQ Working Group had recommended that the NCVQ should carry through its reform work on a voluntary basis. While this was necessary if its proposals were to receive government backing, it meant that in pursuing change the NCVQ had to rely on the strengths of its arguments, the attractiveness of the new system and the voluntary co-operation of educational bodies and employers. Third, the RVQ Working Group had also proposed that, once the national framework of vocational qualifications had been put in place at levels one to four, the NCVQ should be funded by a combination of levy income from accreditations and government grants. The government, however, specified that it should become self-sufficient by 1990–91. These factors might not have been important if the NCVQ had adhered to its original remit. However, the ambiguity of the RVQ Working Group's proposals gave the NCVQ the scope to attempt to initiate change of a more profound kind.

The Development of the NVQ Framework

At its first council meeting in the autumn of 1986 the NCVQ council set up an 'NVQ Planning Group' that would advise on the broad design criteria of the proposed new framework of vocational qualifications. The NVQ Planning Group – which included representatives from industry and the major examining and validating bodies – met on a number of occasions during late 1986 and early 1987, and it eventually reported back to the NCVQ council in February 1987. Discussions in the Planning Group were dominated by the efforts of the employers' representatives to assert that the needs of industry were prominent in the new system. Thus a strong push was given to establishing a modular system of qualifications, akin to the one which was being developed in Scotland with the implementation of the 'Scottish Action Plan'. It was felt that such a system would offer more flexibility to employers, and thus be more attractive to them, insofar as it would allow them to 'pick and mix' units of qualifications in a way that they considered was appropriate. This proposal was opposed by the NCVQ, however, on the grounds that such a modular system would militate against the development of a truly national framework of vocational qualifications – one which offered coherence, transparency and the possibility for comparison with systems in other countries. Related to this was the matter of NVQ 'levels'. Employers' representatives, and some officials, were opposed to the concept of the four proposed NVQ levels. As with the 'pick and mix' approach, their preference was for a less rigid and hierarchical system, not least because of ongoing worries about the potential industrial relations implications of a levels-based framework.

Notwithstanding their failure to establish a modular system based on units, the employers' representatives emphasized – and had accepted – the proposition that NVQs should be founded, as far as possible, upon the assessment of occupational competence in the workplace. This is an important point because at the outset of its work there was a strong feeling within the fledgling NCVQ that its job was, as we have already noted in Chapter 3, to review the provision of bodies such as BTEC, City and Guilds, the RSA and so on, work with them to make their awards more competence-based and then place the amended qualifications within the new national framework. Employers' representatives had, however, expressed their great dissatisfaction with the existing products of these bodies, and their preference was for new arrangements to be put in place, ones which they felt would be more closely related to the needs of employment. One of them argued that they wanted 'entirely new qualifications, by definition they had to be new. Everybody referred to them as new qualifications [and] that their requirements were defined by employment.'

By early 1987, then, there was already pressure on the NCVQ to engage in a more wide-ranging reform of the vocational qualifications system than policy-makers had originally anticipated. Nevertheless, the NCVQ increased its work carefully and as a way of furthering developments it decided, in February 1987, to establish a number of sectoral project groups that would, it was hoped, produce recommendations for awards that could be accredited as NVQs, in line with the broad guidance produced by the NVQ

Planning Group, and thus get underway the process of building the framework of vocational qualifications. In a paper to the NCVQ council on 'Initial Accreditation', Michael Ridley stated that these project groups should be set up 'as a means of testing out the NVQ framework in a number of occupational areas and to look at existing qualifications and consider how they might fit into the NVQ structure'. The project groups met during the spring and early summer of 1987. Comprising representatives from employers, the major awarding bodies and NCVQ development officers, they were set up in a number of areas including: electrical contracting, hotel and catering, motor vehicle maintenance and repair, engineering manufacture, and heating and ventilating, among others.

In the summer of 1987 the various project groups reported back to the NCVQ with the advice that there was little within the existing qualifications' arrangements in their respective sectors that would meet the NVQ design criteria as they were then – somewhat loosely – drawn up.[1] An NCVQ official described the rationale underpinning the establishment of the project groups and the impact of their findings in the following way:

> [B]y then we'd got some idea of the framework . . . but it was in very loose terms, and we said on the basis of that guidance which of the qualifications and training standards would you advise us to adopt? . . . I think we gave them something like four or six months. Most of them reported back in that time, but to our utter amazement all [of the] groups said that there aren't any. They claimed, for whatever reason, that of the existing arrangements there were none they would recommend to NCVQ as being examples of what we should do in the future . . . We thought we were going to choose the best standards, put those in the framework and add to it on a kind of evolving situation as it were. But then we were given the advice that there was nothing to put in the framework.

Although it had been in existence for only a matter of months, pressure from influential employers' representatives on the NVQ Planning Group for new arrangements in respect of vocational qualifications – in particular the notion that they should be based explicitly on standards of competence derived from employment – led to a change in the way in which the NCVQ interpreted its remit. On being advised that, in a number of important occupational areas, there was nothing available that would meet the broad NVQ guidelines that had been drawn up by the Planning Group, the NCVQ began to encourage and oversee the development of new qualifications. In those areas where there had been a paucity of nationally recognized vocational qualifications, the development of new qualifications would have been an inevitable outcome of the NCVQ's work in any event. However, the NCVQ adopted this approach across the board. Indeed, there was also pressure from within the organization itself, particularly among officials, for more fundamental reform. They were also dissatisfied with the nature of existing vocational qualifications, in particular the extent to which they were predicated on the examination of knowledge, and so a 'clean sheet' approach became the favoured way of moving forward. An NCVQ official summarized the organization's change of direction in the following way:

> Certainly civil servants at that time saw the whole enterprise as not so much starting from scratch and developing something completely new, but developing a criteria-driven system into which existing things could fit and perhaps new things could be designed. What we rapidly found, and this was certainly emerging by the middle of 1987, was that that approach would not work. That we had to go back to a much more root and branch way of doing things and the notion of simple criteria wouldn't work.

If it was going to develop properly a system of new vocational qualifications based explicitly upon standards of occupational competence, rather than design a new framework of vocational qualifications and place existing awards within it, the NCVQ needed to do two things. First, it had to construct effective working relationships with the bodies designing occupational standards of competence. Second, it had to establish much more explicit criteria by which the new qualifications could be defined as NVQs.

The Development of the Lead Body Structure

In respect of the first of these tasks, part of the NCVQ's remit had been 'to secure standards of occupational competence and base qualifications on them' (DE/DES, 1986). The MSC, however, held on to the responsibility for managing the occupational standards programme and liaised with the prospective industry 'lead bodies', which would be responsible for producing the standards on a sectoral basis. Given that the MSC had already embarked upon a standards programme in 1986 and had developed close links with employers and their representative bodies, it was considered that the NCVQ should deal solely with the development of the qualifications framework. According to an MSC official,

> [the] NCVQ was a totally new body. It had got no track record, the work on standards was underway and the links with industry were through the MSC. I think it is true to say that the decision was simply not to upset what appeared to be a process that was going pretty well and one that could be managed by good links between the two organisations.

The NCVQ, noting the large amount of money which the MSC deployed through the standards programme and the control this potentially gave it over much of the UK's industrial training, appreciated the MSC's unwillingness to give up the responsibility for the management of the development of occupational standards. Yet by concentrating more explicitly on the development of new qualifications, the NCVQ became increasingly dependent on the products of the standards programme, a process over which it had no control. This might not have mattered so much, had it not been for some of the practical difficulties that accompanied the development of the lead bodies.

The MSC had produced an action plan to stimulate the evolution of a lead body network. MSC officials also held seminars with employers' representatives to discover their views on the prospective bodies and to encourage their participation. By April 1989 about 120 lead bodies had been established (*Educa*, April 1989). They could be classified into three broad groups: those which were part of a surviving ITB (e.g. engineering, construction); those which came under the auspices of an NSTO (e.g. chemicals); and those which were entirely new creations and needed a considerable amount of MSC support, usually in cross-sectoral occupations (e.g. the Care Sector Consortium and the Administration, Business and Commerical Training Group). The emergence of such a large number of lead bodies was a cause of problems from an early stage of the implementation of NVQ policy. While the RVQ Working Group had recommended that industry bodies should be established to develop standards of competence, it foresaw that no more than about 20 of these organizations would need to be set up. An MSC official recalled:

> I think if you'd have asked members of RVQ at the time the majority, almost everyone perhaps, would have said that they did not really envisage industry lead bodies just being the lot that eventually came out of the woodwork, some of them.

Why did so many lead bodies come into existence? To a large degree this was a function of the renewed ethos of voluntarism that began to characterize labour market policy in general in the UK at this time (for example, see DE, 1988).[2] The large number of lead bodies reflected the policy imperative that employers should stipulate their requirements, and come together to develop their own arrangements, in the emerging training market. According to another MSC official:

> It was very strongly felt that wherever employers could get together and argue that they could justify a qualification – almost if they wanted one, that was enough – then the department would work with them. I mean the deal was they had to show willing and believe that they needed the standards and could point to throughput of qualifications.

Furthermore, there was a feeling within the MSC at the time that the existence of a large number of lead bodies was a positive feature because it reflected the enthusiasm within industry about the development of standards of competence and showed that it was not a top-down, bureaucratic imposition. The MSC provided lead bodies with half of the funds for their standards development work (DE, 1991). The contribution of the lead bodies themselves could be, and mostly was, comprised of donations in kind, for example, the time given up by employers' representatives although in some cases, such as the cross-sectoral bodies, where it was more difficult to bring employers together, the MSC had a rather greater input.

The way in which the lead bodies were established, however, militated against the production of broad-based occupational standards, ones that would both reflect and encourage flexibility and transferability in employment. For a start, the effect of having such a large number of these bodies drawing up standards of competence for their particular sectors was that the resulting products became narrowly occupationally specific. For example, an employers' representative who was involved in the implementation of NVQ policy at this time recalled that, while he could 'sell the concept' to the companies in his own discrete sector, they would balk at the idea of having to cooperate with firms even in other closely related sectors. Moreover, the prevailing ethos of voluntarism, to which we have already referred, meant that the individual lead bodies could not be compelled to include broader 'core skills' within the standards they were producing. If employers and their representatives, in a voluntary system, were mandated to develop broader standards that might not reflect the immediate needs of their sector, then the job of ensuring their involvement would be made more demanding. There was also a parallel concern that, if the standards were made too exacting, then this would inhibit access by individuals.

So far, then, we have identified three factors that encouraged the nascent NVQs to become rather narrow and occupationally specific before the NCVQ had even produced its first substantive criteria for the qualifications. First, employers' representatives lobbied effectively for a new system of qualifications in which the interests of employment were privileged over those of education. Second, the large number of industry lead bodies meant that, when occupational standards came to be developed, they did not in the main reflect a broad range of job roles. Third, the breadth that the inclusion of mandatory 'core skills' might have brought about was lost because lead bodies could not be compelled to include them, and therefore mostly did not. Added to all this, the division of responsibilities between the MSC, which managed the occupational standards programme, and the NCVQ, which was trying to elaborate a framework of vocational qualifications based on these standards, did not always run smoothly.

For example, the NCVQ was faced with the problems that accompanied the growth of a 'patchwork' of lead bodies: it was felt that there were too many of them, they were uncoordinated, and in many cases their capacity to do a proper job could be questioned. In its attempt to develop a coherent framework of vocational qualifications, this did not help the NCVQ at all as one of its officials recalled:

> [W]e had a group setting standards for chimney sweeps. We had the Care Sector Consortium who looked after the entire care sector, which doesn't make sense. You know, you might have a couple of hundred chimney sweeps – literally, I'm not joking – chimney sweeps for one standard and millions of people in another. It didn't make sense.

Given the division of responsibilities within the system, moreover, the NCVQ found that its progress in developing the NVQ framework, particularly once it had adopted the policy of encouraging new qualifications, was largely dependent on the quantity and the quality of the occupational standards that the MSC administered programme produced. Indeed an MSC official acknowledged that:

> The important thing was that there was actually quite a distinction between the department, which was very much in the driving seat on this, meaning the department and the MSC, as opposed to the NCVQ. NCVQ were really very passive in this. They were at the end of the process and they had to classify and accredit what came through. They didn't have much chance to influence that.

There was a considerable degree of frustration within the NCVQ that its capacity to achieve its objectives was constrained by a dependency on the MSC. For its part, the MSC, even as late as 1987, was still a powerful body responsible for operating high-profile national youth and adult training initiatives for which it wanted appropriate qualifications. Its officials became concerned at what they felt was a slow throughput of qualifications from the NCVQ, particularly for inclusion in its programmes, perhaps because they still thought that it was reviewing the state of the existing provision and constructing a framework around that. An often strained relationship arose between the NCVQ and the MSC at a high level, something that was exacerbated by personal differences between officials from the respective organizations.

NVQ Methodology and Accreditation

Meanwhile, during 1987 the NCVQ embarked upon the task of developing specific criteria for NVQs. There was no adequate methodology for defining occupational competence, and the assessment of it to produce qualifications, available when the NCVQ considered its first prospective accreditations during 1987. Given the change in the NCVQ's remit – it was now overseeing the development of new qualifications – the production of assessment criteria and guidance was clearly a priority for the organization. In May 1987 Gilbert Jessup was recruited to the NCVQ from the MSC's Quality Branch to become its first Director of Research and Development. With other officials he began work on developing specific NVQ assessment criteria and guidance, and based this work on the 'standard tasks', or 'competence objectives' approach as it had now become known, which the MSC had pioneered within the YTS.

After some months' developmental work, the first NVQ Criteria and Guidance document was published in January 1988, coinciding with a major promotional conference which the NCVQ hosted in London. It was envisaged that, to be accredited as an NVQ, an award would consist of a series of defined 'units of competence' within each of which there would be further 'elements of competence'. In order to attain these elements and units of competence an individual would be required to be assessed on pre-scribed 'performance criteria' in work situations (NCVQ, 1988). Although 'the skills, knowledge and understanding which underpin such perfomance in employment' would be incorporated within the competence-based units, 'this does not imply building into the requirement of an NVQ knowledge and understanding beyond the needs of employment to which the award relates' (pp. 8, 10). The justification for this approach was founded upon the belief that, if NVQs demanded additional knowledge and understanding requirements, this would hinder access to the qualifications by individuals. It also accorded with the preference of influential employers for a system of vocational qualifications based on job-specific standards of competence.

The tightness of the 1988 NVQ criteria further impelled the NCVQ to oversee the development of new qualifications because no existing awards could meet its increasingly rigid specifications. Moreover, the emphasis on the assessment of competence in real work situations excluded many of the huge number of awards delivered through further education colleges.[3] This provoked a substantial amount of disquiet among the major providers of existing vocational awards. There was a considerable degree of support for the concept of competence-based qualifications in general; however, the emphasis that was placed on the need for assessment to take place in the workplace, and what was percieved as the marginalization of knowledge and understanding, provoked accusations of 'zealotry'.[4] An RSA official argued that:

> I think there was a particular kind of ideology permeating some of those people which I don't have a lot of time for because I think it has wasted a huge amount of time, effort and resources. And that is unless it is actually assessed in the workplace at a real job it isn't worthwhile. That seemed to me to be based on no kind of research, no kind of evidence . . . but there was that view around and so almost anything which didn't match that they didn't want to know about.

While this might appear to be a somewhat understandable reaction, coming as it does from the representative of an organization that was potentially having its market threatened by the new NVQs, even employers and their representatives found the criteria somewhat difficult to comprehend. At the promotional conference the NCVQ held for employers and others in January 1988, a considerable degree of scepticism was exhibited about the value of the new arrangements (*Educa*, March 1988, pp. 10–11). Moreover, MSC officials were dissatisfied with the competence-based approach that the NCVQ had adopted, as one who was closely involved with the organization recalled:

> As I see it, it moved increasingly towards what I would term a task-based orientation. With an emphasis on competence being able to do the job as it now exists in terms of the tasks that now need to be done, in order to satisfy the particular skills to undertake the tasks that are required as of the moment. Rather than a competence which was concerned and, in my view, ought to be concerned with the development of those core skills that are more transferable, more generic, and can provide greater adaptability than a task-based operation.

By the beginning of 1988 the NCVQ thus had in place a methodology for the definition of competence and its assessment, albeit one that was to attract widespread critical comment. But it now had barely two years left in which to establish the NVQ framework and meet the target of being self funding by 1990–91. This target had been premised on the much simpler task of developing an NVQ system based largely on existing awards, modified as necessary, whereas now the NCVQ faced the greater challenge of establishing an entirely new competence-based qualifications system. During 1988 the slow pace of accreditations, and the effect this was having on the organization's finances, became a matter of concern to members of the NCVQ council. Both the Treasury and government ministers were unwilling to release the NCVQ from its obligation to become self-sufficient through the charge it made on the awards it would accredit, although the target date was put back to 1992. As an MSC offical recalled, the nascent NCVQ faced considerable pressure to have a framework of vocational qualifications quickly in place:

> The Treasury quickly indicated some pretty serious limitations to the amount of money available and the length of time the Council would be able to carry on without covering costs. There was a jitteryness there which began to develop at quite an early stage. It was a most unfortunate jitteryness because really the Council did need to be given a good solid five years without being pushed up against a wall and told you've got to deliver in terms of thousands of qualifications.

Given that it did not publish its NVQ criteria until January 1988 and that there would inevitably be a time lag before qualifications that met its stated requirements could be produced, the NCVQ decided to accredit qualifications on a 'conditional' basis. Existing vocational awards were approved on the proviso that the respective awarding body, or bodies, would then work to make them consonant with the NVQ criteria. Thus the first accredited NVQs emanated from the work that the sectoral project groups had been undertaking during the spring and summer of 1987. While we have already seen that they could not recommend any existing awards as being suitable for the NCVQ's prospective framework of competence-based qualifications, in June 1987 it was nonetheless decided to approve certain existing awards in Electrical Contracting, Hotel and Catering, Motor Vehicle Maintenance and Repair, and Retail Travel as NVQs.[5]

At this time all of the prospective NVQ awards went to the full NCVQ council for consideration, although towards the end of 1987 a sub-committee of the council – the Accreditation Advisory Committee – was established to examine forthcoming submissions and to advise and make recommendations in respect of their quality. With explicit NVQ criteria now available, it was envisaged that awards that had been conditionally accredited by the NCVQ would be altered over a period of time to meet these specifications. Officials from both the NCVQ and the MSC were unhappy with the concept of 'conditional accreditation' because they were seen as inferior in quality and provided, at the inception of NVQ policy, poor examples of the new qualifications. Although it allowed some BTEC provision in business and finance (see p. 80) into the NVQ framework, for the most part the awards that were given conditional accreditation in this manner were those which the YCB had recommended for use in YTS programmes. As two senior NCVQ figures recalled, the pressure to build the framework meant that:

> [T]herefore there was only one way forward and that was to build on the YTS course . . . So then it was low level stuff and their training was based on low level work.

> [W]e had to take a decision whether we would in fact accept slightly less than perfect NVQ qualifications and accredit them provisionally, or whether we should wait for years until we had qualifications that were really based on these standards . . . rightly or wrongly we decided to go for conditional accreditation, which was of frequently rather narrowly based NVQs.

Therefore not only did the NCVQ adopt a methodology for defining and assessing competence that was derived from the technical work that the MSC had initiated on standards development for the YTS, but the pressure for the rapid establishment of the NVQ framework compelled it to use products designed for the YTS for a large proportion of its earliest NVQ accreditations. Given that a large part of the YTS was targeted at trainees working at low levels in organizations, performing what were often menial tasks (Lee, 1989), this also ensured that the early NVQs became skewed towards a task-specific focus, reflecting the content of many YTS programmes.[6] Moreover, 'conditional accreditation' sent out a message to the providers of existing vocational qualifications that perhaps their awards were suitable for inclusion in the emerging framework of vocational qualifications after all. This was something they found rather appealing, since they believed that the move towards developing new qualifications as NVQs – based on the assessment of occupational competence in the workplace – could be construed as a vote of no confidence in their abilities.

The Awarding Body Network

It was anticipated that providers of existing vocational awards, of which BTEC, City and Guilds and the RSA were the most prominent, would have a major role in the development and implementation of the new NVQ system. Moreover, in the first few months of the NCVQ's existence during 1987, there was strong internal pressure for it to operate more directly through the vocational examining and validating bodies rather than the prospective lead bodies. This was consonant with the policy imperative that existing vocational awards, offered by BTEC, City and Guilds, the RSA and so on, would be amended and if necessary improved, and then placed in the emerging national framework. Yet for the reasons we outlined above, the NCVQ began to encourage the development of new awards as NVQs, ones that would be based on a particular concept of competence. To those working in the vocational examining and validating bodies at the time, the emphasis on the workplace as the sole location wherein competence could be assessed, and the disregard for the role of further education colleges, was typically seen as being another expression of the MSC's distrust of the educational establishment:

> I think there was a feeling . . . that organisations like City and Guilds had lost touch; that they've fallen into the pockets of colleges; that they were exploiting only the easy markets, i.e. the full-time student or students on one day a week apprenticeship programmes; and were all kind of sitting on their laurels.
>
> (City and Guilds official)

However, the examining and validating bodies could not be excluded from the nascent NVQ system. The satisfactory assessment and certification of work-based skills (or competences) was so clearly a crucial element of the new NVQs that the experience and know-how of these bodies had to be employed. According to another City and Guilds official:

Assessment and certification is [sic] a skilled activity and the only way you can get a good assessment and certification system is to use the resources that exist in the nation to be able to do that. [The] MSC had no experience in assessment and certification.

The need for their experience notwithstanding, the response of the vocational examining and validating bodies – or 'awarding bodies' as they became known – to the establishment of the NVQ system was mixed. Of the major national organizations both the RSA and City and Guilds publicly gave the NVQ policy their full support. For example, as early as the summer of 1987 the RSA had embarked on a review of all its awards, with the exception of its single subject certificates, and was beginning to align them with the NVQ levels (RSA, 1987). The most important awarding body support for the nascent NCVQ, however, came from City and Guilds (see Bush, 1993; Stevens, 1993). According to an NCVQ official the backing of City and Guilds was of great significance:

John Barnes [Director-General of City and Guilds] was crucial. I mean John . . . was the only one of the major awarding body chief executives who actually committed himself heart and soul to it and said, this is the way of the future, this is the way we're going to go. It'll cause problems, it'll cost a lot of money, but it's what we must do . . . [H]e did believe it and again that was a crucial element of support.

Importantly for the survival of NVQ policy, senior officials at City and Guilds, like John Barnes, had already recognized the value of vocational qualifications based on the assessment of an individual's competence and, as we have already seen, for a number of years previously, the organization had been adapting its awards accordingly. While City and Guilds were unhappy with the way in which the competence-based approach was coming to be applied by the NCVQ and the emerging employer-dominated lead bodies, particularly the fragmentation that was being encouraged by the MSC, its officials reasoned that it was their job to do their best to make it work in practice – to mitigate the more dogmatic principles about what constituted 'competence' that were then emanating from the NCVQ. There was also a somewhat less high-minded motive present. City and Guilds' officials were concerned with ensuring that their market position, as the UK's largest provider of vocational qualifications, was maintained. While City and Guilds were the most supportive of all the awarding bodies in respect of the NVQ system, internally at least this backing was often grudging.

There was a lot of suspicion about having an organisation which might have a role in regulating awarding bodies, although that word was never used at the time. But there was always this sense of frustration – resentment – at the operational levels that one often had to go outside to another organisation to get approval for what we had been doing for a hundred odd years. But the policy line was very clear. City and Guilds were big supporters of NCVQ and we had to be seen to be flying the flag, but really behind the scenes people were hedging their bets.

(City and Guilds official)

The final comment of this former City and Guilds official is intriguing insofar as it reflects the view among the awarding bodies – at that time widely held – that the NVQ policy was an ephemeral development, another initiative that, like so many that had been instituted by the MSC, was unlikely to have a long life. This was a prominent view within BTEC, which, unlike City and Guilds, was hostile to the NVQ policy from the beginning and for a considerable period of time declined to commit itself to the new vocational qualifications system.

While BTEC had participated in the 1985–86 Review of Vocational Qualifications through its then chief executive John Sellars, who had signed up to the final report, once the NCVQ was established it had developed increasing reservations about the direction of NVQ policy. BTEC submitted its own awards, and placing trust in the quality of their products, assumed that the NCVQ would set about slotting them into the emerging national system of vocational qualifications. BTEC did this on the not unreasonable assumption that the NCVQ's principal priority was to produce a framework within which existing awards could be placed and given the 'NVQ' kitemark. Very soon after coming into being, though, the NCVQ set out on a course of encouraging a new type of qualification, to be known as an 'NVQ'. Accordingly, the NCVQ refused to accredit BTEC's awards as NVQs because they did not meet the tight criteria that it had been developing for the new award. Other major awarding bodies, such as City and Guilds, while they had private doubts about the way in which NVQ policy was being implemented, worked to make the best of the system as it existed. BTEC, on the other hand, largely withdrew its cooperation (Guy, 1991).

BTEC actually submitted, formally, its own qualifications to say, well can we put these in the framework? And the answer was 'no' – scrap those and [develop] new ones. I'm simplifying it, but that's basically the position . . . we had an expectation following the Review of Vocational Qualifications that existing qualifications would be assessed against reasonable criteria and moved into a common national framework. NCVQ started in a very different approach by developing NVQs.

(BTEC official)

Bodies like City and Guilds and RSA by and large accepted the model, even though it didn't carry legislative force, and wanted to work with us, although even within their conception of things there were differences. We were, after all, a quango imposed upon them as they saw it. But other bodies, most notably BTEC, were positively resistant . . . I think BTEC felt they had already done what was required and it was really a matter largely of NCVQ accepting and rubber-stamping their qualifications. Part of the problem there was that some ministers and some civil servants talked as if that's really what they thought NCVQ was about: having a quick look, seeing if the qualification matched the rules and, if it did, stamping it and moving on.

(NCVQ official)

The initial refusal to accredit BTEC's awards as NVQs, and thereby place them within the framework, started a period of considerable tension between the NCVQ and BTEC that was not to be concluded until 1993. BTEC's opposition to the way in which the NCVQ had chosen to interpret its remit was founded on a number of grounds. First, its officials were wary of the threat to BTEC's income that the prospective greater competition in the market for vocational qualifications, particularly at levels three and four, might induce.[7] Second, implicit in the creation of the NCVQ was an intimation that, in the period since its creation as BEC and TEC, BTEC had been ineffectual in initiating and promoting a coherent system of vocational qualifications. An official from another awarding body observed that:

I think they felt that the whole thing was a vote of no confidence in BTEC because, after all, it had been set up to rationalise and be all-embracing in terms of . . . vocational qualifications. Yet here was a body being set up, which effectively was saying it wasn't doing that.

Third, and most importantly, there was a genuine belief within BTEC that the competence-based approach to the assessment of skills that the NCVQ was pioneering was fundamentally misconceived. It must be remembered that, in contrast to City and Guilds and the RSA, BTEC was not directly involved in assessment. Rather, it validated the courses offered by other educational bodies, such as further education colleges and universities, who carried out the requisite assessment themselves. Furthermore, given the nature of its coverage – business, finance and technician awards, many of which, for example, its Higher National Certificates (HNCs) and Diplomas (HNDs), were at tertiary level – BTEC considered itself to be an 'educational' body. It found, therefore, the dominance of the employer-led competence-based approach that was being heavily promoted by the MSC and especially the NCVQ rather more difficult to accommodate than did, say, City and Guilds, which was prominent in craft areas and saw itself as a body serving 'industry' rather than 'education'.

Importantly, moreover, at this time BTEC operated as a quango under the aegis of the DES, though its officials emphasized that it never used its departmental connections to fend off the overtures of the NCVQ and the MSC. Senior BTEC officials hoped that the NCVQ would be only a temporary phenomenon, although they realized that should it prove to be a less transient undertaking, then some cooperative mechanisms might need to be developed. One of them recalled that:

> BTEC was trying to formulate a policy of how they could work with NCVQ, buying themselves enough time to decide how, strategically, they should be positioning themselves to come to [a] sort of accommodation. In the short-term BTEC didn't want to know anything about it.

During 1987 and 1988 Peter Thompson, Oscar De Ville and members of the NCVQ council held informal meetings with the leadership of BTEC in an attempt to reach an agreement. The policy of 'conditional accreditation' of some BTEC awards as NVQs was one outcome of these discussions. Some of the very earliest NVQ accreditations – such as a level three award in Motor Vehicle Repair – had involved BTEC as an awarding body, but this had been in a partnership with City and Guilds and others. The NCVQ had promoted the concept of 'conditional accreditation' because of its desperate need to fill the framework of vocational qualifications in order to begin generating some income. Thus BTEC awards – such as its 'First' awards in Business and Finance – were accredited as NVQs without being adapted to meet the tight competence-based criteria that the NCVQ formally required. Further evidence of growing cooperation between BTEC and the NCVQ became evident during 1988, when they issued a joint statement in September that committed them to working together to improve qualifications. Progress in this area was slow, however, and was not helped by fundamental differences in the outlook of the two organizations over key issues, something that was noted by a joint BTEC–NCVQ working group that met during 1989. It found that, while their relationship was good, differences between the two bodies persisted on matters as significant as: the utilization of standards derived from the lead bodies; the aspiration of the NCVQ to regulate BTEC's awards; the scope of the NVQ criteria; and the rigidity of the system of work-based assessment of competence being promoted by the NCVQ. It was hoped that the appointment of three new NCVQ council members in 1989 – John Capey, Barry Barker and John Spence – who were also members of the BTEC council might have brought about a *rapprochement*. However, in January 1990 the issue of BTEC's continuing reluctance to embrace the NVQ system led Peter Thompson to request an intervention from the then Secretary of State for Education, John McGregor.

BTEC was able to keep its provision largely detached from the NVQ system because of the voluntary ethos that underpinned the NCVQ's work. The NCVQ had no powers to compel awarding bodies to convert their products into competence-based NVQs so that they could be placed in the emerging national framework of vocational qualifications. Nor could the NCVQ prevent the growth of new awarding bodies that began to develop prospective NVQs based on lead body designed standards. Indeed, many of these newly-formed lead bodies chose to award qualifications in their own right.[8] Furthermore, while the construction of working relationships with the principal awarding bodies – BTEC, City and Guilds and the RSA – was clearly a priority for the NCVQ, it soon discovered that a policy decision would need to be taken in respect of the smaller, regional examining bodies, for example the Welsh Joint Education Committee. Thus the matter was raised of how far the NCVQ was able to go in regulating the activity and existence of awarding bodies. Although one of the NCVQ's 'key purposes' was to 'approve bodies making accredited awards' (NCVQ, 1987a), from very early on the council was reluctant to place restrictions on the awarding bodies – presumably because it not only lacked the formal power to regulate them, but was also unwilling to upset them and thus potentially lose valuable income – and the matter was left to one side during 1987 while other tasks dominated its agenda. During 1988, however, the regulation of awarding bodies became a more prominent issue once again, most notably in the context of proposed NVQs in Business Administration.

The MSC had established the ABCTG (Administration, Business and Commercial Training Group), which had taken on the task of developing occupational standards in the business administration sector. Its first offerings, at levels one and two, became available in 1988. The RSA, LCCI (London Chamber of Commerce), Pitmans and later BTEC (with their 'conditionally accredited' First awards in Business and Finance) began to work on producing qualifications based on these standards. All of these bodies could reasonably claim to have experience in producing qualifications in business administration and related areas. However, City and Guilds also developed qualifications based on the ABCTG standards and proposed to have them accredited as NVQs at levels one and two. This caused concern within the RSA, and prompted a considerable amount of discussion within the NCVQ, because this was an entirely new area for City and Guilds. While the NCVQ considered that the rationalization of awarding bodies, and the concomitant diminution of competing qualifications (although not competition between awarding bodies), was a desirable aim, the NCVQ felt that it should not attempt to obstruct City and Guilds from expanding its market. It was held that if a reputable body offered prospective qualifications for accreditation as NVQs, based on standards of competence derived by an appropriate lead body and meeting the NVQ criteria in other respects, then the NCVQ could not turn its submission down.

The case of the Business Administration NVQs prompted the NCVQ to try to seek voluntary agreement among the awarding bodies regarding the establishment of respective 'spheres of influence'. However, in a voluntary system the NCVQ could only move forward by reaching mutual agreement among competing organizations, who were not only protective of their own independence, but were also anxious to maintain, or even augment, their market position and income flow. The presence of these forceful interest groups combined with the lack of powers exhibited by the NCVQ, and its insistence on developing new qualifications as NVQs, led to the early failure to bring about one of the key objectives of the 1985–86 *Review of Vocational Qualifications in England and Wales*: the establishment of a coherent and transparent vocational qualifications system. The NCVQ's desire to establish what it envisaged as a truly national framework of vocational qualifications was also frustrated by the resistance that greeted its attempts to extend its remit to Scotland.

Scotland

Given the scale of change being implemented in the 'Scottish Action Plan', it had been decided that Scotland should be excluded from the remit of the 1985–86 RVQ. Nevertheless, although the implementation of NVQ policy was restricted initially to England, Wales and Northern Ireland, at the time of the 1986 White Paper *Working Together* (DE/DES, 1986) a decision was made to review the relationship between the Scottish system and that being developed by the NCVQ in the rest of the UK after two to three years had elapsed. As early as the beginning of 1988 the NCVQ had begun to anticipate the review that was due later that year, and its officials began to consider ways of extending the NVQ system to north of the border.

> They [NCVQ] had very clear ambitions and in the early days there were extremely . . . strained relationships between SCOTVEC and the NCVQ – we just didn't get on.
>
> (SCOTVEC official)

In line with the promise to review the position of Scotland in relation to the NVQ system, the Scottish Education Department (SED), part of the Scottish Office, published a consultation paper in August 1988. While it recognized the value of having in place a wholly 'national' framework of vocational qualifications and the initiatives that the NCVQ had set in train, it emphasized nonetheless the distinctiveness of the emerging Scottish system and the way in which it was rooted in the sphere of education. Thus the then Secretary of State for Scotland, Malcolm Rifkind, noted that:

> The need to maintain the momentum of these Scottish reforms is as strong as it was in 1986 when the NCVQ was set up. I am clear that

any change must not undermine Scotland's considerable achievements in the field of vocational qualifications.

(SED, 1988)

Nevertheless, it was suggested that, while SCOTVEC might not wish to have its awards regulated by another body, and presumably an 'English' one at that, it might identify additional benefits that might accrue from NCVQ accreditation. Despite the obligation to seek out views formally, the tone of the consultation document itself could not have inspired any confidence in the prospect of the NCVQ unproblematically extending its remit to Scotland.

In early September 1988, Peter Thompson and Michael Ridley travelled to Scotland where they had meetings with representatives of the Scottish CBI and with SED officials. They were encouraged to be flexible in the matter of the extension of the NCVQ's remit and, in the discussions with officials, the concept of a 'Scottish Advisory Committee' was floated as a way of maintaining a distinctive Scottish aspect within a system that applied to the UK as a whole. The notion of just such a dedicated 'Scottish Committee', which would be chaired by a Scottish member of the National Council and composed of Scottish representatives, received more formal expression in the NCVQ's response to the SED's consultation document later that month. The NCVQ also stressed the importance of establishing a unified system of vocational qualifications, to apply to the UK as a whole, the consistency and transparency of which, it was argued, would be of benefit not only to employers, but also, ultimately, to SCOTVEC as well.

Unfortunately for the NCVQ, even these adulterated proposals generated a considerable degree of hostility in Scotland. Indeed only one organization – the Scottish Further and Higher Education Association – expressed approval for the extension of the NCVQ's remit to Scotland, and even it was obliged to rescind its support after protests at its annual general meeting in November. SCOTVEC remained implacably opposed. Its officials considered that the role of the NCVQ would be superfluous north of the border because, in SCOTVEC, there already existed a body that oversaw a single framework of vocational qualifications and was responsible for quality assurance. Nevertheless, SCOTVEC also indicated that it would be willing to work more closely with the NCVQ in developing qualifications that might fit into the newly emerging NVQ framework.

Unsurprisingly, in December 1988 Malcolm Rifkind announced that the NVQ system would not be extended to cover Scotland. Senior NCVQ figures were disappointed about the outcome, although they took some comfort from ascribing it to increasing 'nationalism' north of the border. Given the political climate – during the 1980s resentment at the imposition of Conservative polices in Scotland grew considerably, and this was reflected in rising support for the Scottish National Party (SNP) – perhaps the NCVQ were rather over-sanguine in thinking that Scottish organizations and interest groups would submit readily to regulation by an 'English' body. This was at the same time as the hated 'poll tax' was being piloted in Scotland (Butler et al., 1994). Certainly, government ministers recognized the difficulties inherent in this area of policy:

> I think the Scottish authorities, education authorities and the Scottish Office and so on were never at all sure that they wanted to go along with anything that was invented in England.

The NCVQ considered that it would be pointless to devote much more time to the issue of Scotland. Nevertheless, Peter Thompson was asked by the council to prepare a paper exploring ways of moving forward and, with other senior members of the NCVQ's staff and Oscar De Ville, entered into discussions with SCOTVEC and SED staff during the early months of 1989. Although a paragraph referring to the existence and role of SCOTVEC in Scotland had to be removed from the updated version of the *National Vocational Qualifications: Criteria and Guidance* document that was published in March 1989, it was hoped that a joint NCVQ–SCOTVEC statement might be produced that would indicate how the organizations might co-operate in future. The eventual launch of Scottish Vocational Qualifications (SVQs) is examined in Chapter 5.

The Qualifications of the Professional Bodies

Soon after the NCVQ was established, in April 1987 Lord Young asked it to investigate how the awards of professional bodies could be articulated within the NVQ framework. Following this lead, Peter Thompson held meetings with officials from the Privy Council, the government department responsible for overseeing matters relating to bodies with royal charters, and the UK – Inter Professional Group (UK-IPG), an umbrella organization that represented many of the UK's leading professional institutions. Following these discussions, in August 1987 the NCVQ produced a consultative document – *Professional Bodies, Their Qualifications, and the National Council for Vocational Qualifications* – which proposed that the professional bodies should have a significant role in the evolution of NVQ policy. It noted that:

> The government's concern with vocational qualifications is with the total system and not just parts of it. It would thus not be sensible or appropriate to exclude professional bodies who play a major role in vocational education and training and who determine patterns of qualifications. The National Council therefore invites the professional bodies to play their part in this initiative, and use their considerable experience to ensure the effective provision of vocational education and training, both within their professional domain and beyond.
>
> (NCVQ, 1987b, p. 3)

In particular, the NCVQ hoped that progress on establishing a framework of vocational qualifications at levels one to four would be hastened if the professional bodies would lend their cooperation. At the same time as it produced this consultative paper the NCVQ also established a 'Professional Bodies Advisory Group' under the chairmanship of Sir Norman Lindop. This group had further discussions with the professional bodies and formally reported back to the NCVQ in the autumn of 1987. Although Lindop claimed that his consultation had provoked a favourable reaction, and that the NCVQ's profile had been raised, doubts were raised in respect of the commitment of the professional bodies. There was a recognition that, while they might assist in developments at levels one to four, gaining their support for the extension of the NCVQ's remit beyond this would be rather more difficult. Nevertheless, Lindop's consultation exercise resulted, in early 1988, in the production of an internal NCVQ paper – *Professional Qualifications: The Way Forward*. Although during 1988 the NCVQ continued to discuss the prospect of extending the NVQ framework beyond level four with the UK-IPG, progress was slow. The professional bodies appeared to support the general principles of NVQ policy, but it was apparent that they had no real wish to become involved themselves,[9] not least because they were suspicious of the NCVQ's motives at a time when the government was seen to be hostile to professional interests (see Laffin and Young, 1990). An NCVQ official who was closely involved in the discussions with the professional bodies recalled that:

> They thought we were the evil face of government. At that time the government were getting at professions . . . We were just another device as far as they were concerned, to get at them.

After nine months of negotiations, in February 1989 the UK-IPG and the NCVQ finally produced a joint statement indicating the basis on which they would cooperate in the area of vocational qualifications. Much of the delay was caused by unhappiness within the NCVQ council that earlier drafts of the statement conceded too much ground to the professional bodies, particularly over the issue of their right to draw up standards of competence themselves. Nevertheless, the published joint statement, while it noted – among other things – the value of increasing cooperation between the NCVQ and the professions, the 'need to share experience' and the desirability of rationalizing the system of professional qualifications, still acknowledged the 'right of professional bodies to set standards for professional membership', and that NCVQ would recognize qualifications based upon them (NCVQ/UK-IPG, 1989). Given that at that time the NCVQ was concerned with developing NVQs that were based on extremely tight criteria, and a concept of competence which was largely unfamiliar to the professions, it must be presumed that this statement was largely a public relations exercise rather than indicating a serious purpose of intent.

Such a supposition is reinforced, given the tactics that the NCVQ adopted in the months immediately prior to the publication of the joint statement. Its officials realized that, if they were going to make any progress at all in this area of policy, it would be more productive to identify and work with sympathetic professional bodies, rather than continue to be rebuffed by those which were hostile. Following lobbying from the NCVQ, in February 1989, the Minister of State for Employment, John Cope, announced that the NCVQ's remit would be extended to cover qualifications above level four on this basis. During 1989 NCVQ officials worked, under the aegis of an advisory group reporting to Oscar De Ville, on a further consultation document that would seek out bodies willing to participate in the development of NVQs at the higher levels.

In October 1989 the NCVQ published its latest consultation document relating to the position of professional qualifications in respect of the NVQ framework. It was a notably less forceful statement of aims and objectives than those that had previously characterized the pronouncements of the NCVQ in this area. It was recognized that: the NCVQ's priority should be on building the framework at levels one to four, that the development of NVQs above level four would be a long-term process and need careful monitoring, and that it was likely that knowledge and understanding would need more explicit recognition in any standards of competence that were developed for professional occupations (NCVQ, 1989).

The NCVQ's progress in developing NVQs above level four – at this stage there was still no level five because no final decision had yet been made as to how many levels the NVQ framework would have – is examined further in Chapter 5. At this point in our account, however, it is simply necessary to note the substantial opposition that greeted the NCVQ's attempt to extend its remit to cover the reform of professional qualifications between 1987 and 1989. As we have seen, the NCVQ had encountered a number of obstacles in trying to establish the NVQ framework at levels one to four. Above those levels it was evident that the problems would be significantly greater because professional bodies were determined to protect the independence of their standards and qualifications from what they perceived as the heavy hand of the state. The effort that the NCVQ expended on the matter of professional qualifications is therefore somewhat surprising. For example, large parts of many of its council meetings were taken up with progress reports on, and discussions about, the latest position; and the NCVQ's Chief Executive, Peter Thompson, took a close interest in developing policy in this area. Notwithstanding the enthusiasm of some officials, there was pressure within the NCVQ council for the organization to concentrate on building the framework at levels one to four, and a former minister similarly considered the effort to bring the professions within the framework to be a distraction:

It was probably a step too far, actually, to try and capture them into the machine. There was always the difficulty when you're building up something like this, if you try to get them to do too much then you distract the senior management . . . and before you know where you are they like to be spending all their time talking to the professions and so on, and the rest of it slips. But on the other hand, if you didn't involve the professions then it'd be accused [of being] a second class affair.

Even the minister realized, though, that if the NVQ system was to attract high public esteem, it was important that it applied at all levels and was therefore not seen as something inferior.

Conclusion

The first 'proper' NVQs – based on lead body standards of competence – were accredited in retail distrbution in 1988. Yet progress in building the framework of NVQs was considerably slower than policy-makers had originally anticipated. This was largely a function of the way in which the NCVQ interpreted its remit. At the time it was established, the NCVQ's intention had been to adapt existing vocational awards so that they could be slotted into an emerging framework. However, given the degree of ambiguity with which the RVQ Working Group framed its proposals, and with the backing of influential employers' representatives, NCVQ officials were able to advance a more fundamental reform of the system of vocational qualifications. The NCVQ began to construct a framework of NVQs that would comprise only explicitly competence-based awards. However, the only significant developmental work on the design of assessable standards of competence had been carried out by the MSC for the purposes of YTS certification. This gave the early NVQs a task-based character, something that was exacerbated by the policy of 'conditional accreditation', the higher than expected number of lead bodies, and the way in which the education sector was distanced.

Understandably, therefore, the providers of existing vocational qualifications became reluctant to commit themselves entirely to reform. Given the ethos of voluntarism, they could not be compelled to change their products into NVQs. In fact they frequently looked to offer NVQs in addition to their existing provision, sometimes in new areas. The professional bodies and SCOTVEC were also able to rebuff the advances of the NCVQ. Thus between 1987 and 1989 there was no significant progress towards the establishment of a coherent and transparent structure of vocational qualifications in the UK. Indeed, it could be argued that the addition of NVQs on top of the existing provision made the system more opaque. Given this outcome, the extent to which both the NCVQ council and government departments were capable of ensuring that the organization's remit was carried out properly must be a matter for discussion and is something we will consider more fully in Chapter 8. However, the capacity of the council, in particular, to monitor and guide the work of the NCVQ, so that it fulfils its remit, must be called into question. For the time being we will examine, in the next chapter, the way in which NVQ policy was resuscitated during the early 1990s, given the problems we have identified in this one.

Notes

1 In the retail sector, for example, the National Retail Training Council rejected all existing awards and began to work on developing new qualifications (Morley, 1988).

2 The *Employment for the 1990s* White Paper highlighted the government's commitment to voluntarism in respect of training provision; for example, in the setting of standards of occupational competence for NVQs it maintained that the voluntary approach, whereby it was for employers to come together of their own accord, 'is far preferable to one of regulation and compulsion' (DE, 1988, p. 33).

3 According to an NCVQ information leaflet, assessment 'in the workplace will often provide the only practicable and cost-effective way of assessing performance. Trainers and supervisors in the workplace will frequently be the only people with the opportunity to observe demonstrations of performance required for assessment' (quoted in Wood et al., 1988, p. 3; c.f. MSC, 1988b).

4 It is only fair to note that NCVQ officials defended the NVQ criteria and guidance against the objection that knowledge and understanding had been pushed out. For example, one of them stated that,

> we always understood right from the beginning that possession of knowledge and understanding was a key feature of competent performance. Indeed even the early criteria documents, from mid-1987 onwards, always stressed knowledge and understanding . . . Rather than separating the knowledge and understanding from the context of performance and somehow specifying it separately such as in a set of topics to be covered or a syllabus, we wanted to develop such a clear and comprehensive notion of competence that, by definition, it would include the knowledge and understanding required of performance.

5 The full awards were: Electrical Installation (construction) level three, awarded by the Joint Industry Board for Electrical Contracting in England, Wales, Northern Ireland, Isle of Man, and the Channel Islands in association with City and Guilds, the Construction Industry Training Board and the Construction Industry Training Board (Northern Ireland); Food Preparation and Presentation level two, based on Caterbase modules, and awarded by City and Guilds and the Hotel and Catering Training Board; the National Craft Certificate – Light Vehicle Mechanics, Heavy Vehicle Mechanics – level three, awarded by the National Joint Council for the Motor Vehicle Retail and Repair Industry in association with City and Guilds, BTEC, the Road Transport Industry Training Board and the Northern Ireland Road Transport Industry Training Board; and the Certificate in Travel Skills level two awarded by City and Guilds and the Association of British Travel Agents National Training Board.

6 Even the NCVQ's Gilbert Jessup noted that one 'of the problems with some of the early NVQs created was that they tended to be narrow, focusing on jobs and tasks rather than occupations or functions' (Jessup, 1991, p. 43).

7 BTEC perhaps had genuine cause for concern. Lee et al. (1990) report an NCVQ field representative as stating that an objective of reform was to reduce the 'dominant role' enjoyed by BEC [sic] in further education (p. 177).

8 In the water sector, for example, the industry set up an awarding body before the lead body itself came into existence. Awarding qualifications offers scope for raising income through certification fees.

9 See Massey (1988) for the reluctance of the Engineering Council to cooperate.

5 Embedding the Reforms: NVQ and SVQ Policy 1990–1993

Introduction

Although its remit was to construct a framework of vocational qualifications based on existing awards, the NCVQ had embarked on the development of an NVQ system based on qualifications of a new type, which required competence to be defined in a particular way. They were new products to all intents and purposes. The absence of awards of this type induced the NCVQ to adopt a concept of competence that had been developed with the YTS in mind. In order to begin attracting revenue, however, the NCVQ had given 'conditional accreditation' to certain other products. These were often qualifications that had been designed for use in the YTS. This led to criticism that the emerging NVQs were too task-oriented. The NCVQ also experienced further problems in its attempt to establish the NVQ framework in two other respects. It had almost no control over the process by which industry developed assessable standards of competence, because responsibility for the management of the standards programme was vested in the MSC. Furthermore, the NCVQ possessed insufficient powers to compel other agencies to work with it in establishing a coherent and transparent system of vocational qualifications.

In this chapter we will explore how the NCVQ and the NVQ policy recovered from these initial problems in the period 1990 to 1993. We will begin by examining the reasons for the government's renewed support for the policy at this time, something that was of crucial importance since, having failed to make the anticipated progress on building the NVQ framework, the NCVQ needed an infusion of extra funds in order to continue its work. Most of the remainder of the chapter is then taken up with an analysis of the ways in which the reform of vocational qualifications was embedded: the elaboration of a consistent methodology for the derivation of assessable standards of competence; the evolution of the lead body network; and the attempts to build a single, coherent system of awards. The final substantive section of this chapter will then show that these developments notwithstanding, considerable problems of implementation remained.

The Resuscitation of NVQ Policy

By late 1989 the problems associated with the initial implementation of NVQ policy were becoming increasingly widely recognized as a number of critical appraisals of the new qualifications were published (e.g. CBI, 1989; Prais, 1989), though these tended to focus on their alleged task-based character. At this stage, however, the government was rather more uneasy about the lack of progress the NCVQ had made in establishing the national framework of vocational qualifications itself, than it was about the actual content of the awards.[1] Although 220 awards had received NCVQ approval by the summer of 1990 (*Times Educational Supplement*, 8 June 1990), the majority of these were conditional accreditations.[2]

> It was a sufficiently mature policy for there to be at that stage a whole lot of concern about: one, gaps – there were some sort of slowcoaches in terms of the development of NVQs; two, [the] proliferation of working groups [lead bodies] and the difficulty of managing them. I remember some 180 or something like that is a figure that sticks in the mind; and three, concerns about content were already beginning to surface.
>
> (DE minister)

In early 1990 the then Minister of State for Employment, Tim Eggar, asked the NCVQ to carry out a 'critical path analysis' so that the obstacles hindering progress towards the completion of the framework could be identified and remedial action proposed. For the NCVQ, one of the most tangible obstacles preventing the advancement of the NVQ framework was the fact that responsibility for the management of the development of occupational standards of competence, upon which NVQs were supposed to be founded, was with the Training Agency (TA).[3] NCVQ officials were frustrated at the way in which the TA was handling policy in this area, and with the slowness and unsatisfactory nature of the standards development work in particular. Thus, in order to attract revenue, the NCVQ placed an increasing amount of emphasis on gaining support for its policy of conditional accreditation. This upset TA officials, who were concerned that conditional accreditation was compromising the development of proper, competence-based NVQs.

Given the lack of progress it had made in developing the NVQ framework, by early 1990 there was a growing realization that the NCVQ would not become self-sufficient for the forseeable future.[4] NCVQ officials recognized that, if NVQ policy was to be sustained, they would need to approach the government to ask for more funds. Gilbert Jessup of the NCVQ commented that it was 'unrealistic and undesirable for us to be expected to be self-financing by 1992 without significantly slowing the reform process' (*Times Higher Educational Supplement*, 22 June 1990). The organization was already considering ways of saving money. At first restrictions were placed on discretionary expenditure. This was followed by freezing the research budget and ending recruitment. Although the NCVQ formally requested an extra £1m in 1990-91, and more in the following year, the government delayed its response until a high-level inter-departmental review of the organization's achievements and structures had been carried out and reported in the summer of 1990. While the review's authors noted that progress in implementing NVQ policy had been too slow, they nonetheless recognized that the NCVQ had been faced with a larger task than policy makers had originally anticipated, and that the timescale for it to become self-financing was unrealistic and had compromised the quality of NVQs by forcing it to adopt the policy of conditional accreditation. Moreover, the report acknowledged that the principle of the NVQ policy still attracted widespread support. The report concluded that 'against considerable scepticism, with few resources, and with no statutory or other powers, the NCVQ has gained widespread acceptance of the NVQ system and its underlying principles among its main partners, and in doing so has laid a firm foundation for the further and more rapid development which is now needed' (quoted in DfEE, 1995, p. 14).[5]

While there was an awareness within the government that far too little progress had been made in developing the NVQ framework and that the NCVQ's performance was deeply unimpressive, ministers denied that abolition was ever seriously considered. Yet in reflecting on his period as Chairman of the NCVQ, in 1993 Sir Bryan Nicholson recalled that:

> When I arrived three years ago there were still arguments about whether we should have an NVQ system at all . . . Many didn't want it and believed we would fail . . . As it was the timetable to establish NVQs was hopelessly behind. Nobody really knew when it was going to be completed, and I am sure the Government even considered whether to abandon it and start again.
>
> (NCVQ, 1993b).

Furthermore, an NCVQ official observed that:

> there certainly was a stage there when it was very clear that at ministerial level they were on the brink of getting rid of it all . . . They had lost faith in Oscar [DeVille] I think, and they had lost faith in Peter [Thompson]. So they either had to wind the thing up or they had to effectively tear it up and start again. They didn't quite tear it up . . . but it was close to that.[6]

Regardless of whether or not the abandonment of the NCVQ and NVQ policy was ever seriously considered, the NCVQ's prospects at this time were somewhat uncertain and would be affected by the outcome of the inter-departmental review.

The continuation of NVQ policy can be ascribed to a number of factors. In the first place, as the review noted, despite the concerns about the way in which it was being implemented, the principle of NVQ policy had attracted considerable support (e.g. CBI, 1989). Second, there was growing importance attached to the provision of education and training targets for the UK (see *Financial Times*, 7 December 1989). Targets, however, are useless without some kind of measure of attainment, and this was a role for which NVQs were eminently suited. Finally, perhaps the most important factor was the commitment among senior officials within the TA to the principle of NVQ policy, something that reflected the legacy of the recently wound up MSC. The NCVQ was fortunate, moreover, that Tim Eggar was the minister responsible for NVQ policy during 1989–90 because, somewhat idiosyncratically for a Conservative politician at that time, he was a strong advocate of vocational education and training, and could therefore see the value of a single, coherent framework of vocational qualifications.[7]

After some wrangling the Treasury agreed to release further funds for the implementation of NVQ policy, but only on condition that the NCVQ continue to aim towards becoming self-sufficient. In December 1990 the government gave the NCVQ an extra £11.5m of grant-in-aid for 1990–91 and the following three years up until 1993–94. The NCVQ was expected, however, to assess the prospects for self-sufficiency in 1992. The extra funds came with additional conditions. In December 1990 Michael Howard, the Secretary of State for Employment, notified the NCVQ, by means of a remit letter, of the tasks the government expected it to undertake with its improved resources. The most significant of these was that the NCVQ was requested to focus its energies on the goal of ensuring that the NVQ framework covered 80 per cent of the employed workforce at levels one to four by the end of 1992. The inter-departmental review had recommended that the NCVQ should aim for 100 per cent coverage, but after negotiations its officials were able to ease that obligation. In order to ensure that the respective tasks of the DE and the NCVQ were more closely coordinated, a joint management group of senior officials from both organisations was established to monitor progress towards the 80 per cent target.

The prospect of achieving this objective was made easier by a number of policy developments during 1990 and 1991. For a start, in October 1990 the NCVQ reached an 'agreement' with BTEC regarding the inclusion of the bulk of its awards within the NVQ framework. In the same month the NCVQ and SCOTVEC agreed to recognize each other's awards. Under the influence of a new Chairman, Sir Bryan Nicholson, the NCVQ also put an end to the policy of conditional accreditation. The significance of these developments will be further assessed in later parts of this chapter. They are mentioned here because they give some indication of the extent to which the government and the NCVQ were determined to have the framework of competence-based NVQs in place, once the decision to sustain the policy had been taken. Two other policy interventions deserve to be acknowledged in this context. First, in its April 1991 budget the government announced that from April 1992 onwards individuals would be able to claim tax relief on the costs of their training if they were aiming to achieve NVQs at levels one to four (NCVQ, 1991c). Second, and more significantly as it turned out, the DE gave NVQs a key role in the restructured funding arrangements for the government's employment programmes, such as the new Youth Training (YT), which had replaced the YTS. From 1990 onwards the responsibility for managing these initatives was devolved to the new network of locally based and employer-led Training and Enterprise Councils (TECs).[8] As an incentive for the TECs, and as a way of measuring their performance, a proportion of their funding from the DE, to become known as 'outcome-related funding', was dependent upon the attainment by a trainee of at least an NVQ level two, or a DE-approved equivalent. Clearly, NVQs were perceived to be of considerable value as a device for measuring local delivery against national standards in an increasingly market-based system of vocational education and training (Keep and Mayhew, 1994).

Before we conclude this examination of how the NVQ policy was resuscitated in 1990, however, some reference needs to be made to the way in which the NCVQ itself changed at this time. Oscar De Ville had originally agreed to be the Chairman of the NCVQ for an initial period of a year, although he was subsequently persuaded to extend his period of office to three years and then stayed on for another year until October 1990. He was succeeded by Sir Bryan Nicholson, the Chairman of the Post Office and the head of the CBI's Task Force on Education and Training, who had previously been Chairman of the MSC between 1984 and 1987. In fact Nicholson had agreed to take up the NCVQ post as early as the end of 1989, and during the spring and summer of 1990 he kept a close eye on the internal debate that was going on about the future direction of NVQ policy. His appointment signalled a distinct change in the relationship between the NCVQ and the DE. De Ville had been concerned to make the NCVQ as distant as possible from the department, because he felt that this would give it a greater degree of independence and allow it more chance to survive in the long term, even under different governments. This explains his commitment to the principle of self-sufficiency. Nicholson, on the other hand, had much closer relations with members of the Conservative government and was able to use his connections to advance NVQ policy in a way that his predecessor would have found more difficult. A former employment minister reflected on the substantial influence on training policy that Nicholson had at this time:

Now Bryan Nicholson was a big man in all of this and very, very influential . . . His opinion about all these things was pretty critical. He was a friend who was knowledgeable and in a position to do things. So . . . there was quite a lot of to-ing and fro-ing actually, quite often at the Secretary of State level.

From 1990 onwards, then, a much closer relationship between the NCVQ and the TA and DE developed, particularly because all the parties were committed to meeting the 80 per cent target for NVQ coverage by the end of 1992. The NCVQ's Chief Executive, Peter Thompson, left the organisation in March 1991. For a brief period council member Peter Reay stood in as an acting Chief Executive with John Hillier, who had replaced Michael Ridley as Director of Accreditation a year earlier, as his deputy. In August 1991 Hillier was promoted to become Chief Executive, and the post of Deputy Chief Executive was filled by Gilbert Jessup, the NCVQ's Director of Research and Development. The creation of the post of Deputy Chief Executive was one aspect of a restructuring of staffing at the NCVQ, part of a response to the 1990 inter-departmental review that had found not only that it was under-resourced for the task of developing the NVQ framework, but also that it lacked sufficient staff for the job. Finally, the role of the NCVQ council changed from 1990 onwards. Nicholson emphasized that he expected the council to restrict itself largely to the discussion of broad policy matters, while the detailed work on building the NVQ framework, the accreditation of specific qualifications in particular, was to be left to officials. Meetings of the NCVQ council were convened at quarterly intervals, whereas previously they had taken place on a bi-monthly basis.

Towards a Consistent Methodology: The Emergence of Functional Analysis

When the NCVQ was established in late 1986, no agreed method of designing or assessing competence-based qualifications existed. It soon produced a concept of competence, which, because it originated in the developmental work for the YTS, was quickly acknowledged as being too narrow and job specific. MSC officials realized that existing approaches to the derivation and assessment of occupational standards were inconsistent with their strategic aim of encouraging the development of broad-based skills and employment flexibility. There was also a recognition, moreover, that the establishment of a common approach in this area of policy was a desirable aim (MSC, 1988b). Thus developmental work was initiated, under the auspices of the MSC's newly established Standards Methodology Branch, to explore ways of designing and delivering a methodology for the derivation of assessable occupational standards across all sectors of industry. The principal forum for this work was the Technical Advisory Group (TAG) which met between 1987 and 1989 and comprised officials from the MSC (later the TA), the NCVQ, the main awarding bodies and the leading technical consultants in this area. There were considerable differences between the positions adopted by the NCVQ and the TA on the TAG. In short, and at the risk of considerable oversimplification, while NCVQ officials favoured the wider utilization of the approach that had been developed in the YTS, which involved the analysis of tasks and upon which they had based the first NVQ criteria (the 'standard tasks' or 'competence objectives' method), TA officials and consultants preferred the emerging technique of functional analysis for the purpose of deriving assessable occupational standards. In a series of 'guidance notes' the TA then set out how it anticipated lead bodies should use functional analysis to produce these standards and how they could then be used to underpin vocational qualifications.

The origins of the functional analysis approach can be traced to the development of work-based learning and assessment techniques for use within the YTS carried out under the auspices of the MSC in the early to mid-1980s (see Chapter 2). In 1985 two consultants involved with this work, Bob Mansfield and David Mathews, devised what they termed the 'job competence' model. They had observed that the job of a photocopier operator involves far more than simple task skills. While these were obviously important, the operator was also observed to deploy 'task management' skills and 'job/role environment' skills (see Mansfield and Mathews, 1985). Later, a fourth aspect of 'job competence' was added to the model – 'contingency management' skills. From their research, Mansfield and Mathews deduced that the proper assessment of an individual's competence at work would need to involve considerably more than a simple observation of the successful completion of standard tasks. Officials in the TA found this approach attractive because it appeared to promise that broad-based skills could be acknowledged and certified, thereby encouraging flexibility, and could also be used across a wide range of industries. Thus 'competence' became officially defined as:

> the ability to perform the activities within an occupation or function to the standards expected in employment . . . This is a wide concept which embodies the ability to transfer skills and knowledge to new situations within the occupational area. It encompasses organisation and planning of work, and coping with non-routine activities. It involves those qualities of personal effectiveness required in the workplace to deal with co-workers, managers and customers.
>
> (TA, 1988a, p. 6)

This approach to the derivation of competence became known as 'functional analysis', principally so that it could be distinguished from the narrower 'task analysis' method. Functional analysis, then, rather than being concerned merely with the successful completion of tasks by individuals, though that is clearly one element of it, focuses on the functions they are expected to carry out in employment, which encompasses aspects of the wider social constitution of work. Individual units of competence, and their associated elements of competence and performance criteria, can then be elaborated from the functions.

The TA increasingly made the use of functional analysis a condition of its grants to lead bodies for standards development work and published a list of approved technical consultants who were versed in the approach. Although Stewart and Hamlin (1992) claimed, among other things, that functional analysis could only be used to recognize narrow job or task roles, their critique was vigorously rebutted by Bob Mansfield, one of the leading technical consultants. He argued that task performance was only one aspect of the functional analysis approach and that a concern with identifying and recognizing people's broader job roles was also present within it. Where there was a difficulty, however, was in the limited way in which lead bodies were using functional analysis. Thus he claimed that a 'method cannot be held responsible for those who use it' (Mansfield, 1993, p. 19).[9] The attractiveness of the approach notwithstanding, how realistic was it to expect individual lead bodies, even with the assistance of consultants, to be capable of implementing a full-scale functional analysis of the occupations within their respective sectors – or even understanding what it entailed? As a TAG participant recalled, even he found the extensive technical aspects of the discussions held within it somewhat difficult to comprehend:

> One used to think, well, this is unreal; this is divorced from reality . . . I remember saying to the chairman once, could you explain to me what all this lot means to me, because I haven't got a clue.

The adoption of functional analysis gave the NVQ system a very technicist character. Take the matter of language, for example. In the TAG notes guidelines were provided on how standards should be written so that, rather than reflecting the completion of discrete tasks, they describe the successful realization of functions by an individual. Thus it is recommended, for instance, that lead bodies avoid terminology like 'correct use of lubricant' in the context of servicing machinery. Instead, an acceptable phraseology would be: 'a lubricant appropriate to the application is selected and used. The correct quantity of lubricant is used. The frequency of topping up and changing lubricant conforms to manufacturer's instructions' (TA, 1988b, p. 8). By 1991 one of the principal standards consultants was advising that units of competence be written in accordance 'with the recommended grammatical structure' – active verb, object and condition (Mansfield, 1991, pp. 21, 20). According to one informed commentator, the increasingly 'tightly defined' standards and the prominent role enjoyed by a few technical consultants 'strengthened the tendency of the development process to generate a private vocabulary and conventions which were opaque or incomprehensible to outsiders' (Wolf, 1995, p. 16). The standards were very difficult to comprehend, as an employers' representative noted:

> if you look at those old ones [standards] they're really quite difficult to understand, even if you've been involved in the training world for some time. I certainly can't understand them, but to expect candidates to understand, or shop floor managers or foremen and so forth is really asking too much I think.

It is not altogether clear, moreover, that the majority of employers wanted the kind of broad-based competences that the functional analysis approach was designed to deliver, something that Mansfield (1993) has acknowledged. Aspects of the TAG notes encouraged lead bodies to interpret the functional analysis process, and thus derive occupational standards of competence, in a very narrow way. For example, much was made in the notes of the importance of defining standards in a generic way – that is so that they do not apply just to specific conditions, or to a limited number of organisations. Yet in an effort to ensure that reliability between different assessors and organisations is upheld, it was recommended that the 'perfomance criteria should – be as precise as possible' (TA, 1988b, p. 8).[10] Such a guideline could be used by lead bodies as a justification for the development of narrow, task-based competences.

> the TAG notes were the standards bible and we could not change them . . . If the industry lead body and their consultants looked at those TAG notes, and looked at them in a particular way, then what resulted was a very narrow level of competence.
>
> (NCVQ official)

While the principle that competence-based qualifications should be independent of any mode of learning was one that was adhered to in both the NCVQ and the TA, within the latter organisation there was more of a concern that breadth and knowledge specifications were insufficiently manifested in the initial products. As early as 1987 the place of knowledge and understanding in a competence-based system had been discussed within the TAG, and the TA subsequently established an advisory group and commissioned research into the matter (e.g. Mitchell, 1989). Although its updated guidance stressed that NVQs should recognize breadth and encourage flexibility, the NCVQ held to the view that knowledge could be inferred entirely from successful performance (NCVQ, 1991b).

One of the most interesting features of the TAG notes was the TA's willingness to countenance a variety of assessment techniques, although the observation of an individual's performance in a work situation would usually be the most appropriate (TA, 1989a). This was seen to necessitate, though, the establishment of a structure of 'assessors', usually the candidate's immediate work supervisor, and 'internal' and 'external verifiers' (TA, 1989b). It was clear, however, that the inadequate state of supervisory skills in British industry (TA, 1989c) constituted a major obstacle to such a development. Thus a considerable amount of attention was given to the establishment of a Training and Development Lead Body (TDLB). Not only was the evolving NVQ system given a somewhat technicist and jargon-ridden character, then, but it also became increasingly bureaucratic; neither of which commended it to employers (CBI, 1994).

The Maturing of the Lead Body Structure

Responsibility for designing occupational standards of competence on a sectoral basis was, as we have seen, given to employer-led lead bodies. By 1993, 162 of these organisations had been established (CBI, 1993). Although some of them had got involved voluntarily out of a fear that if they did not then the government might impose something worse, or because of a concern that other bodies might otherwise encroach on their terrain, there was none-theless a widespread recognition that the NVQ policy could have positive results. The increasing elaboration of competence-based vocational qualifi-cations was seen to be beneficial for industrial competitiveness, to improve quality, to give individuals recognition for skills that would otherwise go unnoticed, and to provide an objective measure of a worker's competence among other things.

Despite the requirement that lead bodies match the TA and DE's cash grant with contributions of their own, the adequate representation of employers' interests appears to have been difficult to achieve (Field, 1995).

> I think there has been a concern over the years . . . amongst the employers themselves as to whether the lead bodies adequately reflect or – putting it at its crudest, you know there have been some criticisms that the lead bodies are made up of personnel people who speak the language and the jargon of personnel [but] are fairly far removed from line management requirements, when what we really want is the line management to specify what the standards should be. Because they are the ones who are running the show.
>
> (TA official)

> I would question whether the lead body membership in many instances were really representative.
>
> (awarding body official)

> The lead bodies and the later OSC's [Occupational Standards Councils – see p. 104] were not in many cases fully accountable to the employer community. There were some which were, where they obviously reported in a structure. In other cases they're in isolation. The people there didn't

feel they had a responsibility to report to any representative body within their sector, and that led to decisions being taken which might have seemed right to the narrow lead body, but not necessarily to the employer. So there wasn't the employer feed in there should have been.

(employers' association official)

Given the importance policy makers attached to letting employers have ownership of the NVQ system, why was their adequate representation so difficult to secure? In the first place, the increasing interest of bodies such as the CBI notwithstanding, even by the early 1990s the majority of British companies were neglecting to accord training and development issues strategic importance, despite the frequently articulated message that much of their future competitive performance depended on the skills of their work-forces (Ashton and Green, 1996). Second, although the fact that about 160 lead bodies were eventually established was a reflection of the heterogeneity of industry in the UK, as well as the ethos of voluntarism that underpinned the NVQ system, they still did not adequately capture the diverse nature of employment. Finally, because private sector employers have businesses to run, they tend to find it difficult to give up the time to become involved in extraneous activities, such as taking an active part in a lead body. This was a particular problem for small firms (CBI, 1994). In retailing, for example, while the involvement of the major high-street chains in the activities of the lead body was relatively easy to arrange, this was much less the case for the many smaller concerns. The growing emphasis given to having formally qualified assessors in place, trained to TDLB standards, added to the obstacles faced by those small businesses that wanted to give their staff the chance to attain NVQs, because it significantly increased the cost of the assessment process.

Given the way in which the representativeness of many lead bodies has been questioned, to what extent was the NVQ policy actually employer-led?[11] Field (1995) has contended that the influence of NCVQ, departmental officials and technical consultants in the system has been rather more notable than that of employers. Yet industry did have a significant influence at first. The emergence of a large number of lead bodies can be cited as a reflection of the ascendancy of employers' interests. We have already noted, moreover, in Chapter 4, how influential employers' representatives lobbied effectively for the development of vocational qualifications that were directly work-related, although they could not persuade the NCVQ to adopt a unit-based system. However, given the way in which NVQ policy developed in the late 1980s and early 1990s it becomes more difficult to sustain the contention that it was an employer-led system as both the DE and the NCVQ were increasingly prescriptive about the occupational standards and qualifications they were prepared to support and accredit.

For example, it became a condition of TA and DE support for standards development that lead bodies use the functional analysis method and employ approved technical consultants to aid the process. Given the highly technical nature of functional analysis, there was a concern that the system was being run for the benefit of the technical consultants, who were alleged to be the only ones that actually understood it.[12] Moreover, functional analysis was an entirely new approach for the derivation of standards in employment and had yet to be properly evaluated in practice. This led to alterations during implementation. For example, when departmental officials realized that the early products of the methodology were somewhat narrow in scope, they looked at ways of inserting breadth into the standards. Thus the concept of the 'range statement' was born, when it was realized that individuals should demonstrate each competence in a variety of situations (see Mathews, 1991). While such changes were seen to be necessary, they nonetheless gave rise to accusations by lead bodies that the TA was frequently 'moving the goalposts', a charge its officials readily conceded. In 1990 the NCVQ decided to end conditional accreditation and later, in its updated guidance of March 1991 (NCVQ, 1991b), it specified that NVQ units should offer sufficient breadth to encourage flexibility and progression. Many lead bodies, however, were happy with conditional accreditation, which, as we have seen, not only constituted most of the NVQs available in 1990, but was also largely based on combinations of skills tests and added examinations of knowledge. Such awards were perceived to be too narrow though, and, as an NCVQ official recalled, many lead bodies now began to have their offerings refused accreditation as NVQs:

> We spent at least a year turning down most of the things that were being submitted to us at that stage. Because they were just awful . . . they were either just simple task descriptions dressed up to look like occupational standards. They put all the headings in, but they hadn't actually changed the content. Or the content of them was so infantile because the motivation was simply to produce something you could get your youth training money for.

The NCVQ became increasingly prescriptive about the qualifications it was prepared to accredit in another respect. We have already noted its opposition to a unit-based module system as the basis for NVQs. Some lead bodies, though, had developed a 'core and options' approach as a way of reflecting the diversity of the employment situations in their sectors in the qualifications. That is, in order to attain an award at a particular level, candidates would be required to complete a specified number of mandatory generic, industry-wide units, and also a set of optional units that would apply to the part of the sector in which they were based. The NCVQ would not accept awards based on core and optional units, however, because it felt that this would encourage the development of narrow, occupationally specific awards and militate against progression and flexibility. The core and options approach was promoted particularly heavily in the food and drink industry, where the Biscuit, Cake, Chocolate and Confectionary Alliance (BCCCA) was coordinating lead body developments. It argued that the inclusion of core and optional units had the support of the industry, and was 'the only way of accommodating the diversity of different processes used in the industry' (*Educa*, September 1991). While it was possible to develop units in areas such as food hygiene and health and safety, for example, which could be applied to the food and drink sector in general, the different requirements of, say, baking and dairy production meant that optional units covering such sub-sectors were desirable. The NCVQ rejected the food and drink industry's first set of standards and, although a compromise was eventually worked out, not only was the introduction of NVQs in the sector held up for two years, but they were also not entirely what the industry wanted (see Marshall, 1994).

Perhaps the most interesting example of the tension that existed between an industrial sector and the NCVQ occurred in engineering. The EITB had received conditional accreditation for craft qualifications based on its system of module and segment-based training, and the industry had expressed a wish that 'proper' NVQs should be derived in the same way. This was unacceptable to the NCVQ, however, because they perceived the EITB's system to be too process-based (Senker, 1996), although the engineering body considered that its training system was based on standards, but of a different kind from those the NCVQ wanted. The NCVQ specified that NVQs in engineering should be based on standards of competence derived from functional analysis. The situation was confused by the work of the Marine Engineering Training Authority (META), which, with the help of TA approved consultants, was working on the development of occupational standards based on functional analysis in shipbuilding-related areas. At first the EITB refused to comply with the NCVQ's requirements. This caused a considerable amount of anxiety within the NCVQ because of the size of the engineering sector. If it could not be brought into the NVQ framework then the target of 80 per cent coverage by the end of 1992 would have been jeopardized. In the summer of 1992 the NCVQ and the ENTRA (Engineering Training Authority), as the EITB had become, reached an agreement whereby the latter would alter its provision so that it met the NCVQ's requirements and could thus be inserted into the NVQ framework. The capitulation of the ENTRA came about because, at the request of the NCVQ, ministers exerted pressure on it to comply. Moreover, its capacity to resist had been weakened by the removal of its statutory powers in 1991. An employers' association representative commented that:

> It wasn't employer led. I don't think it was . . . ENTRA was trying to make it more employer led, though one can criticise their results and the way they did it, but they'd have been much more successful if they hadn't had the government, in the form of the Employment Department

(ED), and the NCVQ doing what the ED wanted, they'd have been much more successful if they hadn't had them breathing down their necks and saying this is the way you ought to be doing it.

Given that it was striving to meet its target of 80 per cent coverage, it was bold of the NCVQ to be so willing to reject the initial offerings of the lead bodies. Nevertheless, the way in which it insisted that all NVQs should fit a particular pattern and be derived in the same way caused resentment within lead bodies, even among those that had given the concept of NVQs strong support. It was understood to be at odds with the diversity of employment situations characteristic of industry in the UK, something that made flexibility within an overall framework desirable rather than a prescriptive straightjacket. One lead body official likened the situation to a scene from a well-known film:

> I don't know if you ever saw the film *Amadeus* where . . . the curtain comes down and the Austrian Emperor comes round the back and he says: 'very good piece of work Mozart. Only one thing wrong with it – too many notes.' And Mozart, absolutely flabbergasted, said 'that's exactly the right number you know . . . it couldn't do with more or less.' . . . You need the right number of notes, no more, no less.

As time went on there was an increasing realization within the government that, if the penetration of NVQs was to be improved, employer ownership needed to be strengthened. One of the ways in which policy makers sought to do this was by making the NVQ system less prescriptive. While this is a matter that will be considered more fully in Chapter 7, as early as 1992 pressure was put on the NCVQ to consider ways of instigating unit-based accreditation.[13]

In 1990 the inter-departmental review of the NCVQ recommended that some action be taken to rationalize the number of lead bodies in existence. Thenceforth government policy on lead bodies turned full circle. Rather than encourage the formation of new ones, the imperative was now to get them to work more closely together and if possible to merge. Even the DE was finding that the large number of lead bodies was making the standards development programme somewhat difficult to manage. A DE official noted that:

> We found it very difficult to manage the relationships with all of these bodies – with all of the staff that we could put on to it . . . clearly, if we had fewer bodies to liaise with, we could have spent more time; we could have put more in from our end of the relationship; we could have made it a more effective relationship. So if I had been able to wave the magic wand, I might have waved it and said, 'let's have fewer

of them.' The trouble is that you do have to have some regard to how business people want to gather together. They are not there primarily to fit in with government structures.

While there was an increasing realization, then, that in order to improve the overall integrity of the NVQ system a greater degree of coherence needed to be inserted into the lead body network, care had to be taken not to disturb the principle of employer ownership. Given the importance attached to reaching the target of 80 per cent coverage for NVQs by the end of 1992, the last thing officials wanted was for lead bodies to be distracted from, or put off the main task in hand by the threat of rationalization. Another DE official recalled that:

> We deliberately didn't try and battle in this area . . . because we thought that if we try to shake up all the cards we shan't get the standards delivered. These may not be perfect bodies, but they're the only ones we've got. If we don't let them persist and deliver what they're supposed to deliver we shall never get the standards out and, therefore, never get the NVQ framework populated, and that was the first priority – to get it populated.

Nevertheless, during 1991 and 1992 DE officials explored ways in which the lead body network could be rationalized without mitigating the principle of employer ownership, and came up with the concept of 'Occupational Standards Councils' (OSCs).[14] These were envisaged as broad sectoral bodies that would be responsible for overseeing the development of occupational standards for a wide range of occupations within a particular area. This was a shrewd proposition on the part of the DE because, although the proposed OSCs offered the prospect of rationalization, they did not necessarily threaten the independence of lead bodies, since individual ones could, should they wish to, maintain their individual autonomy within a council. There was another imperative for the establishment of these OSCs. Since 1990 DE officials had been working with a number of professional bodies to develop occupational standards suitable, among other things, for NVQs at levels four and five (see p. 109). However, individual professional bodies, who were careful to protect their autonomy, expected to act as lead bodies in their own right. Not only would such a development, if left unchecked, have given rise to even more lead bodies at a time when officials were trying to reduce their number, but it would also have created artificial barriers to progress within sectors because one lead body would be responsible for standards development at, say, levels one to three, while another had the remit for levels four and five. Although officials pushed the concept of OSCs very hard, and even got Gillian Shepherd to mention them in her remit letter to the NCVQ in December 1992, little progress was eventually made in this area as a DE official explained:

We were encouraging each of the lead bodies to work with related lead bodies. We tried to take that further, to introduce Occupational Standards Councils. That was a notion of having something like 20, and we worked very hard on the principles of that. But that would have been almost a forced rationalisation and when we tried to use logic with the bodies out there they resisted. There was not the ministerial will to push that through and tell them they've got to have it. Of course if we had told them they've got to have it we'd have lost a lot of credibility, because it would have meant that employer ownership would have dropped off.

As this official indicated, employers' representatives and individual lead bodies strongly opposed the DE's attempt to pen the latter into Occupational Standards Councils (Marshall, 1994). Nevertheless, some did become established during 1993 and 1994 on a voluntary basis. The Distributive OSC encompassed a number of individual lead bodies in the retail sector for example, and the Employment OSC was set up to coordinate the work of the Training and Development, Personnel and Trade Union lead bodies.

Building the Framework of Vocational Qualifications

Within the government there was an increasing realization of the importance of having in place a coherent framework of vocational qualifications to cover the UK as a whole. In 1989, then, the Scottish Education Department took the decision to establish a system of Scottish Vocational Qualifications (SVQs), something that would not only provide an analogue with the NVQ framework in England, Wales and Northern Ireland, but would also acknowledge the distinctiveness of education provision in Scotland. This decision was not welcomed by SCOTVEC, however, as its officials considered that the recently instituted National Certificate system already provided a coherent and transparent framework of vocational awards. Indeed, the first SVQ to be accredited by SCOTVEC, in Agriculture, was based on various National Certificate modules. By the beginning of 1992, 185 SVQs were available, many of which were partly based on the same lead body standards as NVQs (*Educa*, March 1992). Although work on the development of the first SVQs had got underway by 1989, under pressure from ministers SCOTVEC was then impelled to negotiate with the NCVQ over the mutual recognition of each other's awards. During 1990 officials from the two organisations worked on ensuring that the specifications of SVQs were compatible with those of NVQs. In October 1990 the NCVQ and SCOTVEC formally reached an agreement to this effect, something that ensured that NVQs were recognized in Scotland.

SCOTVEC appears to have had fewer difficulties in its relationship with partner organisations than the NCVQ. Two factors accounted for this. First, in developing SVQs, SCOTVEC started from a position rather different from that of the NCVQ with NVQs. Whereas the NCVQ aimed to build a framework of vocational qualifications based on the accreditation of new awards as NVQs, in Scotland SCOTVEC established SVQs largely on the existing National Certificate system, although they also incorporated standards of competence derived from lead bodies. Second, unlike the NCVQ, which was just an accrediting body, in Scotland SCOTVEC also acted as an awarding body. This was a situation that generated a considerable amount of adverse comment elsewhere because it made SCOTVEC responsible for both the provision and the regulation of qualifications. Yet it also offered SCOTVEC a great strength because, as an awarding body, it had a good understanding of what was deliverable on the ground. Thus SCOTVEC was able to develop the SVQ framework in a more pragmatic, and arguably less purist, way than the NCVQ was doing with NVQs.

During 1989 and 1990 officials from both BTEC and the NCVQ examined how BTEC products, their First and National Diploma awards in particular, could be brought into the NVQ framework. The NCVQ were particularly keen to work out some kind of compromise because the organization was under pressure to become self-sufficient, and hence needed to have an increasing number of awards accredited as NVQs. The NCVQ and BTEC eventually signed a formal agreement in October 1990 whereby the latter body agreed to revise its awards so that they could be inserted into the national framework as NVQs, though they would retain their broader, more educational content.[15] However, BTEC's participation was reluctant. Its conditionally accredited awards in Business Administration had not been given re-accreditation, when those of other providers were, thus weakening its market position. Moreover, it came under ministerial pressure to reach an agreement with the NCVQ:

> The policy was very much to get them involved, and to apply pressure to do so . . . The BTEC people felt that their qualifications had a better content, but you know there was very strong advice from officials [that] we must get BTEC on board. There was a kind of, I suppose, logic; of saying, well you know there must be a single structure, otherwise you know, the concept of a sort of transparent, universal structure of qualifications is lost.
>
> (education minister)

The NCVQ understood that BTEC First awards were to be replaced by NVQs at level two intially, whereas the revision of National Diplomas and National Certificates as NVQs at levels three and four would be a longer-term development. During 1991 some progress was made in respecifying BTEC awards as NVQs. For example, the NCVQ gave accreditation to BTEC First and National awards in Business and Finance as NVQs at levels two and three, since they were now based on ABCTG standards of competence (*BTEC Briefing*, April 1991). However, the way in which

BTEC was proposing to adapt its awards to the NVQ framework more generally, gave rise to a considerable amount of concern within the NCVQ that BTEC was developing a system of separate certification. That is, students could attain relevant NVQs by successfully completing specified parts of the relevant BTEC approved programme, but to attain the First or Diploma awards BTEC was insisting on additional requirements. BTEC justified this by emphasizing that awards based solely upon lead body standards of competence insufficiently prepared its candidates for entry into higher education (BTEC, 1994). The NCVQ felt that BTEC was trying to establish its own distinctive system of vocational awards outside the NVQ framework, and was therefore implicitly claiming their superiority to NVQs. It then threatened to withdraw its accreditation from all of the BTEC awards that had been recognized hitherto, unless BTEC set about reviewing these arrangements. By this time, in 1991–92, BTEC was under growing financial pressure to comply with the NCVQ's requirements because its unreformed awards were increasingly being rejected by the DE for use in government funded training programmes (House of Commons Employment Committee, 1991).

There was considerable resentment within BTEC because it believed it was being compelled to narrow its awards in order to meet the NCVQ's particular specifications. Perhaps the most prominent expression of dissatisfaction with this state of affairs came in the speech of Parry Rogers, the then chairman of BTEC, at the launch of the organisation's annual report in May 1992. Rogers complained that, in being obliged to offer awards which only met the NCVQ's narrow requirements, the quality of BTEC's more broadly based products was being compromised. He asked:

> Can the skill based training of NCVQ to meet employers' immediate needs be reconciled with the work-related education approach of BTEC, structured to accommodate employers' present and future needs and the requirements of higher education gatekeepers? . . . The present effect of this conflict is that BTEC programmes are having to be rewritten to meet NCVQ skill requirements at the expense of the qualities which make BTEC attractive both to employers AND to the HE (higher education) gatekeepers . . . BTEC wants to offer what it believes the market wants, to compete with others serving the same market segments, to stand or fall on whether it gets that right or not, to have the flexibility to respond quickly to changing market needs, and always to meet (or exceed) the standards laid down by NCVQ.
>
> (quoted in *Educa*, June 1992, p. 9, original emphasis)

Increasingly, however, relations between the NCVQ and BTEC improved, partly because of the joint effort (also with City and Guilds and the RSA) they put into the introduction of the GNVQ (see Chapter 6), and partly because the government did not want to stifle market forces, so where there was a demand for them BTEC First and National awards remained in place.

Although one of the NCVQ's 'key purposes' had been to 'approve bodies making vocational awards' (NCVQ, 1987a), it had no powers to fulfill this aspect of its remit. While it saw some rationalization in the number of awarding bodies as a desirable objective, the NCVQ recognized that this was a sensitive area because organizations relied on delivering qualifications to generate income. The 1990 inter-departmental review of the NCVQ recognized that the growth in the number of awarding bodies offering NVQs had resulted in difficulties and militated against the construction of a coherent framework of qualifications. It proposed that the awarding body network be examined to see how some rationalization could be introduced. This was underlined in Michael Howard's remit letter to the NCVQ of December 1990. A DE official referred to the attention that was given to:

> the problem of the proliferation of all the little [awarding bodies] flying about, most of whom weren't terribly anxious to get locked into a framework that they couldn't see that their funding stream would be guaranteed, and they certainly didn't want to get locked into something where they would be swallowed up by one of the big ones. Whereas from our point of view, we were quite keen for them to be swallowed up by the big ones because it meant that they reduced the jungle.

During 1991 the NCVQ set about exploring ways of fulfilling this part of its revised remit. It was faced with the challenge of bringing about some degree of rationalization, while at the same time paying heed to the importance of allowing market forces to operate, the latter being something that was emphasized in remit letters from successive secretaries of state (see DfEE, 1995). However, the NCVQ made little headway in this area because ongoing discussions with the DES on the matter and the April 1992 General Election delayed a response from DE ministers to its proposals. Where it did make progress, though, was in establishing improved arrangements for ensuring quality assurance in the delivery of NVQs. Thus the NCVQ sought to encourage greater consistency of assessment procedures across the various awarding bodies and better training for NVQ assessors (Ellis, 1993). The most tangible outcome of these efforts came with the publication of the *Awarding Bodies Common Accord* in 1993 (NCVQ, 1993a). The substantive details of this 'accord' had been developed in discussions between officials from the NCVQ and the larger awarding bodies during 1992, and it was publicly launched at the end of that year. The *Common Accord* recommended that bodies awarding NVQs should work to certain guidelines. These included: a common approach to the assessment and verification of NVQs; agreement on the respective roles of assessors, internal verifiers and external verifiers; the use of approved centres for the delivery of NVQs that met certain agreed criteria; and the requirement that assessors and verifiers be properly competent to fulfill their roles. While awarding bodies could not be compelled to meet the specifications of the *Common Accord*, it was considered unlikely that they would be able to deliver proper NVQs without so doing.

In early 1990 professional bodies were consulted about the NCVQ's proposals to extend the NVQ framework above level four. Although the NCVQ claimed that the overall tone of the replies had been positive, there was some notable opposition to the prospect of having NVQs in place for the professions, including from the Engineering Council and the Institute of Chartered Accountants in England and Wales. The NCVQ recognized that progress could be slow given the complexity of the area, the inherent political sensitivities, and because there were no additional funds available for the work; although a part-time consultant was appointed to follow up the consultation exercise. The UK-IPG, moreover, remained hostile to the development of NVQs for professional occupations. The main impetus in this area in fact now came from the DE.[16] In December 1990 it established a steering committee, with NCVQ and SCOTVEC officials, to coordinate policy developments at level five and to link them with the work being done at levels one to four. The steering group oversaw work on a number of exemplar projects – in accountancy, chemistry, construction, engineering, law, management, pharmacy and psychology – which were charged with developing assessable standards of competence for use in vocational qualifications at level five. This initiative on the part of the DE notwithstanding, progress was difficult to achieve, as an NCVQ official observed in an unpublished document:

> It took a great deal longer than was expected to convince the Professional Bodies concerned that there was any benefit from undertaking the work. Two of the bodies were reluctant to share their experiences with the Steering Group and others were slow to begin work. This very attitude highlighted the main difficulty in involving Professional Bodies in developing competence-based qualifications, namely that they had other things to do, they saw the new competence movement as a threat to the independence of their institutions and they found the process intellectually suspect.

Perhaps the most positive, albeit atypical, sector was management. Occupational standards in management were developed by the Management Charter Initiative (MCI), which had become a recognized lead body in April 1990. The MCI had been established two years before as a business-led body, whose objective was to improve the standard of management education and training in the UK after a number of influential studies had shown it to be somewhat weak (Constable and McCormick, 1987; Handy, 1987). The first level five NVQ in Management (awarded by the Institute of Industrial Managers in association with BTEC) was accredited by the NCVQ as early as March 1992. Elsewhere, headway in developing NVQs at level five was much slower, and no others were accredited until 1995, when some became available in the museums sector, an area that had not even been part of the programme of exemplar projects. There was a recognition within the DE and the NCVQ that the establishment of a lead body for education would be desirable, in order that standards of occupational competence and N/SVQs could be developed for teachers. Although the DES exhibited some initial interest in this area, to the extent that it organised a conference on the matter in November 1991, progress was very slow, and the idea was ultimately shelved, principally because education ministers were resistant to the concept. Elsewhere, progress was slow for three reasons. First, the developmental work itself was complex and time-consuming. Second, while the professional bodies saw the elaboration of occupational standards as being of benefit in their own right, for example in continuing professional development, the prospect of founding their qualifications' arrangements upon them was less attractive.[17] Even the MCI regarded the development of NVQs as an off-shoot of its major work on the establishment of management standards. Third, the complexity of the pattern of professional coverage, and the potential for boundary disputes this causes, impeded reform in some instances. The DE initially funded four separate standards development projects at level five in accountancy, until the various bodies could be persuaded to cooperate in a 'common issues group'. The participation of bodies in engineering and construction can be ascribed, in part, to the imperative to protect their terrain from the possibility of encroachment by industry bodies, the CITB and ENTRA respectively.[18]

The Progress of the Reforms 1992–93

Despite having encountered difficulties in some areas, the engineering sector for example, the NCVQ met its target of having sufficient NVQs accredited at levels one to four to cover 80 per cent of the employed workforce by the end of December 1992. In the end, some extra effort towards the end of the year notwithstanding, the NCVQ found it a relatively easy achievement, although there was a feeling among its officials, perhaps unfounded as we will shortly discover, that departmental officials did not share their commitment.

> I don't think anybody in the department thought we were going to make that target. It was set, as they thought, absurdly high.
>
> (NCVQ official)

> I think they were completely astounded that we managed to do it, and I wouldn't be surprised personally if that target had been set for us to fail.
>
> (NCVQ official)

It would be unfair, however, to accuse departmental officials of being uninterested in the NCVQ's progress. If the 80 per cent target had not been met they would have borne the responsibility of informing ministers that one of the government's policies was not succeeding. As a DE official emphasized, there was 'a highly specific target to hit, which was the one about 80 per cent of the sectors being covered up to level four . . . by the end of 1992. We were determined we were going to hit that bloody target.' Such was their concern that the target was met, senior DE officials took a considerably greater interest in the implementation of NVQ policy than they had exhibited hitherto. In his remit letter of December 1990 Michael Howard had demanded that a Joint Management Group comprised of senior NCVQ and DE officials be established to monitor progress towards the 80 per cent target. One of its departmental members recalled that it turned out to be:

> a monthly meeting . . . to assess progress and to pick out areas where we saw problems, and where there were problems deciding between us how we were going to tackle them . . . One of the reasons that we did it of course, was that one important aspect of the process, the sort of supply chain, was actually something that we were responsible for and they [NCVQ] weren't, which was the relations with the Industry Training Organisations that developed the occupational standards that were needed to underpin the qualifications. So if we didn't get the links between that work . . . and the vocational qualifications right they were never going to hit the target.

In fact, such was the level of interest they took in the implementation of NVQ policy at this time, DE officials felt sure that the NCVQ must have resented it; although there is no evidence that the NCVQ's officials recognized it as a particular problem of this period. Nevertheless, once the 80 per cent target had been met the Secretary of State for Employment, Gillian Shephard,[19] delivered a new remit letter to the NCVQ in which she proposed that such guidance would subsequently be provided annually. In this new correspondence Shephard gave the NCVQ a revised target for 90 per cent coverage at levels one to four by the end of 1995 and asked it to assess the prospect of financial self-sufficiency again during 1993.

Although the NCVQ had been successful in reaching the 80 per cent target, further concerns about the progress of NVQ policy arose between 1991 and 1993. Policy makers faced the difficulty not only of getting employers to use NVQs for workers in their establishments, but also of making them aware of the new qualifications in the first place. The slow penetration rate of the awards was increasingly being acknowledged by external studies (e.g. Callender, 1992). Of course, the NVQ policy had been in place only since 1987, and after something of a false start, it really became established only in 1990–91. How realistic was it, then, to expect NVQs quickly to achieve high levels of penetration, particularly in a voluntary system where employers were under no compulsion to offer their employees the opportunity to take them, and where existing, alternative vocational qualifications remained widely available? A rational assessment of the success of NVQs in finding a market would perhaps have allowed the system some years to establish itself. The problem was, however, that ministers, having given the NCVQ additional money to advance NVQ policy, pressed for early results. Although, according to a senior NCVQ official, there were 'lots of people panicking' about this, there was a realization, especially within the NCVQ, that once the product was in place then market penetration would accelerate.

Nevertheless, the 1990–93 period was characterized by largely unsuccessful attempts to promote NVQs among employers. In 1990 DE officials realized that employers needed to be better informed about the NVQ system if it was to be a success and, in his remit letter of December that year, Michael Howard had asked the NCVQ to explore how the qualifications could be publicized, though no additional funds were allocated for this task. When, during 1991, the NCVQ got around to discussing how to pursue this aspect of its remit, it encountered problems. Consultants had recommended that the NCVQ should undertake a two-year marketing campaign. Yet it had sufficient funds only for a one-year initiative, in 1991–92, and could not afford to employ a Communications Director to coordinate developments.[20] The NCVQ asked the DE for extra resources so that it could undertake a publicity drive, and it was given funding for this, on a contract basis, for 1992–93 and 1993–94. A newly established NCVQ Communications Group then developed a strategy that began, in January 1992, with a major national conference on the theme of 'World Class Britain', which was addressed by the Prime Minister, John Major.

This new communications strategy notwithstanding, during 1992 there was growing concern that the NVQ system was being insufficiently publicized (CBI, 1994). The importance of raising the awareness of NVQs was attested to by government and NCVQ officials, and even the Secretary of State for Employment herself.[21] Perhaps the most expressive requests for better publicity, however, came from supportive employers' representatives, as at a special CBI conference on lead bodies in October 1992 (see CBI, 1993). For example, Ted Willmott, Chief Executive of the CITB, was reported as saying that:

> We maintain faith in NVQs and believe in their vision for the future, but for Christ's sake please come to our help to promote them in our industry.
>
> (*Times Higher Education Supplement*, 30 October 1992)

Although Michael Howard had asked the NCVQ to investigate ways of 'marketing' NVQs more effectively, when it came to implementing a strategy, the organisation could only mount a 'communications' campaign. This was because until 1995 the DE formally retained responsibility for leading the marketing of NVQs.[22] While this was in part a reflection of the DE's reluctance to give up any of its functions, there was also a more profound cause of the unwillingness to give the NCVQ a remit for marketing NVQs. At the inception of the NCVQ it was tacitly conceptualized as a regulatory body, despite its lack of powers to regulate, and charged with ensuring that vocational qualifications met certain stated criteria and were included in a national framework. The way in which the NCVQ interpreted its remit, however, led it to oversee the development of one particular type of award – the NVQ – around which the framework was built, when there were numerous other awards also available in the marketplace. Given its implicit regulatory function, responsibility for marketing one particular type of award would clearly have been an inappropriate function for the NCVQ (see DfEE, 1995). Nevertheless, following the extensive concern that NVQs needed to be better publicized, the DE did take action to raise awareness of them during 1993. In her new remit letter of December 1992 Gillian Shephard promised to launch 'a major campaign to put NVQs on the map'. An initiative to publicize NVQs and the new Investors in People standard was started by the DE in the spring of 1993, although the NCVQ council was disappointed about the number of responses for information that the promotional campaign generated. There also appears to have been some frustration that the DE's lead role in promoting NVQs, especially the way in which it funded the NCVQ to 'communicate' on a contract basis, was too constraining.

Among DE officials there was a further concern that the perceived poor quality of NVQs was a major obstacle to improving their take-up. Concentrating on the achievement of the 80 per cent target, while it had focused efforts, had not only meant that there was little effort to increase the penetration of NVQs, but also that measures to secure quality had been overlooked. The 1995 Quinquennial Review of the NCVQ found a widespread recognition 'that insufficient attention had been devoted to the quality assurance issues in the effort to complete the National Framework and to get the qualifications within it in place' (DfEE, 1995, p. 32). However, by the beginning of 1993 a number of measures had already been taken to improve quality assurance in the NVQ system, including the publication of the updated NVQ criteria and guidance in March 1991, the ending of conditional accreditation and the development of the Awarding Bodies Common Accord. There was an increasing realization, moreover, that two related aspects of the way in which the NVQ system was organised had potentially damaging effects on the quality of the NVQs.

One of these was the nature of the competence-based assessment regime that was a central feature of NVQs. There was a growing recognition that not only was the assessment process burdensome, over-complicated and rather bureaucratic, but that it was also difficult to establish consistency, given the criterion-based arrangements. While this was an issue that DE officials identified as an area for improvement in itself, their concern was amplified because of the impact of outcome-related funding in government employment programmes. In Youth Training, for example, the proportion of the total fee paid by the TEC to the training provider once an individual trainee had successfully completed a scheme (by gaining a recognized qualification or obtaining a job) rose from 10 per cent of the total amount in 1990–91 to between 25 per cent and 40 per cent in 1993–94. It has been recognized that the elaboration of a funding regime based on payment by results can be an efficient and effective way of organizing publicly funded training programmes (Bennett et al., 1994; Steedman and Hawkins, 1994). However, the competence-based nature of the NVQ system gave rise to a concern that the people directly responsible for assessing trainees had a financial interest in ensuring that they were successful. One observer has noted that it 'is obviously unsatisfactory if . . . people are placed in a position where their income or the resources of their organisation are affected by whether or not they judge a trainee to be competent' (Stanton, 1996, p. 7). An NCVQ official reflected at some length on the potential for trouble caused by the combination of a results-oriented funding regime and the competence-based approach to assessment:

> I think that the one thing I under-estimated severely was the impact of funding regimes on quality. I always remember when we first heard that NVQs were going to be a required outcome for Youth Training, which must have been in 1990 . . . We all said, isn't that terrific, wonderful, great news, guaranteed market, how could we fail? And we never said, yes, but what are the other consequences of that? And it took a long time for that to sink in; and it still hasn't to some extent. I mean . . . [it's an] unresolved policy tension between output related funding and a devolved qualification system. I mean they are irreconcilable ultimately. And it doesn't mean that either of them are wrong, but when you put them together it's an explosive mixture.[23]

Although the take-up of N/SVQs was to rise significantly from 1993 onwards, the perception that the qualifications were insufficiently rigorous and deficient in quality also shaped N/SVQ (and GNVQ) policy in this period.

Conclusion

In this chapter we have examined the resuscitation of NVQ policy in the period 1990–93. In the summer of 1990 its future looked uncertain because the NCVQ had run out of funds, and government dissatisfaction with the slow pace of reform had brought about a major review of the policy and its implementation. However, the DE was able to secure additional resources for the NCVQ to enable it to focus its energies on establishing the NVQ framework, and a specific target was set – for coverage of at least 80 per cent of the workforce at levels one to four by the end of 1992. In striving to meet this target, which it eventually achieved, the NCVQ was assisted by a number of factors. They included among other things: the signing of an agreement with SCOTVEC regarding the mutual recognition of SVQs and NVQs; the way in which BTEC was increasingly compelled to adapt its products to the NVQ framework; the development of a consistent approach to the development of assessable standards of competence by industry lead bodies; and a greater degree of cooperation with the TA and the DE.

Clearly, then, a much more sustained and coordinated effort went into implementing NVQ policy between 1991 and 1993 than had been the case hitherto. Indeed, perhaps the most striking difference in the way in which NVQ policy was advanced during this time was the notably greater degree of interventionism by the government and its agencies. Both the DE and the NCVQ established increasingly prescriptive and highly technical criteria for what was acceptable for accreditation as an NVQ and sectoral industry training bodies, such as ENTRA for example, were put under considerable pressure to comply. Moreover, DE officials started to evince an interest in rationalizing the number of lead bodies and awarding bodies; hitherto, the prevailing view had been that this was something that should be decided by the market. Yet it would be a mistake to make too much of this change in emphasis. While there was undoubtedly a shift in the assumptions and actions of policy makers towards a more interventionist approach, it was nonetheless bounded by the government's belief that market forces should operate in this area of public policy. Finally, while the NCVQ and the DE had expended a considerable amount of effort in establishing the NVQ framework, there was a growing realization that not only was the slow take-up of the qualifications an issue that needed to be addressed, but also that their quality needed to be improved.

Notes

1 For example, see the evidence of the then Minister of State for Employment, Tim Eggar, to a House of Lords Select Committee in 1990 (House of Lords, 1990).
2 Sir Bryan Nicholson, who was to take over the chairmanship of the NCVQ in 1990 (see p. 94), later reflected on the way in which the policy of conditional accreditation had militated against the progress towards a proper NVQ framework. He observed that 'existing qualifications which were clearly not up to NVQ standards were being accredited largely unchanged, and this was completely undermining the system. The critics were having a field day' (NCVQ, 1993b).
3 The Training Agency (TA) replaced the MSC (the Training Commission from April 1988) in October 1988. In December 1990 it was taken into the DE as the Training, Enterprise and Employment Directorate (TEED).

4 In its original plans the NCVQ had anticipated receiving some £1.9m of revenue from accreditations in the financial year 1990–91. Given the slow progress in building the framework of NVQs, it was having difficulty in getting even a tenth of this amount (*Times Educational Supplement*, 8 June 1990). The NCVQ's Director of Finance and Administration, Mervyn Unger, observed that the 'income arising from certification has taken longer to build up than envisaged and therefore the process of creating NVQs has taken longer' (*Financial Times*, 15 June 1990).

5 Interestingly, given the content of the RVQ report and the subsequent 1986 White Paper, the review also suggested that the NCVQ's lack of statutory powers may need reviewing in due course.

6 See Ellis and Lee (1995) and the interview given by Gilbert Jessup to the *Times Educational Supplement* (7 April 1995) for indications that the government was considering drastic changes.

7 The importance of the support given to vocational education and training policy by another Conservative minister, Lord Young, was discussed in Chapter 3.

8 Local Enterprise Companies (LECs) in Scotland.

9 In a later work, *Towards a Competent Workforce*, Mansfield and his co-author, Lindsay Mitchell, return to this theme, although here they also point to the way in which N/SVQ policy has been dominated by the government's training programmes, and the compromising effect this has had on the proper development of broad-based standards of competence (Mansfield and Mitchell, 1996).

10 Alison Wolf has written at length about how there is an inherent tendency within the competence-based approach for the designers of standards to 'strain' after 'unattainable levels of precision' (Wolf, 1995, p. 112).

11 Trade unions have managed to gain increasing representation on lead bodies. Occasionally, in the care sector for example, their influence has been considerable. The development of occupational standards and vocational qualifications for trade union officers from 1993 onwards is an important example of the way in which union leaderships have embraced NVQ policy.

12 Consultants stressed that they had a partnership with lead bodies, and that while they were the ones who understood how to apply functional analysis, industry representatives, given that they had a detailed knowledge of their sectors, performed a key role.

13 See the Secretary of State for Employment's remit letter of December 1992.

14 Rationalization was, cleverly, presented as a way of increasing employer ownership of the standards programme. In advocating the establishment of OSCs, John Fuller of the DE argued that they would potentially be more secure and long term entities, less reliant on the department for funds than many lead bodies and, implicitly, therefore more independent of government (CBI, 1993).

15 The pressure on the NCVQ notwithstanding, this was only possible because the NCVQ was increasingly occupied with enhancing the breadth of NVQs (see NCVQ, 1991b).

16 Policy makers in the DE and the NCVQ envisaged that there would be only one NVQ level above level four – a level five. Some ambiguity about the exact number of levels to comprise the NVQ framework persisted during 1991, however, leading the NCVQ to clarify the situation.

17 Note, for example, withdrawal of the Law Society and the Royal Pharmaceutical Society of Great Britain from the programme of exemplars.

18 The Engineering Council oversaw the establishment of a number of standing conferences to pursue the development of occupational standards: the Standing Conference on Engineering Manufacture (SCEM); the Engineering Services Standing Conference (ESSC); the Standing Conference on Extracting and Processing

(SCEP); and the Construction Industry Standing Conference (CISC). CISC made the most rapid progress, getting a level five NVQ/SVQ in Construction Project Management accredited in December 1995.

19 Shephard had succeeded Michael Howard in April 1992.

20 The NCVQ finally appointed a Director of Communications in March 1993.

21 The then Permanent Secretary at the DE, Sir Geoffrey Holland, reportedly said in June 1992 that 'there is a huge job to be done in marketing National Vocational Qualifications. Unless this is done within the next 12 months, then all is lost' (*Education*, 8 January 1993). Sir Bryan Nicholson, the NCVQ's Chairman, claimed that a dearth of funds was responsible for the low profile of NVQs (*Education*, 18 December 1992), while Gillian Shephard indicated her dissatisfaction with the lack of employer knowledge about the qualifications, and at the CBI conference in November 1992 promised to take steps to raise it (*Financial Times*, 29 July 1992; *Education*, 13 November 1992).

22 According to an NCVQ official, 'it was always made very clear to us that our role was not marketing; it was communications, which was different. And there was always a lot of tension about . . . what that responsibility meant, because some of us felt that we needed to go further and we actually did need to market and advertise and everything like that.'

23 From 1994–95 onwards the outcome-based element could rise to as much as 100 per cent in some cases. We will further consider the implications of such an arrangement in Chapter 8.

6 Coherence for 16- to 19-Year-Olds: The Origins and Development of GNVQ Policy

Introduction

At this point in our account it is necessary to consider the origins and development of GNVQ (General National Vocational Qualification) policy. GNVQs were developed as broad-based vocational qualifications appropriate for young people, to be delivered in schools and colleges in a number of occupational areas and to prepare candidates for employment and/or higher education. Their essential characteristics were noted in Chapter 1, as were some of the major problems that emerged once they came on stream from 1992–93 onwards. Concerns were raised about the heavy burden of assessment in GNVQs, the reliability of the assessment and grading procedures, and the high drop-out rates among other things. In this chapter we will show that these problems can largely be ascribed to the way in which GNVQ policy was originated during the late 1980s and early 1990s.[1] GNVQs themselves, though they were then known only as 'general NVQs', were formally launched in the 1991 White Paper, *Education and Training for the 21st Century* (DES/DE, 1991). But we shall go back further than that to examine how they were orginally conceptualized as a separate policy aim of both the DE and the NCVQ. We will then go on to investigate how the proposals came to appeal to ministers and officials in the DES. They then provided the impetus for the advancement of GNVQs, and with the cooperation and input of three major national awarding bodies, the NCVQ was subsequently given the remit to develop and design the new awards.

The Limitations of NVQs

The origins of the GNVQ policy in England and Wales cannot be disentangled from the way in which NVQ policy had progressed in the period 1986 to 1989. As the new NVQs came on stream, a considerable amount of criticism was directed at the way in which they appeared to recognize only narrow, job-specific skills and failed to take into account knowledge and understanding that individuals might accrue outside their immediate workplaces. This was, to a large extent, an expression of the employment-led character of the new qualifications; predominantly educational bodies, further education colleges and some of the providers of existing vocational awards in particular, found that their expertise was unwanted. There was an increasing realization among TA and DE officials, and even within the NCVQ, that the scope of the newly instituted NVQs was too narrow and that there was a concomitant need to add breadth.

> There had been a lot of discussion within NCVQ about NVQs and whether NVQs were providing the sufficiently broad base for people who were not necessarily committed to a specific role.
>
> (NCVQ council member)

> Putting NVQs in place meant that we took a big step in terms of a system that did assess and certify people with actual competence. The traditional qualifications, even though we played them down . . . I don't think that we were recognizing that there were people who also needed to develop, and help assess the knowledge and understanding based thing.
>
> (DE official)

There was also a parallel concern that the emphasis placed on the assessment of NVQs in the workplace restricted their take-up too much because it largely militated against delivery in further education colleges. While the new qualifications derived in part from the great amount of dissatisfaction with the existing system of vocational qualifications exhibited by the government and the MSC, once the more employment-based NVQs came on stream there was a feeling within the DE that the pendulum had perhaps swung too far away from education. Moreover, within the NCVQ there was also a realization that not only might some mitigation of the requirement for delivery through, and assessment in workplaces lessen the opposition of educational bodies to the new system, BTEC in particular, but would also help to increase access, something that the emphasis on the workplace was supposed to have brought about. An NCVQ official recalled that NVQs were designed as:

> an on-the-job thing . . . I think there were two problems with that. One was that vested interests in the education and training community wouldn't allow it, or would resist it; but also the fact that there is a theoretical difficulty with plunging people into the workplace and having them learn in this work-based way from day one.

There was an increasing recognition, then, of the part that could be played by colleges in delivering NVQs, particularly given the large share of the vocational education and training market that they covered. Policy makers thus began to consider how greater breadth could be introduced into the new awards. Continuing their longstanding commitment, when part of the recently dissolved MSC, to the establishment of greater vocational relevance in education and the construction of a 'permanent bridge from school to work', TA and DE officials resumed their quest for the establishment of a more coherent framework of vocational qualifications that could be attained in colleges, as well as in workplaces – a role that the developing NVQ system was patently not fulfilling. One former DE official conceded that this was becoming increasingly recognized as a 'fatal gap' in the NVQ framework. As a result, in 1989 officials had cautious and unproductive discussions with BTEC to see if there was some way of including its awards within the emerging national framework of vocational qualifications.

During 1989, NCVQ officials carried out a similar task when they participated with BTEC officials in a joint study that examined how non-occupationally specific vocational awards could be incorporated into the NVQ framework. This study was an outcome of the desire of NCVQ officials to instill greater 'breadth' into NVQs, given the recognition that the early awards were too job-specific (Jessup, 1991), and an internal NCVQ working group was also established to look at ways of bringing this about. The duplication of work in this area – both DE and NCVQ officials were in discussion with BTEC – is an indication of the uncertainty about where responsibilities in the new system resided. Nevertheless, in exploring ways of increasing the knowledge and understanding base and thus the breadth of NVQs, the motives of the two organizations were different. While DE officials looked at ways of improving the quality of NVQs out of a longstanding (strategic) commitment to the improvement of the skills base of the economy, the activity of the NCVQ in this area arose from rather more immediate concerns.

The NCVQ was eager to bring non-occupationally specific awards, those offered by BTEC and delivered through further education colleges in particular, into the NVQ framework in order to attract revenue from their accreditation. We have already noted the way in which the NCVQ was willing to compromise the principles of the NVQ criteria in order to accredit qualifications, which did not meet those criteria, on a 'conditional' basis. These further discussions with BTEC in 1989 can be interpreted in the same way in that they represented an attempt by the NCVQ to broaden the requirements for NVQ accreditation as a way of gaining some revenue from the insertion of other vocational awards in its framework. Following the discussions with BTEC and the meetings of the NCVQ's working group on 'breadth', early in 1990 Peter Thompson proposed to the NCVQ council that the organization should begin work on the development of 'general NVQs', in addition to the more occupationally specific qualifications based on lead body standards that had then started to come on stream. At this time no blueprint for what were later to emerge in 1992 as GNVQs existed. Rather, the proposal for 'general NVQs' merely represented a further attempt to insert a greater degree of flexibility into the NVQ system so that vocational awards that were not competence-based, and thus did not meet the NCVQ's stated criteria, could be placed within its framework and thus provide it with some accreditation revenue.

The 'general NVQ' proposal was received cautiously by the NCVQ council. Members requested further work to be done on the outlines of the suggested award before any development work was undertaken. There was greater opposition to the NCVQ's initiative, however, from its principal sponsoring department – the DE. This was not on any grounds of principle. As we have already noted, DE officials were well aware of the difficulties that had arisen from the introduction of occupationally specific NVQs, which lacked sufficient recognition of knowledge and understanding acquired away from the workplace. Nevertheless, they felt that it was not an appropriate time – in the early months of 1990 – for the NCVQ to be expanding its activities, given the then 'precarious' condition of the organization. Yet by the spring of the following year (1991) the introduction of 'general NVQs' had become one of the government's key policy initiatives (DES/DE, 1991). While they clearly acknowledged the desirability of developing such a qualification, NCVQ officials were nonetheless taken aback by the rapidity with which it was to come about, as one recalled:

> I said one day the idea would be resurrected. It happened within twelve months. I hadn't realised it would be so fast.

Better Provision for 16- to 19-Year-Olds[2]

In order to understand why the 'general NVQ' policy was launched in May 1991, barely a year after the NCVQ's proposals had apparently been shelved, and, moreover, after BTEC had come to an agreement with the NCVQ about the inclusion of its awards within the NVQ framework, it is necessary to refer to the debate about the reform of education provision for 16- to 19-year-olds, which, between 1988 and 1991, had become increasingly pronounced both inside and outside the government. After the 1987 General Election the government established a committee of inquiry, under the chairmanship of Professor Gordon Higginson, to explore possible changes to the teaching and assessment of A levels. It reported in June 1988, and in its report, *Advancing A Levels* (Higginson, 1988), the committee recommended among other things: that there should be a reduction in the number of different A levels; that a greater emphasis should be placed within the examinations on the acquisition of skills; that students should take a greater number of A levels and thus broaden their portfolio; and that as a consequence the A level syllabi should be subjected to considerable reform, largely to reflect the broader range of examinations that it was envisaged that students would take.

The government, however, rejected the proposals of the Higginson Committee. Its official view was that with the recent introduction of both the GCSE (General Certificate of Secondary Education) at the conclusion of the compulsory stage of education and the A/S (Advanced/Supplementary) level, there was enough change taking place in the educational system anyway, and that any more reforms were impractical for the time being. However, Richardson (1991) has noted that there was 'a sense of dissatisfaction within the education system that necessary change was forestalled for political reasons' (p. 2); principally the commitment of senior government ministers, including the then Prime Minister Margaret Thatcher, to the maintenance of the A level 'gold standard'. Nevertheless, it became increasingly evident to policy-makers that the existing situation in respect of education provision for 16- to 19-year-olds was unsatisfactory and that some form of reform, however minimal, was desirable, particularly as the government was under increasing pressure to boost participation rates in post-compulsory education (see CBI, 1989, for example). Thus both Kenneth Baker in February 1989, and his successor as Secretary of State for Education, John MacGregor, later that year, expressed an interest in exploring ways of altering provision for 16- to 19-year-olds, without disturbing the perceived primacy of A levels, their much-attested weaknesses notwithstanding (Richardson, 1991).

At this stage, the principal way in which they sought to do this was by promoting the development of generic core 'skills' or 'studies' within the post-compulsory curriculum. Following a speech on this by Baker to the Association for Colleges earlier in the year, in July 1989 the DES issued a paper that sought to expand on and formalize the government's position. It identified the core skills that could be incorporated within the assessment of post-16 learning programmes as being: oral and written communication; problem solving; practical skills; personal and social qualities (team working, for example); and possibly, an understanding of industry and information technology (DES, 1989). At this stage, however, the possibility of establishing a common set of core skills that could apply equally to vocational courses, A/S level examinations and A levels was deemed to be impractical. Nevertheless, following on from this initiative, in November 1989 John MacGregor asked the recently established NCC (National Curriculum Council) and SEAC (Schools Examination and Assessment Council) to investigate ways in which 'common core skills' could be delivered and assessed within the A and A/S level syllabi, since there appeared to be growing official concern about rising failure and drop out rates (Richardson, 1991, p. 13).

Thus during 1989 there was a growing realization within the government that some reform of the education provision for 16- to 19-year-olds was desirable, largely because it was recognized that the existing system, based as it was on a sharp distinction between narrowly 'academic' A levels and vocational awards, could not adequately cater for the growing numbers of individuals staying on in full-time post-compulsory education.

> We recognized that, in a rather crude way, the qualifications framework . . . had evolved against a background of rather limited post-16 participation in full-time provision, and we needed to ensure that we had a framework . . . which could cater for all potential participants.
>
> (DES official)

> The big problem was not the academic high-fliers; it was the bulk of people . . . above the bottom 25% and up to just below the top 25%. It was that group which I thought we had seriously short-changed for a long period of time . . . It was also leading to problems in schools, in that however good the schools there was a group of quite able kids who simply weren't switched on by the fare they were being given.
>
> (education minister)

Until about the middle of 1990, the principal policy objective of the government, in trying to broaden the scope of education suitable for a greater number of potential participants in the post-compulsory stage, was, first, to promote the recently established A/S level and then, second, to encourage the development of common core skills within the 16-to-19 curriculum. In April 1990 the NCC published its recommendations in respect of core skills in A and A/S levels – to encompass communication, problem solving, personal, numeracy, information technology and modern languages skills within existing syllabi – without compromising the A level 'standard' that the Prime Minister was reportedly 'determined to preserve' (NCC, 1990; Richardson, 1991, p. 14). The NCVQ, meanwhile, brought out a report on 'common learning outcomes', largely the work of Gilbert Jessup, which argued, contrary to the views expressed by the NCC, that they should be assessed and accredited in isolation from any specific courses and thus form the basis of an integrated, credit-based system of vocational and academic qualifications (NCVQ, 1990). This work did much to raise the NCVQ's profile, at a difficult period in its history, and was accorded considerable praise by the organization's council.

Outside government there was growing pressure for a more fundamental reform of post-compulsory full-time education provision. The IPPR's (Institute of Public Policy Research) 'British Baccalaureate' proposals in July 1990 (Finegold et al., 1990), which called, among other things, for the replacement of A levels by a single advanced diploma that would encompass both academic and vocational curricula, received widespread publicity. The Labour Party was later to come out in favour of such a single award, with its suggestion of an 'Advanced Certificate of Education and Training' for 16- to 19-year-olds, within which significantly reformed advanced level academic curricula would be given parity of esteem, and interchangeable with, vocational units (Labour Party, 1991). Government ministers, however, were less convinced of the desirability of marrying academic and vocational qualifications in such a manner. For a start, there was a continuing unwillingness to interfere with the A level 'gold standard', something that was further confirmed by the appointment of the right-wing traditionalist Michael Fallon as a junior DES minister in July 1990. But ministers were also sceptical about the espoused benefits of a single, all-embracing qualification for 16- to 19-year-olds. Not everybody in the government considered that the recent introduction of the GCSE had been a success. Moreover, as one former minister pointed out, the emphasis on the reform of A levels could be seen as a distraction:

> Whatever was wrong with A levels, they were nothing compared to how you dealt with [the] great bulk of people.

Nevertheless, the 'retention of A levels was the central point at issue in the educational part of the debate' (Richardson, 1993, p. 13). The incremental and tentative approach that government agencies took regarding the question of A level reform, which had hitherto mainly involved the promotion of core skills, slowed from the autumn of 1990 onwards. In September of that year, the proposal of SEAC to increase the amount of coursework assessment allowable in A level examinations met with a considerable amount of ministerial hostility. It was reported that not only had the Prime Minister herself 'poured cold water' on the reforms, but that Michael Fallon had also stated that any reforms to the A level would have to be 'over his dead body' (*Times Higher Education Supplement*, 2 October 1991; *Education*, 20 October 1991). Thus the strong opposition of many in the government to what was presented as the dilution of academic standards, reinforced by influential lobbyists such as the Headmasters' Conference, impeded officials in their attempts to make even marginal reforms to the A level system. As we have already seen, however, rising staying-on rates had induced a realization among ministers and officials that the maintenance of the *status quo* in respect of 16 to 19 provision was unsustainable. From about the middle of 1990, then, rather than looking to broaden the appeal and constituency of A levels, policy-makers in the DES sought to improve the vocational options for full-time students in post-compulsory education. According to one senior DES official, Nick Stuart, the government's 'strategy was to increase the number of 16-year-olds in education largely by extending vocational courses' (*Times Educational Supplement*, 15 March 1991).

In the summer of 1990 a high-level joint DE–DES working group was established to explore ways of enhancing the vocational aspect of full-time post-compulsory education for 16- to 19-year-olds. It included two government ministers – Tim Eggar (DE) and Robert Jackson (DES) – and a number of senior civil servants from both departments – Geoffrey Holland (DE), Roger Dawe (DE) and John Vereker (DES), among others. One of the participants reflected on the imperative for the working group's formation:

> Higginson got turned down, but we were then left with this kind of, you know, rather difficult policy of defending a traditional academic qualification at 18: narrow, decreasingly deep, although we tried to pretend that it wasn't, at a time when everybody was saying it ought to be broadened, and at a time when there were increasing numbers of people staying on in school . . . Those who were attempting A levels had quite a high failure rate and there was a feeling that, you know, something had to be done.

In some ways, the setting up of this group represented a considerable achievement as the relationship between the DE and DES had previously been rather poor. Remember that one former DE official had likened it during the 1980s to that which existed between North and South Korea. Two factors, however, combined to bring about a greater degree of cooperation in 1990. One of them – the need to improve (vocational) educational provision for young people – we have already discussed. Given such a policy imperative, it was clearly necessary to instigate greater cooperation between the two departments. Second, it is also evident that the ministerial reshuffle of July 1990, when Tim Eggar moved from the DE to the DES and Robert Jackson moved the other way, induced a less adversarial inter-departmental climate. Importantly, Eggar appeared to take with him to the DES a firm belief in the value of further and vocational education (Richardson, 1993), an area that had hitherto been somewhat marginalized in that department. The working group met during the later months of 1990 and early 1991, and the member of it quoted above recalled that:

> The answer that emerged from this working party was that we would have two qualifications at the A level standard. We would keep the A level, which we would hope [would] revert to being really focused on university entrance . . . But we would sit alongside it a new vocational qualification which would . . . have parity of esteem, would fit into university entrance if that was so wanted, would be mixed with A levels . . . but would also be linked in some way to the NVQ system.

Thus the working group revived the 'general NVQ' proposals that had previously been circulating within the DE and the NCVQ. The joint departmental constitution of this group notwithstanding, it is important to bear in mind that it was the DES that took the lead in promoting the 'general NVQ' idea from the autumn of 1990 onwards. DE officials had become interested in developing less occupationally specific vocational qualifications out of a concern that NVQs, as they were coming on stream, were incapable of contributing to its strategic aims in respect of the upskilling of the workforce.

As we have shown, the NCVQ initiated policy developments in this area largely because its immediate financial constraints compelled it to try to reach compromises with providers of existing vocational qualifications that were not competence-based. DES officials and ministers, however, were more concerned with setting in place appropriate curricula for the growing number of young people aged 16 to 19 who were staying on in full-time education and for whom unreconstructed A levels were deemed unsuitable. A DE official noted about the DES officials that:

> They had another agenda which was that increasing numbers of young people in schools were not suited to the A level curriculum. Ours was about a qualification which fed into employment.

We shall return to the tension between the 'educational' and 'employment' imperatives within 'general NVQ' policy later as they resurfaced during its development and implementation. Nevertheless, innovation in this area was made slightly easier by change at the top of the government. In November 1990 John Major replaced Margaret Thatcher as leader of the Conservative Party and as Prime Minister. His supporters claim that at this time he took an interest in vocational education and training policy, perhaps reflecting his non-academic background. While fundamental reform of the full-time education system for 16- to 19-year-olds, such as the replacement of A levels with a unitary vocational and academic award, could still not be countenanced, policy-makers nonetheless felt that they had enhanced scope to innovate in respect of vocational education and to provide, in the words of one former minister, 'a real parallel to A levels'. Indeed, the DE–DES working group's proposals appear to have been discussed and honed at a weekend meeting at Chequers, the Prime Minister's country residence, in March 1991 (Hogg and Hill, 1995). The most important thing to note about the way in which 'general NVQ' policy originated, then, is that for the most part it was not progressed on account of a rational analysis of its merits, rather its advancement was contingent on the coming into existence of a particular set of institutional and political circumstances. Reflecting on this, an NCVQ official observed that:

> When you're dealing . . . close to government logic plays no part in what you do at all. It's actually political will and money . . . Politicians should listen to logic, but they don't. They're about their own agenda, and the GNVQ story is a good illustration of that. It was perfectly logical. It was a natural development. But it was not supported because there was no political will behind it and no money. Until it was politically re-born nothing happened.

The 'general NVQ' proposals were included in a major statement of the government's policy aims and objectives in the area of education and training, the May 1991 White Paper, *Education and Training for the 21st Century* (DES/DE, 1991).

The Development of the GNVQ

For what was to become such a major policy development, affecting many schools and most colleges, the section in the White Paper that launched 'general NVQs' is surprisingly brief, comprising just three paragraphs. In the document it was recognized that there was a need for general vocational qualifications as occupationally specific awards could restrict the opportunities of young people, and that while other awards existed that fulfilled this need, most notably those offered by BTEC, it was desirable for them to be 'clearly related to the NVQ framework' (DES/DE, 1991, p. 18). 'General NVQs', it was noted, should 'cover broad occupational areas', 'offer opportunities to develop the relevant knowledge and understanding' and give students 'an appreciation of how to apply them at work'. More specifically, the awards should:

- offer a broad preparation for employment as well as an accepted route to higher level qualifications, including higher education;
- require the demonstration of a range of skills and the application of knowledge and understanding relevant to the related occupations;
- be of equal standing with academic qualifications at the same level;
- be clearly related to the occupationally specific NVQs, so that young people can progress quickly and effectively from one to the other;
- be sufficiently distinctive from occupationally specific NVQs to ensure that there is no confusion between the two;
- be suitable for use by full-time students in colleges, and, if appropriate in schools, who have limited opportunities to demonstrate competence in the workplace.

(DES/DE, 1991, p. 19)

At this point, we can already identify two significant areas of ambiguity contained within the 'general NVQ' proposals. The first concerns the purpose of the new qualifications. Were they primarily to be taken by individuals to prepare them for employment? Or were they to be used to facilitate entry to higher education, as an alternative to A levels? Of course these need not necessarily be mutually exclusive objectives. Yet we have already discovered that the principal imperative for the introduction of 'general NVQs' had shifted from how they might act to raise skill levels in the workforce to the way in which they could provide a vocational alternative to A levels in schools and colleges. It became difficult, moreover, to promote the qualification on the basis that it could fulfil both roles. Employers were to become sceptical about the value of GNVQs since it soon became apparent to them that the new qualifications were largely an educational initiative, administered and directed by the DES. One education minister dwelt on this matter and recalled that he:

> always used to call GNVQs a Janus qualification – looking both ways they've got a head forward and a head back . . . It comes back to the joke I saw quoted the other day by John Gummer about you can sell a shampoo because it makes your hair lustrous, or because it cures dandruff, but it's rather difficult to say it does both.

The second area of ambiguity in fact echoes one aspect of the way in which NVQ policy was initially implemented. The proposals for the 'general NVQs' contained within the White Paper are vague to the extent that they do not specify clearly whether the suggested awards were to be entirely new qualifications, or were to be existing products, those offered by BTEC in particular, suitably altered to meet the government's specifications. With this in mind, then, it is clearly not a trivial point to emphasize that not only did the White Paper refer to the need to introduce 'general NVQs' – not GNVQs – but also that the relevant part of the document was entitled 'general qualifications within the NVQ framework'. This perhaps suggests that at the time of the White Paper a major imperative for the introduction of 'general NVQs' was to stimulate the NVQ system, not the erection of a system of entirely new qualifications.[3] As a former senior NCVQ official observed, even at the post-White Paper stage, most policy-makers envisaged that the 'general NVQ' initiative was simply the latest, and most prominent effort, to bolster the NVQ framework by trying to get BTEC awards included:

> I don't think anybody thought at the time that there was much thought behind it, other than a sort of desire to tidy up the system and to try to bridge the BTEC–NCVQ gap. I don't think there was any more to it than that.
>
> (NCVQ official)

It might seem odd that a body that had been experiencing great difficulties in carrying out its core remit should have been given the responsibility for managing a new policy initiative. Yet it was stated in the White Paper that the NCVQ, in liaison with other bodies, should be responsible for developing 'criteria for accrediting more general vocational qualifications' (DES/DE, 1991, p. 18). However, if the aim of policy-makers was simply to further the progress of NVQ policy, then this should not be considered as being too much of a surprise. But as we have already seen, given the direction in which 'general NVQ' policy was proceeding under the aegis of the DES, there was a strong sense that it would become a more wide-ranging affair, and be much more related to the educational sphere than NVQs had ever been. With this in mind, the central role of the NCVQ in the development and implementation of the 'general NVQ' has to be further explained, particularly given the difficulties it had encountered in ensuring that its core remit was fulfilled properly.

Indeed, prior to the publication of the White Paper there was a feeling within the DES that BTEC, as one of 'its' quangos, should be given the responsibility for developing the proposed 'general NVQs'. Such a view was consonant with the department's initial belief, as it considered ways of improving the vocational options for young people in schools and colleges during late 1990 and early 1991, that an expansion in the coverage of existing awards, such as BTEC Firsts and City and Guild's Diploma in Vocational Education (previously the CPVE), would be an adequate arrangement. Officials from these bodies certainly thought that their products were suitable, as broad-based vocational qualifications that attested to knowledge and skill as well as workplace capability.

The NCVQ was, however, given the remit for developing 'general NVQ' policy for a number of reasons. First, as we have just noted, for a considerable period of time the need for the 'new' qualifications arose from an imperative to establish the NVQ framework properly. Despite the NCVQ's much acknowledged problems, once the government had decided to develop the 'general NVQ' initiative, this clearly made the policy fall within the NCVQ's sphere of responsibility. Second, policy-makers were aware that neither BTEC, nor indeed any other of the vocational awarding bodies, was even close to being monopoly providers of broad-based vocational qualifications for young people. It would have been difficult for a government that was ostensibly committed to the introduction of market forces and competition, not just in education and training but in all areas of public service provision, to have offered just one of the major national awarding bodies the remit to develop the new qualifications. Third, the DE would have been very resistant to the idea of allowing 'education' quangos such as the SEAC, which, among other things, had responsibility for regulating A level provision, to have had a role in progressing vocational qualifications policy, although the recent, substantial experience in operating through quangos that the DES had accumulated since the institution of the National Curriculum for 5- to 16-year-olds meant that it was comfortable about the prospect of working through the NCVQ. Fourth, following its highly regarded work on core skills proposals in 1990, not only had the profile of the NCVQ been raised, but under the chairmanship of Bryan Nicholson it was also able to exhibit greater political influence. NCVQ officials lobbied effectively to be given the responsibility for taking the lead in shaping the vocational qualifications system for 16- to 19-year-olds, and bringing into being a 'qualification which was better than BTEC, although it borrowed many of its features, and was designed to be complementary to the NVQ, which BTEC never was' (NCVQ official). Another NCVQ official recalled that:

On GNVQs we were quite proactive. The initial policy was to promote BTEC qualifications and City and Guilds in schools, and we were only something marginal, the NVQs. So we had a meeting and we agreed that we would bring it forward.

Finally, and perhaps most importantly, while policy-makers were fully aware of the nature of the existing vocational awards for young people, they considered that a more coherent and rational system of provision was desirable. Regarding the origins of 'general NVQ' policy, a DES official noted that:

I don't think it was based on a sort of evaluation of the existing qualifications so much as the need to have a clearer framework within which the options would be more clearly presented, and so the choices for individuals were clearer.

Thus the government considered the NCVQ to be the most appropriate body to take on the 'general NVQ' proposals. Despite the way in which NCVQ officials lobbied for this work, there was a large degree of apprehension about it within the organization's council. Members were concerned that the new initiative could lead to the work-based NVQs being compromised, or be a distraction at the very least. There was resentment, moreover, that the decision to develop 'general NVQs' was taken outside the council. Two NCVQ council members commented on this:

[T]he idea of the general vocational qualification worried me no end. Because no sooner [had] we got the pukka vocational qualifications with the idea of it being tested on the job, of being an absolute functional thing, and doing not knowing, [it] muddied the whole business with something that was general.

My perception is that the council didn't want GNVQs; it was a distraction from NVQs.

Nonetheless, during the summer of 1991, after it had received more detailed guidance from ministers regarding the proposed new awards, the NCVQ swiftly began to work on the development of the proposed 'general NVQs'. Peter Reay chaired a Policy Group that was to oversee, and advise on, the broad guidelines and structure of the new initiative. A Development Group was established to advise on more specific aspects of the proposed 'general NVQ' criteria. Finally, five Occupational Working Groups were also set up. These were concerned with developing the new qualifications in the broad occupational areas within which it was proposed that the first five 'general NVQs' would initially be available: business, art and design, health and care, leisure and tourism, and manufacturing. In addition to

NCVQ officials, these groups contained representatives of industry and the major national awarding bodies – BTEC, City and Guilds and the RSA. Although the DE, in its original proposals for 'general NVQs', had envisaged that the industry lead bodies would largely be responsible for determining the form and criteria of the awards, once the policy lead was taken up by the DES, it was anticipated that educational bodies were to be charged with the major role in establishing their content, in association with the NCVQ. BTEC, City and Guilds and the RSA were given the 'monopoly rights' to award 'general NVQs' and, according to a DE official, 'had their market protected'. While this might be seen as contradicting the imperative to allow markets and competition to apply in the area of vocational qualifications, it was nonetheless essential if the new awards were to become established because the expertise and resources of the three major awarding bodies were thought to be crucial in this respect. They were also being asked to commit a considerable amount of time and resources to the development of 'general NVQs'. As an NCVQ figure observed, though, in the meetings of the NCVQ's Policy Group the representatives of the awarding bodies, their chief officers in fact, made sure they followed developments closely:

> Crucially, you had the three top people from City and Guilds, BTEC, and RSA, and it was fascinating because in a sense they were competitors. But they were . . . being asked to modify their qualifications . . . They sat there like three wise men . . . always at the end of the table together, and I used to watch them like hawks to see which way the wind was blowing.

Clearly, in its determination to make progress with 'general NVQs' the government, while ostensibly committed to supporting competition between providers of vocational qualifications, was not averse to taking a *dirigiste* approach if it was considered necessary. The commitment of BTEC, however, was somewhat grudging (Gokulsing et al., 1996). Unlike City and Guilds, and to a certain extent the RSA, BTEC's market principally comprised full-time, broad-based vocational awards designed to aid progression into higher education and employment – very much the proposed characteristics of the envisaged 'general NVQs'. Thus BTEC, in an echo of the way in which they initially received the implementation of NVQs, could not help but see the institution of the new 'general NVQ' policy as constituting a further vote of no confidence in its abilities. Indeed, rather than having its position enhanced by being given sole responsibility for developing 'general NVQs', as some had initially envisaged, BTEC now became exposed to competition from City and Guilds and the RSA, albeit heavily regulated competition, in a market in which it had previously been dominant. Two informants from the DES commented on the difficulties BTEC had in committing itself to supporting 'general NVQ' policy:

> BTEC commanded a vast majority of the territory of full-time vocational education and further education, and they had enormous business interests in maintaining that. So it's not surprising that they found GNVQs hard to stomach.
>
> (DES official)

> As I recall, they'd got BTECs, which were a bit of currency, and people knew what BTEC was. And they were very worried about having to lose all that.
>
> (education minister)

The government, however, managed to allay BTEC's anxieties that they might be put out of business by the new awards. Once it had made a progress report on the broad shape of the proposed 'general NVQ' framework to DE and DES ministers in September 1991, the NCVQ embarked on a rapid consultation exercise in order that the new awards could be ready for piloting during the 1992–93 academic year. The responses to this exercise revealed a considerable degree of support for the 'general NVQs', as they were still known, from educational bodies, employers and their representatives and other interested parties (NCVQ, 1992).[4] As an NCVQ figure pointed out:

> The most astonishing thing about GNVQ was that we could in three months, from a standing start, have put together a group and got an agreed framework in 12 weeks. Then having carried out the consultation in the next four months [we] had . . . an amazing degree of support.

The positive responses to the consultation exercise notwithstanding, there were two contentious aspects pertaining to the way in which GNVQ policy progressed during 1991–92. The first of these relates to the NCVQ's proposition that 'general NVQs should maintain the primary characteristics of NVQs' (NCVQ, 1991a, p. 6). Indeed, in September 1991 Bryan Nicholson, in a speech to the Institute of Careers Officers, remarked that the 'NCVQ's position is that general NVQs should as far as possible adhere to the same criteria as are required for the existing NVQ framework, except where there are essential reasons for them to be different' (*Times Educational Supplement*, 27 September 1991). Thus it was suggested that, among other things, the new qualifications should be 'specified in the form of the outcomes to be achieved', unit-based, and independent of the learning process – 'general NVQs should be awarded to those who meet the required standards, irrespective of the time taken to achieve them or the mode of learning.' Nevertheless, it was envisaged the proposed awards would differ from NVQs in two key respects. First, the 'general NVQs' should 'assess the skills, knowledge and understanding that underpin a range of NVQs within a broad occupational area'. Following on from this, while the employment-based NVQs were founded upon a 'statement of competence', the proposed new qualifications, in recognition of their broader educational base, would be based on 'statements of attainment' (NCVQ, 1991a, pp. 6–7). Evidently, it was anticipated that other major principles of the NVQ system, the absence of any grading requirements and lack of any form of external assessment, could be carried into the new GNVQs. In effect, the distinction between 'statements of competence' and 'statements of attainment' and the lead role of the DES notwithstanding, the NCVQ was endeavouring to reproduce much of the NVQ model within the new qualifications.

> When GNVQs were introduced you still had the main protagonists of NCVQ who had driven and forced the whole design model . . . and they were quite determined that the model was transferable.
>
> (awarding body official)

> The whole policy development was being driven by the DE and the NCVQ, by people who had a clear idea themselves of what they wanted and [were] simply not prepared to see what was on the ground . . . Which was where I think the policy went fundamentally wrong. I mean it wasn't looking at practice first and establishing what was wrong with it. It was starting with an NVQ model and trying to adapt it to a completely different requirement.
>
> (DES official)

Although the consultation exercise had revealed a major division of opinion over whether or not GNVQ units should be graded and subjected to external assessment, these were features whose presence DES ministers and officials considered to be essential if the new qualification was to have credibility. While the NCVQ and parts of the DE had been responsible for policy innovation in this area and were committed to advancing a qualifications model which derived from what they saw as the needs of employment, it must be remembered that the DES (From April 1992 the DfE – Department for Education) had become the lead department in respect of GNVQs. During the spring and summer of 1992, then, there was a sustained effort made by the DfE to ensure that external assessment specifications, in particular, were included within the nascent GNVQs, in order to make them more rooted in educational imperatives.

> A lot of them, I think, in NCVQ had produced this theology – it had to be competence-based. And I think some people in education, and I wouldn't say it was actually an attempt to recreate A levels . . . but I think it was more an attempt to put on drag anchors and stop it from becoming too wacky, or indeed too theologically driven.
>
> (education minister)

Thus the first GNVQs were piloted during 1992–93, and launched nationally a year later, as a curious blend of the competence-based NVQs and the features of more traditional educational awards – such as grading and external assessment requirements. Perhaps it is no wonder that as a result many schools, colleges and students found the arrangements relating to the provision and awarding of GNVQs so complex and confusing (e.g. OFSTED, 1993).

These implementation difficulties might have been addressed and mitigated during the development phase were it not for the haste with which GNVQ policy was implemented – the second of the contentious aspects to have affected its development. The onus was on the NCVQ to complete its consultation exercise and have concrete proposals in place by January 1992, with a view to embarking on the pilot year in September of that year, so that the Prime Minister, John Major, could then formally launch the initiative as a major part of a speech on his vision of a classless 'society without barriers' in the run up to the General Election that had to be held sometime within the forthcoming six months. Among officials in both departments there was a strong feeling that the design of the GNVQ framework was pushed through too rapidly:

> The pity of it was that ministers, having been enthused, which was a good thing, and then they got so enthused they aimed to have it done very quickly indeed, probably far quicker than it should have been done . . . We certainly should have had more time to do it.
>
> (DE official)

> [It's] true of educational policy that the political timescales are always at odds with proper planning timescales, and new qualification systems are an extremely good example of that. They are long term developments, but inevitably, and this isn't criticism, ministers have to be able to demonstrate short term gains. And there's no doubt that in an ideal world, you'd have spent more time developing and implementing GNVQs.
>
> (DfE official)

Former ministers, however, defended the short timescale within which GNVQs were prepared for two related, and largely pragmatic, reasons. First, it was considered important to make early, rapid progress in order to build up the pace of change.

> I think this needs to be said about the GNVQ thing, that if you went back in history and said, what would be the ideal speed, I suspect that we would still be piloting and just about introducing. We could have taken 10 years and have got it all right before we started,

but you can't do that realistically, and you'd have lost momentum if you had.

(education minister)

Second, given this imperative for 'momentum', it was emphasized by the same erstwhile minister that in politics there is a 'tension which is that the best is the enemy of the good', while another argued that there is 'always a trade off in government between being determined to get something happening and delivering the perfect animal' and that electoral considerations were 'exaggerated'. We will consider further the relationship between ministers' objectives, their careers and the quality of public policy outputs in Chapter 8. At this point, however, it is useful to note simply that the quality problems that were to affect the initial implementation of GNVQs were perhaps not unexpected. Furthermore, while there was clearly an implicit recognition that any difficulties with GNVQ policy could be mitigated during the implementation phase, such a course of action was somewhat unfortunate for many of the initial GNVQ candidates, who experienced less than satisfactory provision.

Conclusion

In this chapter we have observed that the concept of the 'general NVQ' was initially favoured by DE and NCVQ officials as a way of introducing non-occupationally specific awards into the emerging NVQ framework, although the motives of the NCVQ had rather more to do with the need for income from accreditations than a consideration of long-term skill needs in the economy. Little progress was made, however, until DES officials and ministers picked up the 'general NVQ' proposals and pushed them forward as a way of improving education provision for 16- to 19-year-olds, given the political reluctance to reform the A level system. The 'general NVQ' policy was then formally announced in the 1991 White Paper, *Education and Training for the 21st Century* (DES/DE, 1991), although the scale of the proposed innovation envisaged at that time is not entirely clear. Nevertheless, under considerable pressure of time, the NCVQ and the three major national awarding bodies – City and Guilds, the RSA and, with reservations, BTEC – began to work on the design of, and delivery mechanisms for wholly new qualifications in a number of broad occupational areas. It is evident that the NCVQ council were not all that happy with this expansion of the organization's remit. While the NCVQ aimed to base the new GNVQs, as they had become known, as closely as possible on the criteria it had employed for NVQs, pressure from DES officials and ministers ensured that grading and external assessment specifications were added to the awards.

Two issues arising from this account of the origins and development of GNVQ policy require further consideration. First, in Chapter 1 a number of problems were identified that had a deleterious impact on the implementation of GNVQ policy from 1992–93 onwards. While these can be ascribed in part to the rapidity with which the new qualifications were developed, their manageability was also adversely affected by the nature of the assessment arrangements – a combination of the NVQ criteria, which had been criticized for being overly bureaucratic and burdensome in their own right, and external testing requirements. Second, the extent of government intervention in this area of policy is striking. Perhaps the most noteworthy aspect of this was the government's willingness to act to regulate vocational awards. We have already seen that one of the most notable aspects of the way in which NVQ policy progressed was the prevailing ethos of voluntarism. The NCVQ was designed, implicitly, to act as a regulatory body. Yet it possessed no powers to compel other bodies to work towards the establishment of a single national framework of vocational qualifications. An examination of the case of GNVQ policy, however, reveals the presence of a significantly more interventionist ethos, and a willingness on the part of government to interfere with the market for vocational qualifications, in that three bodies were given the sole rights to award, and with the NCVQ design, the new qualifications.

Notes

1 In Scotland GSVQs were also launched, although their impact has been slight, not least because the existing structure of National Certificates has made them largely superfluous.
2 Much of the background to this section is drawn from William Richardson's detailed account of policy developments in post-compulsory education and training in the period 1988–91: *Education and Training Post-16: Options for Reform and the Public Policy Process in England and Wales*, Centre for Education and Industry, University of Warwick, June 1991.
3 The new products did not formally become known as 'GNVQs' until March 1992 (see p. 132). In a later interview with the *Times Educational Supplement* (7 April 1995) the NCVQ's Gilbert Jessup recalled that he was lobbying for 'a new qualification'. The fact that the NCVQ was given no additional money to develop 'general NVQs' further suggests that the original intention was to relax the NCVQ's specifications so that existing non-competence based awards could more easily be placed in the NVQ framework. Indeed much of the expense of the development and implementation of GNVQs was borne by BTEC, City and Guilds and the RSA.
4 There was some opposition to the name 'General National Vocational Qualification' (GNVQs) in the consultation process, largely from a concern that they would become confused with NVQs. In March 1992, however, the government decided that the new qualifications would be formally known as 'GNVQs' (NCVQ, 1992). From here on in our account, then, we will refer to them as GNVQs.

7 Rigour, Review and Relaxation: Vocational Qualifications Policy 1994–1997

Introduction

After a somewhat shaky start the NVQ policy made a considerable recovery during the early 1990s. SVQs were developed and launched in Scotland; a consistent approach to the elaboration of occupational standards of competence was established; work on the formulation of higher level vocational qualifications accelerated; the 80 per cent target for NVQ coverage by the end of 1992 was achieved; and with the introduction of the GNVQ the NCVQ greatly increased its coverage in the school and college sectors. This progress notwithstanding, there were increasing concerns that in the rush to make the qualifications available other problems had been sidelined: notably the slow rate of N/SVQ penetration, for example; and the perceived deficiencies in the assessment process. There was also a more general acknowledgment that the imperative to have the new awards in place had compromised their quality (see DfEE, 1995). In this chapter we will examine the attempts of policy-makers to improve the qualifications between 1994 and 1997, hastened as they were by significant political interventions. Moreover, the institutional environment within which the alterations to the N/SVQs and GNVQs were advanced was also transformed during this period, something that further affected the change process. Because the review activity was frequently characterized by extensively detailed descriptions of the respective qualifications' arrangements and structures, and the proposed changes, we will be necessarily selective in our own treatment.

Rigour

By 1993 officials had become increasingly concerned about the way in which NVQ policy was progressing, despite the achievement of the 80 per cent target for coverage of the workforce that was attained by the end of 1992. The perceived lack of quality of NVQs, particularly in the assessment process, was the subject of growing attention. Not only was the competence-based approach to assessment propagated by the NCVQ considered to be overly bureacratic, complex and restrictive, but there was also a realization that outcome-related funding was beginning to have a deleterious impact on the delivery of the vocational qualifications. A later substantial review of the implementation of N/SVQ policy found that such a funding mechanism was 'not conducive to rigorous assessment' (Beaumont, 1996, p. 28). Moreover, a DE official noted that:

> What hasn't stood the test of time, for some good reasons and some bad reasons, is the sort of detailed way in which they [NCVQ] thought assessment would take place. That has proved to be a very substantial Achilles heel for NCVQ . . . I greatly regret that we didn't actually grip the assessment part of it as quickly as we should have done.

Clearly, DE officials regarded the way in which NVQs were assessed, as well as the imperative of having effective quality assurance mechanisms in place to ensure consistency, to be matters for improvement. However, in December 1993 the perceived deficiencies of the NVQ system, and also those of GNVQs, were given a considerable amount of publicity by a highly critical Channel Four *Dispatches* television programme and an accompanying report by Professor Alan Smithers (Smithers, 1993). The NVQ system had already been the target of adverse comment (see CBI, 1989; Prais, 1989), but Smithers' criticisms were, by virtue of their presentation on network television, given a considerable amount of publicity, especially the reported claim that the government's promotion of NVQs and GNVQs constituted a 'disaster of epic proportions' (*Financial Times*, 15 December 1993). In *All Our Futures* Smithers derided the 'bureaucratic procedures', 'unfamiliar jargon', and the 'outcome-related funding' element that accompanied NVQs, accusing the NCVQ of employing a 'schematic framework derived from behavioural psychology ruthlessly applied' (p. 9). Perhaps the most notable criticism made by Smithers was his argument that knowledge and understanding were marginalized in the competence-based NVQs, particularly because of the lack of written examinations. Focusing on the plumbing and electrical industries, Smithers compared NVQs unfavourably with other awards, the City and Guilds craft certificate in plumbing and the Joint Industry Board apprenticeship scheme for electricians, and with practice elsewhere in Europe in these sectors, formation skills training in the Netherlands and Germany in particular. According to Smithers:

> The root of the problem is that in seeking to develop an education which is distinctively practical the National Council for Vocational Qualifications has departed from established educational practice. It has insisted that students should be assessed solely on what they can do rather than including also what they know and understand.
>
> (Smithers, 1993, p. 9)

The NCVQ responded by calling the television programme and the report 'damagingly inaccurate' and contested Smithers' claims in a 36-point statement. Among other things the NCVQ asserted that a 'separate assessment of knowledge' was permissible if it was necessary to attest competence and that written examinations continued to be used in many NVQs (NCVQ, 1994).[1] The veracity or otherwise of Smithers' claims notwithstanding, the public attention that they generated had an impact on the progress of vocational qualifications policy in two important respects. First, they helped to reinforce a perception, widely held in education, industry and the professions, that NVQs were insufficiently rigorous. One lead body representative noted the significance of:

> the adverse comments about NVQs. And that's certainly been a problem for us because it's been very difficult . . . to go to our chief executives and say we ought to be doing this because they say, hang on a minute . . . I saw the Channel Four programme, Alan Smithers said you know and I read an article . . . They remember the bad news.

Second, and perhaps more importantly, Smithers' criticisms received attention within the government and reaffirmed the scepticism that existed there about the direction of vocational qualifications policy. While the government was, understandably, embarrassed that one of its policies was the subject of a high profile attack, ministers sympathized with the views that Smithers expressed. An employment minister recalled that:

> It was taken very seriously and there were some loud voices almost . . . I mean certainly questioning the very fundamentals of NVQs and almost suggesting, I don't think it was ever quite put in these terms, but almost suggesting that we should tear the whole thing up and start again.

Although the *Dispatches* programme, and the accompanying press comment, raised concerns within the government about the direction of vocational qualifications policy, DE officials, who generally supported the principle of NVQ policy although they could see that improvements needed to be made, particularly the way in which the competence-based assessment regime operated, were nonetheless able to sustain it at that time. As one recalled:

> There was a hell of a lot of briefing on this called for . . . [and] a lot of things that were in the programme we were able to take apart . . . There was an attempt to recover some of that ground and that obviously went into the briefing of ministers. And I think the ministers then present wished it wasn't all happening, but they basically accepted the advice they were getting from the officials.

Things were to change later in 1994 after Michael Portillo became Secretary of State for Employment in July. Portillo was hostile to NVQ policy. Another official observed that:

> The genuine worries, and there were some, then got mixed up with the politics of the thing. We found ourselves with a deeply sceptical [Secretary of State] who sometimes we thought was prepared to throw everything away.

Portillo was not the first minister in the DE to have been equivocal about the value of NVQs, but hitherto officials had managed to persuade sceptical ministers that it was a worthwhile policy that should be sustained. In 1990, for example, officials convinced the then Secretary of State for Employment, Michael Howard, that the NCVQ should be supported and extra resources were procured from the Treasury as a result. However, not only was Portillo reportedly concerned about the amount of money spent by the DE on supporting training programmes in general (*Financial Times*, 22 August 1994), but he was also opposed to NVQs on ideological grounds as two informants revealed:

> Portillo wasn't in favour of it because it wasn't elitist; because he thought that the assessment process [was] weak; that they were a soft option . . . [and] knowledge and understanding, in his view, were a good deal more important than implied in the structure of NVQs as he perceived them.
>
> (DE official)

> We had a rough ride with Michael Portillo. He was . . . an educational right winger who just believed in proper examinations and all of the things that you associate with that kind of education, and therefore had no time at all for any of this really.
>
> (NCVQ official)

For the first time in the case of NVQ policy, a minister declined to accept the advice of DE officials that, while there were problems about the implementation, the principle of NVQs should be supported. Two approaches were employed by officials to try to persuade Portillo to mitigate his scepticism. First, some individual NVQs were examined in a considerable amount of detail, the one in Electrical Installation for example. This was an NVQ in which, contrary to the claims of Smithers, the appropriate knowledge and understanding required was quite well specified. Second, meetings with a representative group of employers were also arranged so that Portillo could gauge a cross-section of views about NVQs, both critical and supportive, in the hope that a constructive way forward could be arranged. These tactics notwithstanding, Portillo's antipathy towards NVQs could not be diminished. However, he did not remain in the DE long enough to alter radically the direction of NVQ policy. In the Cabinet reshuffle of July 1995 Portillo was moved to become Secretary of State for Defence, and was succeeded by Gillian Shephard, who had already been Employment Secretary in 1992–93, and who now became Secretary of State in a new, merged Department for Education and Employment (DfEE). Although the NVQ policy survived the year spent by Michael Portillo as Employment Secretary, the way in which it was advanced was affected in two respects. First, review processes to explore ways in which NVQs could be improved, particularly their assessment, which had been conceived before Portillo moved to the DE, took on a greater significance as a way of channelling criticism and weathering the attack on the policy; and, second, Portillo's concern to make NVQs more akin to traditional academic qualifications, generated work on the possibility of enhancing the scope for externally set examinations within the awards (see p. 143–6).

While Michael Portillo's concerns about NVQs represented the most prominent scepticism about the direction of vocational qualifications policy within the government, in the DfE, which was responsible for leading on GNVQ policy, there were also increasing anxieties that these qualifications were insufficiently rigorous. There is evidence that GNVQs were welcomed within the schools and colleges where they were delivered (see Jackson, 1995). Moreover, during 1993 the new awards garnered increasingly strong support from the DfE itself, where vocational education had not hitherto been accorded high priority. For example, the Secretary of State for Education, John Patten, made public his backing for the GNVQ. In a speech to the Institute of Directors in April 1993 he called for the faster introduction of GNVQs into schools and colleges, and envisaged that the awards had the potential to be undertaken by up to half of the 16 to 19 age group (*Educa*, April 1993). In September 1993 GNVQ piloting began in three new subject areas – Built Environment, Hotel and Catering, and Science. Much of this enhanced interest in vocational qualifications can be ascribed to changes in the senior personnel at the DfE. In January 1993 Sir Geoffrey Holland, who earlier in his career had been director of the MSC and was a noted advocate of vocational education and training, moved from the DE, where he had been Permanent Secretary, to the analagous position in the DfE. Some months before this the then Director of TEED, Roger Dawe, had also moved to take up a leading position in the Education Department. These movements by senior officials 'made a big difference' according to one official in the DfE. Moreover, the junior minister in the DfE responsible for policy in this area, Tim Boswell, was sympathetic to the policy of improving the vocational options for young people in schools and colleges.

This support for the concept of GNVQs within the DfE notwithstanding, the limits of its acceptance must be recognized. Although the notion of GNVQs originated in the DE, out of a recognition that formation skills training needed enhancing to enable young people to enter employment more easily and thus make a contribution to their firms' competitive success, it became increasingly apparent that, under the jurisdiction of the DfE, educational imperatives came to govern the direction of policy. The level three award was increasingly promoted in respect of its capacity to provide an alternative route into higher education (HE). The renaming of the GNVQs as 'foundation' (level one), 'intermediate' (level two) and 'advanced' (level three) awards can therefore be regarded as significant, as can the July 1993 announcement by the DfE that the qualifications were to be henceforth known as 'vocational A levels' (*Educa*, September 1993). It is interesting to note that when occasional attempts were made to reassert the role of the GNVQ in providing employment opportunities, and to play down its function as an HE entry mechanism, such as in a February 1994 speech by the NCVQ's John Hillier, it was reportedly a matter of some surprise (see *Times Higher Educational Supplement*, 25 February 1994).

The strong support for the principle of the GNVQ within the DfE and its popularity on the ground notwithstanding, there was a growing realization that the delivery of the awards needed considerable improvement. The rapidity with which GNVQs were implemented in schools and colleges led to serious difficulties during the pilot year of 1992–93. There were two major problems. First, the new qualifications had been introduced so quickly that there was a lack of appropriate teaching materials and other resources. Second, teachers and lecturers found the assessment and grading specifications difficult to comprehend and apply consistently. These findings were prominent in a November 1993 OFSTED (Office for Standards in Education) report, which examined how the GNVQ pilot phase had fared in schools during 1992–93 (OFSTED, 1993). It noted the extent of the popularity of the new vocational qualifications, welcomed the way in which they encouraged students to develop their own learning strategies and observed that the 'quality of teaching made a positive contribution to learning and standards of achievement' (p. 11). However, it also found that supporting materials and external tests had been late in arriving in schools; that schools were inadequately prepared to offer the new qualifications; and that, although standards at the advanced level were satisfactory, and sometimes better than that, those at the intermediate level were more inconsistent and that 'sometimes they were unsatisfactory' (p. 3). Moreover, 'many teachers found the GNVQ assessment procedures required by the performance criteria, range statements and grading criteria hard to understand' (p. 12).

Perhaps more importantly in political terms, in his *Dispatches* television programme and accompanying report Alan Smithers had also criticized GNVQs (see p. 138). The popularity of the GNVQs was recognized, but a number of problems in their delivery were highlighted, including: the lack of specified knowledge and understanding content; the absence of syllabi, so that teachers had difficulty identifying what subjects needed to be covered; the uncertainties generated by the assessment and grading criteria; the lack of evaluation of the new qualifications that had been undertaken and the speed with which they had been introduced; and the 'ambiguity' over their purpose (Smithers, 1993, pp. 31–5).

Although vocational education was accorded a higher priority by the DfE in 1993 than had hitherto been the case, these critical appraisals of the GNVQs, particularly the Smithers television programme, were received with a high degree of seriousness. Supporters of the policy in the DfE, who themselves recognized that the qualifications needed to be improved, found they were having to fight an 'internal and external battle' to sustain them. According to one senior figure in the DfE, the Smithers programme 'had a very considerable impact within the department'. It reinforced the perception held by supporters of traditional academic forms of education, principally the A level in this context, that the vocational qualifications were inferior and were leading to a dilution of educational standards. Not only, therefore, was it clear to policy-makers in the DfE, and also to NCVQ officials, that improvements needed to be made to GNVQs, but there was also a political imperative present, given that critics of the qualifications within the government needed to be appeased. In March 1994, therefore, at a CBI meeting on education and training, Tim Boswell announced that he would be looking to the awarding bodies and the NCVQ to improve GNVQs in six areas, in what subsequently became known as the 'Boswell six-point plan'. They were asked to: 'clarify the knowledge and understanding required in GNVQ units; improve the assessment regime; review and clarify the basis for grading; extend training for external verifiers; provide more and clearer guidance for teachers; and tighten the criteria for accrediting schools and colleges' (quoted in Dearing, 1996, p. 76).

Hence, during late 1993 and 1994, the direction of NVQ and GNVQ policy in England, Wales and Northern Ireland became the subject of much discussion in both the DE and DfE. The comments of Alan Smithers, in particular, reinforced the perception, often held by senior government figures such as Michael Portillo, that the vocational qualifications were insufficiently rigorous and were deficient in quality, particularly when they were compared with academic awards. Policy makers in both departments had recognized that the respective qualifications needed to be improved, especially the assessment specifications, and were actively considering ways of moving forward. Political interventions substantially accelerated the process.

Review

DE officials were already concerned with making N/SVQs more accessible in order to improve their take-up among employers. The delivery of the awards in workplaces was hampered by the purportedly bureaucratic and costly competence-based assessment regime, the arcane language in which the occupational standards were written, and the reluctance to allow employers to choose appropriate, specific N/SVQ units that were relevant to their operations and to disregard those that were not (CBI, 1994). A minister recalled that he 'spent quite a lot of time out talking to various people, seeing it being done and the one message that was coming out loud and clear was that employers liked the idea, but they did not like what was happening'. The CBI lobbied for a greater amount of flexibility to be inserted into the N/SVQ system, and were particularly keen for the 'core and options' approach to be made formally acceptable. Although the NCVQ was reluctant to accept this, because it would militate against progression and transferability, it was under DE pressure to concede some ground in this area. The concept of 'company specific' qualifications was floated, for example.

DE officials successfully bid for resources under the Department of Trade and Industry's (DTI) Competitiveness initiative to conduct two concurrent reviews of the N/SVQ system. The original intention was that all the then existing NVQs and SVQs would be examined and enhanced by April 1996 – the 'Review of All'. However, there would also be a more intensive analysis of the 100 most popular awards to be completed by the end of 1995, which would look in particular at how assessment was delivered within them and the extent to which the required knowledge was specified (DTI, 1994).[2] A DE official described how the reviews came about:

> [W]e had the opportunity of a White Paper and – it's the usual way these things happen – we wanted to do things about qualifications and address some of the concerns. And we worked up, under quite a bit of time pressure . . . the notion of having a good solid re-look at qualifications. The natural thing to do was [to do it] in two parts in a way: to take an intensive look at a few qualifications and to have an increase in the rate of activity on all qualifications.

Preparatory work on the two reviews got underway during 1994. Although it had been envisaged that the two reviews would be carried out concurrently, this soon changed, and the 'Review of All NVQs and SVQs' was postponed until the outcomes of the 'Review of 100 NVQs and SVQs', the 'Beaumont' Review, were known. Another DE official recalled that:

> I think it was recognized that the review of 100 was going to probe some early, fundamental conclusions and that the emphasis then ought to be on improving all NVQs and SVQs to reflect those findings.

The Beaumont Review took on greater significance, in part because it was employed by officials as a way of ensuring that vocational qualifications policy was sustained despite a more hostile environment; that is, to deflect internal and external criticisms:

> They started getting more importance as the political line became more hostile . . . I mean when they were set up they were very much about

managing day to day business and . . . getting implementation right. Anyway, they became very, very important in this very hostile environment from Portillo.

(DE official)

We felt Smithers was actually attacking the very fundamentals and we thought . . . that the best way of responding to his attacks was actually to get the thing right and try to ensure the credibility of the system, which was so essential and which was seriously being questioned.

(employment minister)

The Beaumont review of NVQs and SVQs formally commenced in April 1995, with much of the research and evaluation work contracted to the NCVQ and SCOTVEC. Its stated objectives were to 'evaluate and report on the effectiveness of approximately 100 of the most used NVQs and SVQs in fulfilling the occupational competence requirements of employment', which would include the 'breadth of competence; the specification and assessment of knowledge and understanding; [and] the quality and cost-effectiveness of the assessment process'; 'highlight good practice and inform the development of guidance in order to promote improvements in NVQ and SVQ development and assessment methods'; explore how 'external assessment might be included in NVQs and SVQs';[3] and to produce recommendations that would inform and underpin the subsequent Review of All NVQs and SVQs, which was now due to begin in April 1996 (Beaumont, 1996, p. 8). In the end, 111 vocational qualifications (93 NVQs and 18 SVQs) were examined; they were chosen to be representative of a range of sectors, levels and awarding bodies and were not necessarily those that were the most widely used (p. 9).

Echoing the earlier findings of the CBI in its *Quality Assessed* report (CBI, 1994), the Beaumont group, in its report of January 1996, found that, while there was 'widespread support for the NVQ/SVQ concept' among employers, there were also 'widespread criticisms of implementation' (Beaumont, 1996, p. 5). In particular, the assessment regime was thought to be excessively bureaucratic and costly, with too much inconsistency evident, and criticism was directed at the 'complex, jargon ridden language' in which the occupational standards were written (p. 13). It was recognized that some employers found NVQs and SVQs too narrowly specified for their needs, while others thought them to be too broad. Therefore there was 'some resistance to take-up where the specification does not fit closely with employers' needs' (p. 13). The review group considered that, on the whole, the qualifications contained sufficient breadth, but it also noted the 'strong support for the mandatory and optional unit approach', something which 'encourages breadth in a flexible way' (p. 5).

Beaumont's review of NVQs and SVQs was an important policy initiative for two reasons. First, on a practical level it was established as a way of

responding to the concerns of employers in particular that the implementation of the vocational qualifications in their firms was proving to be difficult.
Second, on a political level, the review could be presented as a tangible recognition of, and response to, the influential internal and well-publicized
external criticism of the awards that had been circulating. However, the
timing of the review was somewhat unfortunate in one major respect. The
NCVQ published its updated NVQ criteria and guidance in January 1995
(NCVQ, 1995b), in which it addressed many of the problems of implementation that had been raised since the last edition had been produced in 1991.
The NVQs examined in the Beaumont review were largely those which had
been developed in accordance with the old criteria. Work on the preparation
and drafting of the new criteria and guidance took place during 1994, and the
most striking theme of the document is one of greater flexibility in what could
be accepted for accreditation as an NVQ.

Three aspects of the revised criteria and guidance are worth noting. First,
there was a formal recognition that qualifications could comprise core and
optional units. Second, the importance of knowledge and understanding
was attested more explicitly. Thus the 'NVQ statement of competence'
must henceforth 'be accompanied by a knowledge specification' (NCVQ,
1995b, p. 26). Third, the revised criteria contained, according to one of its
developers, other 'important keys for unlocking the door to professional
bodies'. It was accepted that: some professional qualifications came under
a European directive that mandated that awards could only be made after
a specific period of time had elapsed; where the 'mode and duration of learning, or other aspects of the learning process' was specified by legislation, then
the NCVQ's requirements must accede to them (p. 31); and a minor change
was made to the regulations governing awarding bodies, which made it easier
for professional bodies and universities to award the qualifications.

These changes point to the extent to which the NCVQ was willing to relax
some of its earlier principles in order to bring the qualifications offered by
professional bodies into the NVQ framework at the higher levels. Although
by 1995 the 'exemplar projects' had been running for a number of years, progress had been fitful. Perhaps the most advanced sector in this respect, other
than management, was construction, where by 1994 CISC had prepared a
complete suite of occupational standards in Construction Project Management (*CISC News*, September 1994). While there was some evidence of
a softening in the attitude of professional bodies towards N/SVQs – the
Engineering Council appeared increasingly well-disposed, for example (see
Engineering Council, 1995) – for the most part they were suspicious of the
drive to produce higher-level qualifications, and their cooperation was predicated upon a desire to control developments themselves and thus prevent
other organizations from intruding on their terrain. Otherwise, trying to
get the professional bodies interested was, according to a former employment
minister, like 'banging your head against a brick wall'.

Two factors affected the advance of vocational qualifications policy at the higher levels at this time, one was technical the other political. The formal view of the DE appears to have been that the format and structure of occupational standards and N/SVQs as they existed before the 1995 revisions were universally suitable (see CBI, 1993). Yet the considerable amount of DE-sponsored research and development work that examined how occupational competence could be defined and assessed in professional work (e.g. Eraut and Cole, 1993), and how appropriate knowledge and understanding specifications could be included (e.g. Mitchell and Bartram, 1994), perhaps shows that this was not in fact the case. Although the view that lead body designed standards of competence could underpin N/SVQs at levels four and five, as they did in the rest of the framework, was restated in early 1995 in the *Vision for Higher Level Vocational Qualifications* paper (DE, 1995), the way in which the NVQ criteria was revised in 1995 points to the adjustments needed if the awards of professional bodies were to be accepted in the national framework. The 'Vision' document was the outcome of two years of meetings by a 'Higher Levels Strategy Group', comprising DE, NCVQ and SCOTVEC officials. While it was a somewhat vague statement of government policy in this area, perhaps reflecting the numerous redrafting it appears to have been put through, there is nonetheless a distinctly belligerent tone to the document's call for professional bodies to participate in developing vocational qualifications as a way of vindicating their positions and privileges. A profession:

> needs openly to be able to justify its own conception of professionalism, and to stand up to the public scrutiny exercised by a society increasingly mature and well-informed, and certainly less deferential than in the past. A cohesive set of qualifications derived through a public process involving clearly defined partnerships and resulting in agreed occupational standards could benefit existing structures and increase public confidence and accountability in the 'professions'.
>
> (DE, 1995, p. 11)

The apparent seriousness of the DE's intent in the matter of higher level NVQs and SVQs at this time did bring some results. The senior accountancy bodies, for example, came together to establish a 'Professional Accountancy Qualifications' (PAQ) group out of a recognition that a united front was desirable if potentially threatening policy initiatives were to be managed effectively.

The determination of the DE, and the NCVQ and SCOTVEC as well, to establish the qualifications at higher levels was a clearly matter of interest for the HE sector. Although a lead body for education had failed to take off, universities were increasingly becoming affected by developments in vocational qualifications policy – through the provision of training for

TDLB standards in some cases. Moreover, the 'GATE' project had been set up to explore the ways in which individuals with Advanced GNVQs could access higher education. In 1993 the Committee of Vice Chancellors and Principals (CVCP) convened a working group to examine vocational education, an initiative that resulted in the publication of a strategy paper (CVCP, 1995). In addition to providing an overview of developments in vocational qualifications policy, the paper noted the importance of monitoring developments and maintaining a dialogue with relevant bodies. However, outside a small number of 'new' universities, the increased interest of the CVCP in this area – it was described as a 'priority' for 1993–94 (CVCP, 1994) – did not stem from a genuine desire to assist the reforms. Rather, it was a pragmatic response to what appeared to be an important government initiative, and was a reflection of the importance attached to influencing policy developments from within. A well-placed informant observed that 'HE didn't want anything to do with NVQs', and that attitudes ranged 'from scepticism to hostility'.

GNVQ policy, meanwhile, was advanced in a number of ways. During 1994–95 the number of available GNVQ subjects increased. Awards in Engineering, Information Technology, Management, Media Communication and Production, and Retail and Distribution were piloted, while GNVQs that had been tested out the year before – in Construction and the Built Environment, Science, and Hospitality and Catering – were offered nationally. Perhaps the most significant indicator of the perceived success of GNVQ policy was the willingness of the government to expand it in two directions. In his proposals for the reform of the National Curriculum in schools, Sir Ron Dearing had recommended that there should be greater scope for students to take a vocational option at key stage four (14- to 16-year-olds) (Dearing, 1994). The NCVQ and the School Curriculum and Assessment Authority (SCAA), a new body that had replaced the NCC and SEAC, established a joint working group in January 1994 to consider ways in which this could be advanced, and in the summer of that year they produced proposals for a new qualification – the 'GNVQ Part One' – to be delivered in schools. It was suggested that the award could be made available in three subjects – Business, Health and Social Care, and Manufacturing – and be ready for piloting in September 1995. Later in 1994, ministers gave the go-ahead for piloting the GNVQ Part One. This was a major development in vocational qualifications policy, extending as it did the NCVQ's remit into the area of compulsory schooling. It was not done without some reservations (see the *Times Educational Supplement*, 4 November 1994), but according to an education minister these were outweighed by its more positive attributes: it might encourage greater commitment to schooling among academic low-achievers; broaden the options available for schoolchildren; and it would help to formalize a situation in which some GCSEs were increasingly vocational in their character anyway. The NCVQ had already been asked, in 1993, to consider whether GNVQs could be developed at higher levels, analagous with levels four and five of the NVQ framework. It took the NCVQ a considerable amount of time to prepare a consultation paper – it finally appeared in the summer of 1995 (NCVQ, 1995a) – largely because of the numerous other tasks that the NCVQ was then responsible for undertaking.[4]

These developments notwithstanding, following pressure from the DfE the NCVQ and the GNVQ awarding bodies looked at ways of simplifying the qualifications' assessment and grading procedures. The principal response of the NCVQ was to establish a review group to consider, and make recommendations in respect of these matters. Among other things the Capey review, which reported in late 1995, recommended that: schools and colleges should seek to reduce the amount of unnecessary assessment; the assessment regime should be based on whole units rather than on the elements that comprised them; the opacity of the language and terminology in the GNVQ system should be reduced; and that the grading criteria should be simplified so that assessors would make their judgements in just two broad areas, 'quality of outcomes' and 'process' themes (only the former at Foundation level GNVQ) (Capey, 1995).

Finally in this section, it is important to note that the NCVQ itself was in a state of some flux during 1994–95 because it had also taken on the lead responsibility for marketing NVQs and, again, had its work jeopardized by a shortage of cash. We have already noted how the absence of a single, clear focus for marketing NVQs had been perceived as a weakness. Those who viewed the NCVQ's remit as primarily being akin to a regulatory body were not convinced that this was an appropriate role for it to undertake.

> I can understand those who wanted to see NCVQ having a clear respon-
> sibility for marketing, but I never felt entirely happy with that. If you're
> regulating the system you can't always be marketing it at the same time,
> because sometimes you're going to have to say to people, sorry that's not
> good enough. Whereas on the other hand as a marketeer you're saying
> this is a wonderful product.
>
> (NCVQ council member)

Nevertheless, on succeeding Sir Bryan Nicholson as Chairman of the NCVQ in the autumn of 1993, Michael Heron sought to propagate a change of organizational culture, reportedly to make it less like a technical research laboratory and more outward looking (*Guardian*, 19 April 1994). Effective marketing of NVQs was seen to be an important part of this process. The government agreed that the NCVQ should play a more prominent role in this area, and from April 1995 onwards it was funded by the DE to develop and implement a campaign to increase the awareness of NVQs. Perhaps the most significant aspect of the 'Establishing the Benchmark' initiative, as it was known, was the institution of a network of regional NCVQ field offices. The job of the staff in the regions was not only to promote NVQs among local employers, but it was also to help ensure that the increasingly robust quality assurance arrangements for assessment set out in documents like the *Common Accord* (NCVQ, 1993a) were being maintained on the ground.

Despite the expansion of its role, the renewed problem of underfunding afflicted the NCVQ during 1994–95. Grant-in-aid was used to support the NCVQ between 1990–91 and November 1994, when it was due to cease. Grant-in-aid was a flexible funding mechanism for the recipient in that it came with few strings attached and NCVQ officials had been satisfied with the financial settlement.[5] Yet the Treasury would not permit the self-financing objective to be dropped – indeed a revised target date of April 1995 had been specified – in spite of it being quite evident that income from the NVQ and GNVQ levies would not be sufficient for the NCVQ to survive without continued government support. Moreover, there was strong pressure from within the NCVQ itself for the levy on GNVQs to be withdrawn since it made these vocational qualifications more costly than equivalent academic awards and thus impeded their take-up.[6] As the NCVQ's grant-in-aid came to an end, then, it became increasingly short of money and the Treasury was unwilling to release any more (see DfEE, 1996c). NCVQ officials held discussions – 'forthright exchanges' according to one informant – with the DE to try to secure some extra funding and raised the possibility of insolvency by the end of 1994 if additional resources were not forthcoming. An agreement was eventually arrived at whereby the Treasury allowed the NCVQ to carry over up to 10 per cent of its non grant-in-aid income from 1993–94 into the following financial year. Fortunately for the NCVQ, the higher than anticipated take-up of GNVQs had brought in considerably more levy income than had been expected, and this money was used to tide the organization over. It could only be a short-term solution, however, because it had been decided to end the GNVQ levy. The NCVQ's funds were then derived from three sources: a grant from the DfE to fund work on GNVQs (to replace the loss of the levy income); DE support for particular projects, such as the Beaumont Review; and cash brought in from the levy on NVQs and the NCVQ managed National Record of Achievement. Although these sources of income were all no doubt welcome to the NCVQ, they were unlikely to bring about stability and security to the organization. An NCVQ official commented on the difficulties caused by the uncertainty and complexity of the different funding regimes:

> And we had two years of absolutely crazy funding regimes . . . we had an absolute nightmare of funding for two years when we had some output-related funding, some grant-based funding and something else as well I think. I mean it was just a nightmare and we never knew from one month to the next whether we could pay the bills, and there were some months where we couldn't pay the bills.

There are three further points to be made regarding the vicissitudes of the NCVQ's funding arrangements. First, the increasing proportion of the NCVQ's money coming from departmental grants – for GNVQ development and improvements, for the NCVQ's marketing stategy, its field office network, and the work of the Beaumont review among other things – indicates an interesting shift in the locus of control over the direction of vocational qualifications policy. Contract funding, rather than grant-in-aid, reduced the autonomy of the NCVQ because it was bound to follow more closely the specifications laid down by the sponsoring departments. Second, it is perhaps significant that twice in its relatively brief existence the work of the NCVQ was imperilled by the lack of sufficient funds. To what extent does this reveal an ambiguity within the government – though not, it has to be noted, among DE officials – about the value of the reforms to vocational qualifications? Third, the funding problems of 1994–95 at least showed the importance of securing long-term funding arrangements if the NCVQ and its work were to prosper. As it turned out, though, the NCVQ did not have a long-term future in its own right.

Relaxation

Although measures had been set in train to improve the quality of N/SVQs and GNVQs, by 1995 the failure to establish a single, coherent system of vocational qualifications was an increasing concern of policy-makers in the DE. Although measures were in place to encourage the take-up of N/SVQs, the outcome-related funding mechanism in government-supported training programmes in particular, elsewhere (for example, in the further education sector) demand for more traditionally assessed awards continued to be robust. In England and Wales the 1992 Further and Higher Education Act instructed the newly established Further Education Funding Council (FEFC) to support courses that led to the awarding of NVQs and GNVQs. Schedule 2A of the act, however, permitted the Secretary of State for Education to issue a list of other vocational qualifications that would also attract funding. In this way in 1994–95 awards, such as BTEC First Certificates and Diplomas, and their National Diplomas, City and Guilds' awards, Pitmans' certificates, and RSA certificates, were recognized for funding purposes (DfE, 1994). In 1995–96 the FEFC funded the provision of nearly four million qualifications: 27 per cent of which were GCSE, GCE A or A/S levels, 4 per cent GNVQs, 8 per cent NVQs and 61 per cent other vocational qualifications (*Educa*, February 1996). The government's own figures show that in the same year over a half of all the vocational qualifications awarded were not N/SVQs or GNVQs (DfEE, 1998a). During 1995–96 the preponderance of other vocational qualifications was increasingly highlighted (see Beaumont, 1996; Dearing, 1996; DfEE, 1996c; Robinson, 1996a).

The awarding bodies found that their non-N/SVQ and GNVQ products attracted a considerable and continuing demand, and accordingly continued to offer them. The RSA, for example, was reportedly committed to keeping its established certificates available alongside its NVQs (Pickard, 1996). BTEC had agreed to phase out its First and National Diplomas (and the part-time Certificates) in favour of GNVQs. Yet demand for these products remained high; indeed it was rising for the National awards. Perhaps unsurprisingly, then, BTEC, which had become independent from the government in October 1993 and was now operating as a more explicitly commercial organization, chose to keep its National Diplomas and Certificates as well as GNVQs. It put up various justifications for this reversal of policy, including the need for more time to effect the changes needed and the claim that GNVQs were not adequate replacements for some of its products (see *Educa*, March 1995; *Educa*, April 1995). Nevertheless, as a BTEC official acknowledged, the principal cause of his organization's decision to keep the National awards available was their continuing popularity:

> There's considerable demand for BTEC Nationals . . . and if you take the market forces, then, providing what customers want, then why should we give up the BTEC National?

Although government officials were keen to get the awarding bodies to 'play down' their non-N/SVQ and GNVQ awards, they could not compel them to do so. There was, then, a clearer recognition that few powers existed to force providers of vocational awards to modify their products so that they could be inserted into the framework of vocational qualifications (see DfEE, 1996c). While the government could have made greater use of its powers to remove qualifications from the FEFC's approved list, it was recognized that, because the market was expressing a clear demand for other awards, they clearly possessed attributes that N/SVQs and GNVQs did not. There was also an unwillingness to interfere (too obviously anyway) in the way in which awarding bodies, which were largely commercial organizations, operated. By 1995–96, therefore, policy-makers in the newly established DfEE, comprising the merged DE and DfE (see p. 141), recognized that if a coherent and comprehensive framework of vocational qualifications was to be established, some way would have to be found of including awards which were not N/SVQs or GNVQs. A DfEE official pointed out that:

> [the] intention was that the NVQs would be good enough to drive out all traditional qualifications and that ministers would stick with that firmly, over a consistently long period, to make that actually happen. There's a variety of reasons why that's actually changed now. I don't think anybody expects that NVQs will drive out other qualifications or that that is the policy intention.

Even within the N/SVQ system itself, considerable incoherence and fragmentation had arisen, given the number of different awarding bodies. Qualifications based on the same occupational standards could be offered by more than one, and sometimes several different awarding bodies. The inconsistency between the products offered by separate awarding bodies was identified as a problem by the NCVQ itself in respect of Management NVQs, and was something that employers reportedly also found undesirable (Pickard, 1996). Beaumont noted that competition 'is valuable, but without effective regulation, has led to far too many variations of the same qualifications. ABs [awarding bodies] have widely different systems, procedures and styles: not all are efficient, some are overly bureaucratic and some have still to learn they are providing a service to customers' (1996, p. 24). Although the NCVQ and the major awarding bodies had devised the *Common Accord* (NCVQ, 1993a) in an attempt to standardize assessment procedures and structures, a widespread feeling existed that the high number of bodies involved in offering NVQs not only caused confusion, but also led to variable quality (Dearing, 1996). An official of a major awarding body commented that:

[O]n the one hand the government and everybody in the country seems to be talking about parity between vocational and academic qualifications . . . When you have 100 plus awarding bodies for NVQ, how can that ever be possible? And . . . let's take the motor vehicle sector, [with] something like five awarding bodies – would you be able to say that quality was standard across those five awarding bodies for NVQ level two, for level three, [and] are comparable? We know darned well they are not.

In areas where the providers of awards were particularly thick on the ground, lead bodies were compelled to establish structures – awarding body committees for example – to ensure that the delivery of qualifications based on their standards was consistent. Beaumont recommended that policy-makers consider the establishment of 'Managing Awarding Bodies' offering a 'one-stop-shopping' type of service as a way of rationalizing the awarding body network (1996, p. 24). The DfEE did not favour such an approach, however, and the NCVQ also reportedly rejected the idea (Pickard, 1996).

DE officials had already begun to explore ways of bringing non-N/SVQs and GNVQs into the vocational qualifications framework, and had identified the fact that their greater requirement for knowledge and understanding was a major source of their continuing popularity. Thus in early 1995 the NCVQ was asked to consider the development of 'Part One' NVQs (DTI, 1995). It was envisaged that such a title could be given to awards that were not strictly competence-based, but that gave individuals knowledge and understanding that would act as a foundation for NVQs. Beaumont's review group, which had also been asked to consider 'how knowledge and understanding might be separately certificated and the desirability of doing this' (Beaumont, 1996, p. 6), identified the development of Part One N/SVQs as a way of bringing 'traditional vocational qualifications', albeit suitably modified, into the framework (p. 27). The NCVQ rejected the concept of Part One NVQs for reasons that are not wholly clear.[7] Nevertheless, following the January 1996 publication of the Beaumont report, the NCVQ expended considerable effort on exploring ways in which it could oversee non-N/SVQs and GNVQs within a single framework. It eventually came up with the concept of 'Related Vocational Qualifications' in early 1997. Under pressure from the DE and DfEE, then, in 1995–97 the NCVQ increasingly focused on how a coherent, single framework of vocational qualifications could be devised, one that could include non-N/SVQs and GNVQs so long as they met certain defined specifications. Clearly, there was an increasing emphasis on the regulatory aspect of the NCVQ's remit, an aspect that had hitherto been somewhat sidelined. An awarding body official remarked that:

> NCVQ is now taking a rather different tack. It's now looking at a framework into which qualifications will be fitted against criteria. And that was always the intention of the *Review of Vocational Qualifications*; that they should establish a framework and qualifications should go into that framework.

Perhaps the most notable example of the aim of policy-makers to progress the development of a broad framework of vocational qualifications, as opposed to the advancement of just NVQs and SVQs, concerned the higher-level awards. The somewhat belligerent tone of the 1995 'Vision' document was distinctly absent from a further 'position paper' issued by the DfEE in late 1996. In this later document it was recognized that 'the relationship between professional accreditation and vocational qualifications is complex and politically sensitive'; that 'there would be little point in attempting to supplant existing and adequate professional accreditation arrangements with NVQs/SVQs which performed much the same function'; and that there were anxieties among professional bodies about 'submitting themselves to the quality assurance requirements of the accrediting bodies [NCVQ and SCOTVEC]' (DfEE, 1996b, pp. 18–19). At the higher levels, then, it was envisaged that progress would now be largely confined to areas where existing arrangements were deficient in some way. Indeed, the NCVQ and SCOTVEC had already sponsored a number of small-scale developmental projects to explore ways of establishing NVQs and SVQs among sympathetic professional occupations (see NCVQ, 1997c).

The increased emphasis given to building a broad-based framework of awards was one way in which the character of vocational qualifications policy was relaxed between 1995 and 1997. Moreover, the N/SVQ and GNVQ products themselves were also made less prescriptive during this period. Following the Capey review of GNVQs, and with extra funds provided by the government, the NCVQ and the awarding bodies took steps to improve these awards. In November 1996 the NCVQ announced changes to the structure of GNVQs, modifications that were designed to ease the assessment requirements while at the same time ensuring that rigour was enhanced. A greater emphasis was given to the external scrutiny of GNVQ assignments, for example; there was a switch from assessment based on elements to a unit-based assessment approach; and there was to be an end to multiple choice tests. Not only was the number of tests to be reduced, but those that remained would be broader in scope and would encourage students to provide lengthier, written answers (see *Times Higher Educational Supplement*, 8 November 1996).

Dearing's review of educational provision for 16- to 19-year-olds made recommendations regarding the broad structure of GNVQs (Dearing, 1996). It was noted that the size of the award, particularly at Advanced level, where the candidate had to complete twelve units and three additional core skills units, was problematic in two respects. First, it gave students insufficient scope to combine the GNVQ with another qualification, a single A level for example. Second, it encouraged non-completion. Thus the review proposed that the Advanced GNVQ, renamed as the 'applied A level', should be restructured. The full twelve-unit qualification, plus the three core skills (or key skills) units would remain in place as the Applied A level (Double Award), but there should also be an Applied A level in itself, comprised of six full units and the key skills units. Further, 'detailed consideration should also be given' to the establishment of a three-unit award, to be known as the Applied AS level (Dearing, 1996, pp. 69–72). Proposals for more fundamental reform of the GNVQ structure, however, were postponed by the incoming Labour government in 1997, and further comments on the broader reform of qualifications for 16- to 19-year-olds were invited (DfEE, 1997b).[8]

In early 1996 the government endorsed the majority of Beaumont's proposals for the improvement of N/SVQs, many of which had in any case already been addressed by the accrediting bodies (e.g. NCVQ, 1995b), and accepted action plans that had been devised by the NCVQ and SCOTVEC. The Review of All NVQs and SVQs, which had been postponed so that it could take Beaumont's findings into consideration, then got underway in April 1996. The NCVQ had already broadened its criteria for NVQs in 1995. This came too late, though, to deflect ministerial criticism that the competence-based approach to assessment was insufficiently rigorous. Consequently, before he left the DE, Michael Portillo asked the NCVQ to consider how 'an element' of external assessment could be introduced into NVQs.

Following research, Beaumont's review concluded that 'the independence of the assessor' was the 'key factor of externality' and that external assessment was desirable insofar as it is the 'combination of methods which create rigour' (Beaumont, 1996, p. 18). During 1996, then, the NCVQ followed up this aspect of the Beaumont report, and it was increasingly accepted that a range of assessment methods could, as long as they were appropriate, be used to attest competence. Thus the previous reliance on the direct observation of performance in the workplace was diluted. For the NCVQ and the Scottish Qualifications Authority (SQA),[9] 'the value of independent assessment', as they preferred to call it, rested upon the way in which it 'lends rigour and boosts public confidence'. 'Independent assessment' was considered to mean that a 'significant *part of the assessment* for an NVQ/SVQ is carried out in a manner that is demonstrably independent of anyone who might have a vested interest in the outcome of the assessment decision'. While this could include 'centrally determined and assessed tests or assignments', it might also mean the deployment of a 'visiting assessor' or the utilization of an 'independent centre or assessment location' (NCVQ/ SQA, 1997, p. 6 original emphasis).[10]

Although NCVQ officials stressed that, if it attested to competence, such 'independent assessment' had always been permissible in the NVQ system, there can be little doubt that, following DfEE pressure, the changes to the NVQ criteria that were developed during 1996–97 constituted a significant move away from the rather prescriptive competence-based approach to assessment that had hitherto characterized vocational qualifications. Indeed, the degree of flexibility that was increasingly being encouraged in assessment methods became a matter of concern within the NCVQ. For example, its Chief Executive, John Hillier, warned against 'throwing the baby out with the bathwater' (*Update*, August 1997, p. 6), while another former senior NCVQ official observed that the criteria were now 'frighteningly loose'. Although the revision of the NVQ criteria and guidance was initiated and mostly carried out by the NCVQ, the task of publishing the new version was to fall to its successor, the Qualifications and Curriculum Authority (QCA; see p. 159).[11]

During the period 1995–97, then, there was a notable shift in the direction of vocational qualifications policy. In particular, more attention was given to the regulatory aspect of the NCVQ's remit, and the way in which it, and the QCA, could effectively oversee a coherent framework of awards, rather than just develop and promote NVQs and GNVQs. Moreover, the assessment criteria for the NVQs and SVQs themselves were loosened, and the GNVQs were made less prescriptive. It is important to recognize that these developments took place in the context of substantial institutional reform: the merger of the DE and DfE in July 1995 to form the DfEE; and the lead-up towards the establishment of the QCA, from an amalgamation of the NCVQ and SCAA, in October 1997. The immediate impact of the departmental merger was that Michael Portillo was moved to the Ministry of Defence and was succeeded by Gillian Shephard, who thus became the first Secretary of State at the new DfEE. Although the formation of the DfEE may have been the outcome of short-term political imperatives (see House of Commons Employment Committee, 1995), the fusion of the education and employment departments had long had influential advocates. Such institutional reform, it was envisaged, would encourage a more coherent and strategic approach to the way in which education and training policy was developed and implemented, as Sir Geoffrey Holland, a former Permanent Secretary in both departments and Director of the MSC, acknowledged in evidence to a House of Commons select committee (see House of Commons Employment Committee, 1996a). Thus the prospects for vocational education, training and qualifications could be enhanced in a department in which education and employment matters were dealt with together.

Paradoxically, however, the effect of the departmental merger has arguably been to diminish the impetus behind vocationalism that had hitherto been a characteristic of the DE, and was a residue of the MSC. In the DfEE issues relating to schools and academic education, areas that were perhaps more politically sensitive, appear to have been prioritized.

> [T]he NVQs went into eclipse a bit, because when the departments merged the DfE won the battle if you like.
>
> (NCVQ official)

> There was a belief, I think, that the, if you like, the old ED [Employment Department] culture would affect the DfEE culture more than the DfE culture would affect [the] ED. That hasn't happened.
>
> (DfEE official)

> [T]he merger of [the] ED and DfE . . . was the right thing to do . . . and they were a hell of a long time in getting things going, getting the people appointed and so on. When they were appointed it became rapidly clear that all the people in charge of policy and strategy and so on were ex-DfE people with no sympathy at all for the vocational idea and precious little for the NVQ idea.
>
> (DfEE official)

Although we have noted the greater attention vocational education received in the DfE, both in 1990–91 when GNVQ policy was initiated and in 1993–94 when, under sympathetic official and ministerial guidance, the department promoted GNVQs increasingly heavily, the prevailing climate nonetheless remained strongly imbued by a culture in which academic education was accorded a high priority. The relaxation of the N/SVQ criteria and the increased attention given to the way in which other vocational qualifications could be brought into the framework might suggest a weakening of the commitment to vocational education and training within the newly established DfEE. However, there are two problems with such an analysis. First, the origins of these developments in fact predated the departmental merger. Second, given the difficulties of implementing N/SVQs and the continuing preponderance of other awards, it could be argued that such changes were crucial if the N/SVQ policy was to be sustained at all. They can, therefore, be interpreted as constituting a strengthening of vocational qualifications policy in the DfEE. Another NCVQ official noted the large amount of vocational provision that the DfEE now oversaw. He observed that:

> The DES thought it had taken care of vocational qualifications by inventing BTEC . . . All they thought about were O levels and GCSEs and A levels and the National Curriculum when that came along. There was no vocational impact on what they were doing. Now if you look at the extent of the impact that it has: you have the GNVQ . . . running at Key Stage four, legally as part of the National Curriculum; you probably have more teenagers doing GNVQs than are doing A levels; you have . . . a respectable work-based route in the Modern Apprenticeship developing . . . So I don't regard that as marginalising at all – I think that's a profound change in the way things used to be.

Nevertheless, the concern that, putting it crudely, employment interests were in danger of becoming subordinate to those of education in the newly established DfEE was evident in the preparatory phase of the QCA.

Since early 1994, a close relationship on matters of mutual interest – principally in respect of provision for 14- to 19-year-olds – had developed between the NCVQ and SCAA. For example, they jointly oversaw the evolution of the Part One GNVQ, the piloting of which commenced in September 1995. In early 1996 relations became formalized with the establishment of a joint NCVQ and SCAA working group to advise on and coordinate matters pertaining to curriculum and qualifications policy in schools and colleges. Dearing welcomed the increasing collaboration of SCAA and the NCVQ on matters affecting the curriculum for 14- to 19-year-olds in his review and suggested that there were three options for further reform. He discounted the idea that SCAA should take over the reponsibility for GNVQs, not least because it would be an unpopular move among employers, who already felt that the awards had become too educationally oriented. The other two options – a merger between SCAA and the NCVQ to form a single organization, or the establishment of two new bodies to replace them, one to be responsible for qualifications, the other to look after curriculum developments – would require legislation. Although Dearing set out the possible advantages and disadvantages of each, he left it as a matter for ministers to decide (Dearing, 1996, pp. 30–34).

The government not only supported the increasing collaboration between the NCVQ and SCAA, but also considered the full merger of the two organizations to be a desirable objective. It embarked on a consultation exercise during the summer of 1996. Apart from highlighting the government's preference for the NCVQ and SCAA to be combined within a single body, the consultation document – *Building the Framework* (DfEE, 1996a) – was notable in two other respects. First, and following the findings of the Quinquennial Review of the NCVQ that had recently been undertaken (DfEE, 1995; DfEE, 1996c), there was an explicit recognition that the NCVQ had been given insufficient powers to fulfil a key aspect of its initial remit – the establishment of a single, coherent framework of vocational qualifications. This provides a further indication of the extent to which the government was increasingly seeking to promote the regulatory aspect of the NCVQ's role. Second, it was also noted that care would have to be taken to ensure that employment interests were not marginalized in a single qualifications and curriculum body. Following the consultation exercise, in the autumn of 1996 the government announced that a new body would be established – the Qualifications and National Curriculum Authority (QNCA), later to become the Qualifications and Curriculum Authority (QCA). The new organization, which succeeded the NCVQ and SCAA, was eventually founded in October 1997 under the provisions of that year's Education Act, with the former SCAA Chief Executive, Nick Tate, at its head.

As early as the summer of 1996, however, anxieties were expressed at a high level within the NCVQ about the difficulties of securing sufficiently strong employer representation in a single NCVQ–SCAA body, and these concerns were also evident within parts of industry. Institutionally at least, it would seem that the predictions of those who suggested that employment interests would be marginalized in a merged body have been borne out in two respects. First, in June 1997 the names of the first members of the QCA were announced, and employers' representatives were in a minority.[12] Second, at its inception the QCA's senior staff was heavily dominated by figures from the former SCAA; only one former NCVQ official – Alan Bellamy – secured an appointment at director level. Another former NCVQ official remarked that 'NVQs will find it hard to flourish' in such an environment, while a prominent lead body representative was concerned about the degree to which the QCA was 'going to be driven by the academic education lobby'. The extent to which the QCA manages to promote vocational and academic qualifications equally remains to be seen, and such a matter is beyond the scope of this book. Nevertheless, as a member of the NCVQ council recognized, having in place one body to oversee all qualifications, both academic and vocational, might bring important benefits:

I was one of those who started off by being opposed to amalgamating NCVQ with SCAA but was persuaded that we should do it because of the greater degree of authority and coherence that comes from having a single, national qualifications authority. I think that we have had a problem with there being a differential value placed on different types of qualification. One way of cracking that problem is to have a single authority that deals with all types of qualification. That was basically what persuaded me.

Three aspects of the new organization's remit are worth noting. First, in April 1998 the QCA took over the management of the occupational standards programme from the DfEE. The previous division of responsibilities had been acknowledged as less than satisfactory, not least because of the confusion it was seen to have generated (CBI, 1994; DfEE, 1995). Although there had been some persuasive reasons for not allowing the NCVQ to manage the development of standards – its absence from Scotland for example – it appears that the most important factor was the department's reluctance to relinquish its work in this area to another body. With the establishment of the QCA, however, it would seem that the DfEE lost the 'battle', as one of its officials put it, to look after the standards programme.

Second, a much greater emphasis was placed on the regulatory character of the QCA's work than had been the case with the NCVQ. Although the NCVQ had, under government pressure, begun to explore how non-NVQs could be brought into a single, coherent system of vocational qualifications during 1996–97, one of the major early priorities of the QCA was to establish a common framework, something on which the NCVQ was supposed to have started over 10 years earlier. The QCA carried on with the work on defining assessment criteria and developing quality assurance arrangements that could apply to all vocational awards within a single framework that the NCVQ had started in the final year of its existence – in its proposals for 'related vocational qualifications' for example.[13] The new body, however, would have powers, under the 1997 Education Act, to advise the Secretary of State for Education on the suitability of qualifications to attract public funding, particularly in the further education sector. Thus the QCA would have greater scope than the NCVQ had ever enjoyed to press the providers of vocational qualifications to adapt their products to the specifications required for inclusion in a single framework. Indeed, even before the QCA came into existence, one major awarding body – the RSA – expressed concerns about the extensive powers that the regulatory body would have in this regard (see *Educa*, April 1997). There was a recognition within the DfEE, moreover, that the QCA's powers over vocational qualifications were potentially 'far reaching'.

The regulatory aspect of the QCA's remit will potentially be assisted by two other institutional developments. In April 1996 the government initiated a renewed attempt to rationalize the lead body network. It was anticipated that the new sectoral National Training Organisations (NTOs) would not only undertake the duties of a lead body, in particular the development of occuptional standards of competence, but would also have a strategic remit to promote and improve skills training in their respective constituencies, a role hitherto undertaken by the ITOs. Although there were some suspicions that the NTO initiative was conceived by DfEE civil servants in order to make the system easier to manage, and was not a reflection of the the heterogeneous interests of employers, the first set of these bodies was recognized by the government in July 1997.[14] There was also increasing interest in ways of rationalizing the awarding body network. Unlike the lead bodies, which were mainly dependent upon government grants, awarding bodies operated more commercially and relied upon income derived from certification fees for their existence. Thus there was less scope for increased regulation that would interfere with the commitment to the operation of market forces. The government's priority, moreover, was to reduce the number of bodies offering academic awards, particularly A levels, so that variability was diminished, greater consistency established and standards thus improved (DfEE, 1997a). Encouragement has also been given to the merger of bodies offering academic and vocational qualifications. BTEC, for example, joined up with the University of London Examinations Board and became EdExcel in 1997.

Third, the QCA was established with no remit for marketing NVQs. This might be considered a somewhat surprising development, given that the NCVQ had only acquired the lead responsibility for promoting the qualifications in April 1995. In fact it reflects the dominant regulatory role expected of the QCA. Not only was there no longer any expectation that NVQs, and GNVQs, would come to replace all the other existing qualifications, but it was also felt to be inappropriate for an organization that was concerned with developing a framework within which different awards could be posted, also to be promoting a particular type of award.

Conclusion

The principal aim of this chapter has been to trace how the direction of vocational qualifications policy in the UK shifted between 1994 and 1997. Although widespread concerns about the delivery, quality and penetration of N/SVQs already existed, and the way in which GNVQs were initially implemented had also provoked criticism, the pressure for review was boosted by significant political interventions. Two broad changes were then formulated and progressed. The strongly prescriptive criteria that had hitherto characterized the NVQs in particular began to be relaxed. Additionally, a greater degree of flexibility was gradually introduced in the GNVQs. The second change concerned the broader institutional setting, rather than the structure of the qualifications themselves. The NCVQ had originally been established to oversee the development of a coherent, transparent and single framework of vocational qualifications. For two reasons in particular – the stipulation that awards could only be included if they were founded upon a particular competence-based approach to assessment, and the absence of regulatory powers – the NCVQ was unsuccessful in fulfilling this aspect of its remit. Indeed, albeit through little fault of its own, it had not even attempted to do so.

Despite the interventionary mechanisms that policy-makers had devised to promote the spread of the new qualifications, for example the provision of tax relief, by 1995 there was an explicit recognition that, in a voluntaristic, market-based system, the persistence of demand for alternative vocational awards, and the willingness of providers to meet it, was a matter that needed to be addressed if the creation of an adequate framework was to be accomplished. Increasing attention was directed, then, at how the system of vocational qualifications as a whole, not just N/SVQs and GNVQs, could be effectively regulated. This was a matter that became a priority for the QCA, with its potentially greater regulatory powers, after it was founded in October 1997.

Notes

1 Additionally, the NCVQ stated that what it 'and its partners in the development of the NVQ and GNVQ systems do not need, but received with damaging effects in the Dispatches programme and associated report, was polemic presented as fact and unrepresentative perceptions presented as if they were widely held' (*Times Higher Educational Supplement*, 14 January 1994).
2 Since the chairman of the review's Evaluation Advisory Group was the industrialist Gordon Beaumont, it became known as the 'Beaumont Review'.
3 NCVQ officials always claimed that, if it attested to an individual's occupational competence, any one or a combination of assessment methods could be used.
4 Although the higher level GNVQ initiative was subsequently shelved.
5 For example, the development of GNVQs had initially been funded out of the NCVQ's grant-in-aid.
6 The GNVQ levy was ended in September 1995. Thenceforth the NCVQ's GNVQ work was funded by a departmental grant.
7 Although the NCVQ's John Hillier reportedly commented that they needed 'another qualification like a hole in the head' (Pickard, 1996, p. 26).
8 In April 1998 it was announced that revised Advanced GNVQs would become available in 2000. The full twelve-unit award, equivalent to two A levels, was to be maintained; but there would also be new six-unit and three-unit GNVQs available, equivalent to one A or AS level respectively (DfEE, 1998b).
9 The SQA was formed from the merger of SCOTVEC and the Scottish Examinations Board in March 1997.
10 Lead bodies were also now expected to specify appropriate assessment methods.
11 Given this background, it is interesting to note that the QCA subsequently pronounced that while 'performance (including simulations and assignments) provides an important source of knowledge evidence, it is unlikely that it will satisfy all the requirements. It cannot be assumed that because some aspects of knowledge have been demonstrated the rest can be inferred' (QCA, 1998,

p. 20). Thus the relaxation of the NVQ criteria continued under the auspices of the new body.

12 See QCA (1997b) for a list of board members and their positions.

13 Although the development of the criteria for these awards was held up by the ongoing revision work pertaining to the N/SVQs and GNVQs.

14 Eighteen bodies were given NTO accreditation in the first wave, including the Engineering and Marine Training Authority (EMTA – the successor to ENTRA) and the Board for Education and Training in the Water Industry. A further 19 NTOs were recognized in December 1997.

8 The Reform of Vocational Qualifications: An Anatomy of Policy

Introduction

In the main body of this book we have provided an account of how the reforms to vocational qualifications were planned, developed and implemented in the UK during the 1980s and 1990s, up to the establishment of the QCA in October 1997. There are, however, a number of key, overarching issues that have had a significant effect in shaping the way in which the reforms progressed. They are: the low status accorded to vocational forms of education; the renewed ethos of voluntarism in labour market policy; the extent to which the authority and power of the state have become centralized; and the matter of coherence and consistency in the formulation and delivery of policy within government. The analysis of each of these themes that now follows has three purposes. First, it will allow us to highlight not only those factors that have impeded the progress of the N/SVQ and GNVQ policies, but also those responsible for the resilience of the reforms despite the considerable amount of criticism they have attracted. Second, the example of vocational qualifications policy can be presented as an instructive case study of the significance of the above issues in the advancement of education and employment policy, indeed public policy more generally in some instances, during the 1980s and 1990s. Third, the more analytical, thematic approach adopted in this chapter points to the importance of institutional and political factors in determining the way in which vocational qualifications policy progressed, something that will be further explored in the conclusion of this book.

Youth Training and the Politics of Vocational Education

In the early 1980s the elaboration of an improved structure of vocational qualifications, more closely related to the needs of employers, was identified by the MSC as an important means of enhancing vocational education in the UK, and of improving the effectiveness of skills training. Although there was a desperate short-term need to improve the quality of the YTS, there was also a concern that opportunities for adults should be improved. According to one highly placed individual:

> What we wanted was to have parity of esteem between technical and academic qualifications . . . [the] ultimate objective would be if somebody decided to go down the technical route [and] could at some time switch to go down the academic route; or the other way round.
>
> (employment minister)

The ambitions of policy-makers in this respect, however, were to be frustrated in two respects: by the coupling of the reforms of vocational qualifications with the short-term concerns about how to manage youth unemployment, and by the political significance of the low esteem accorded to vocational forms of education.

Although the MSC considered the reform of the vocational qualifications system to be a desirable policy objective in its own right, the need for provision suitable for the YTS programmes offered the necessary pretext. However, the association between vocational qualifications policy and youth training undermined the later reform process in three important respects.[1] First, the competence-based approach that the NCVQ used to underpin NVQs from 1987 onwards was derived from development work that had been carried out in the context of the YTS. Given the task-based character of many YTS programmes (Lee, 1989), this made the NVQs very narrow in scope. Second, the bulk of the take-up of NVQs has been stimulated largely by government programmes for the unemployed, such as YTS, YT, and their equivalents for adults (Field, 1995). This led to problems of credibility, particularly in sectors where skill requirements were deemed to be higher. The representative of one lead body, involved in developing and promoting N/SVQs at higher levels, commented that 'the perceived wisdom that created the criteria was based mainly on lower level NVQs because that's where the bulk of the work is. It's just happened. There's nothing you can do about it; it just causes tensions and challenges that you have to try and work around.' Crouch has observed that 'most governments have integrated work with the unemployed with strategies for advanced VET (vocational education and training). However, this is often unrealistic as the two sets of activities are very different. There is then a danger that the stigma attached to remedial VET extends to the whole public policy component and that government agencies are simply not taken seriously within advanced areas' (1998, p. 377; c.f. Chapman, 1994; King, 1993; Mansfield and Mitchell, 1996). Third, added to this the outcome-related funding element of government supported training programmes has arguably also had adverse effects on the delivery and quality of N/SVQs (see p. 185). Even the GNVQ, although it was originally formulated by DE officials as a way of complementing the NVQ, by thus helping to raise skill levels in the economy, was progressed by the DES as a way of improving provision for 16- to 19-year-olds in full-time education; not out of a recognition that vocational education was of value in its own right. The more strategic aims of some officials (and occasionally ministers) notwithstanding, government policy on vocational education and training in general, and the reform of vocational qualifications in particular, was dominated by the political imperative to manage the diminution of employment opportunities for young people. According to a DE official, 'most ministers first and foremost wanted kids kept off the streets – there's no argument about that.'[2]

The progress of vocational qualifications policy was also impeded by the absence of sustained political commitment by the Conservative administrations of the late 1980s and the 1990s. NVQ policy was largely originated under the auspices of the MSC, a body that strongly advanced vocationalism during the 1980s (Ainley, 1988). The political climate, moreover, was favourable because the well-placed Lord Young was committed to such a policy (see Young, 1990). However, once Young moved on – he switched from the DE to the Department of Trade and Industry (DTI) after the 1987 general election – political support for the reforms to the vocational qualifications became more intermittent. Generally, incoming Conservative ministers in the DE, who tended to have had no previous experience of non-academic education, needed to be apprised of the merits of the vocational qualifications policy by officials. Although the intensity of Michael Portillo's antipathy towards NVQs was an isolated affair, a more general suspicion of vocational education existed within the government. The presence of enhanced vocational options notwithstanding, education policy under the Conservative administrations of the late 1980s and the 1990s became increasingly focused on the reassertion of 'traditional' values and academic 'standards', with the 'Gold Standard' A level held up as the pinnacle of educational excellence (Richardson, 1993). People working on the development and promotion of vocational qualifications felt that for this reason support from Conservative ministers for their efforts was often lacking.

> I have a certain difficulty . . . because I am a lifelong Conservative . . . I had the impression that Tory politicians, that they paid lip service to the value of VQs [vocational qualifications], but were wedded to the Gold Standard of A levels and to the primacy of degrees and the traditional educational route. They saw that as excellence. And although they would never say it in public, I got the distinct impression that they perceived the VQs as being given to less gifted mortals; they were almost for the menial class.
>
> (employers' association official)

The key question is the extent . . . that the Tory Government really supported vocational training and education as a policy, and my own view is that they didn't support it as much as they should.

(NCVQ council member)

I think there was always . . . a certain ambiguity. They [the Conservatives] didn't want it to fail because it was their initiative; but they didn't want it to succeed either, because it was actually contrary to their deepest instincts.

(NCVQ official)

Well there have been times when we've been disappointed, and one doesn't want to sort of moan too much here because there are a lot of very dedicated people in the department who've been doing a lot of excellent work. But I think at the political level we felt that ministers haven't given the push to this.

(employers' association official)

It would be unfair, though, to characterize Conservative attitudes towards N/SVQs and GNVQs, indeed towards vocational education and training in general, as being entirely indifferent or antagonistic. From time to time individual junior ministers – of whom Tim Eggar, Tim Boswell and James Paice were the most notable examples – at the employment and education departments did take care to advocate an enhanced role for vocational education.[3] A former (sympathetic) minister recalled, however, that he was 'carrying the banner' for vocational provision largely on his own (in the education department). He elaborated: 'I don't think it was shared by any of the other ministers. I mean they went along with it . . . but without any enthusiasm.' Given the political context, moreover, within which the more traditional, academic and elitist aspects of education were held to define excellence and rigour, ministers who supported the extension and improvement of vocational provision had to be careful not to leave themselves open to the criticism that they were reducing educational standards. For political reasons there was a strong interest, then, in preserving the notion that achievement in education was analogous with the attainment of academic qualifications. A DfE official noted that, even under the premiership of John Major, when GNVQ policy was being developed, this 'constrained the policy options enormously. And you know those of us who were involved at all in qualifications had to understand very clearly what you know was acceptable to Number Ten and what wasn't.' One minister, who had had some experience in both the employment and education departments, regarded the prioritization of academic forms of education as less an expression of Conservative ideology than a reflection of the social composition of the policy making elite under any administration:

I think it suffers from you know a great problem which is one, one encountered in all sorts of ways; and that is that you know we're all as it were to some extent victims of our own training and background. And all the people handling these issues are people who've been to university and thought about issues in university terms, and were thinking about their own children when they thought about children at all.

Although parity of esteem between academic and vocational qualifications was continually promoted as a desirable policy aim, both societal and, more importantly, political factors meant that, other than at a rhetorical level, commitment to its achievement was intermittent – at best – within the Conservative administrations of the late 1980s and the 1990s.[4]

The 'British Way': the Renewed Ethos of Voluntarism

Although both education and labour market policy in the UK have historically been characterized by the primacy of voluntarism (Green, 1990; MacInnes, 1987), the scale and scope of the interventionary mechanisms established by the MSC were considerable, particularly in the area of vocational preparation. The powerful influence of the MSC in the 1980s has been the subject of considerable comment. Evans, for example, observed that its 'authority was at its peak' at this time (1992, p. 196; c.f. Ainley and Corney, 1990; Ainley and Vickerstaff, 1993). This was largely because the MSC was the 'only institution through which a politically acceptable response to unemployment could be delivered' (King, 1993, p. 227). Yet soon after the NCVQ was established and the NVQ policy launched, the MSC was wound up.[5] The Conservative government had become increasingly hostile to tripartite methods of policy formulation and implementation (Evans, 1992), and once unemployment ceased to be a major poitical priority – according to official figures it was in decline from January 1986 onwards – the MSC was living on borrowed time (Ainley and Vickerstaff, 1993). The dismemberment of the MSC had an adverse impact on the nascent NVQ policy. An MSC official noted that:

> In a sense what happened with [the] RVQ I suppose, was here were a set of instruments – through RVQ and NCVQ – that have been thought up and presented really within a strategy for an organisation like the old MSC, which had power and an interest in strategy, to use and deliver. Just at the time these instruments were delivered the MSC was weakened, and indeed disbanded.

Following the winding up of the MSC labour market policy in the UK came to be characterized by a renewed ethos of voluntarism (see DE, 1988; Evans, 1992). From 1989 onwards, for example, the government moved to fill the vacuum created by the demise of the MSC with a network of ostensibly employer-led TECs and LECs. The NCVQ was expected to develop a national framework of vocational qualifications without the authority either to compel providers of existing awards to cooperate or to get employers to participate. It was expected to achieve its objective without any legal powers. An NCVQ official recalled that legislation:

> was a dirty word. I always felt, and later it became possible to say it, that really what we needed was a legislative push, a fairly light touch . . . but legislation that this is going to be the UK's national framework. Now you must come in and you must find your way within it . . . I think the council was hampered from its earliest days in being seen as purely a voluntary regulatory body.

Progress was not made impossible, but the credibility of NVQ policy was damaged and making any headway was slow work.

> I still personally regret that we didn't put the NVQ framework on a legislative basis. I think if that had been done, if that nettle had been grasped . . . then an awful lot of the problems that NCVQ have admittedly had would have been greatly reduced. By legislative framework let me be clear, I don't mean impelling people, for instance, to offer nothing but NVQs; but giving it the cachet and the sort of recognition.
>
> (DE official)

> If you'd had a statutory base then you might have got more resistance, but it would have been an established part of the scene – like the German system . . . A voluntary system – this is the British way I have to say – a voluntary system means that it takes a lot longer.
>
> (City and Guilds official)[6]

The accent on voluntarism, and the importance attached to the operation of market forces, meant that the NCVQ had no powers, other than persuasion, to secure the cooperation of the providers of existing vocational qualifications. Many of these bodies had built up solid reputations for the delivery of awards, often over many years, and had commercial interests to defend. The early difficulties of the NCVQ were caused in part by the paucity of mechanisms to encourage the providers of existing vocational qualifications to adapt their products to fit in with the NVQ framework; bearing in mind, of course, that the reform embarked upon was more radical than policy-makers had originally anticipated. Although some awarding bodies accepted the changes, City and Guilds in particular, their qualified support for NVQs was by no means universally shared.

There have been some interests in the economy who have not welcomed NVQs *per se*, because they've seen it requiring changes in what they need to do . . . Awarding bodies . . . in many cases had their own qualifications . . . and as a consequence they quite understandably said, look here we are, we're a growing body. We are selling more and more of these qualifications to employers and individuals, and yet we're told we've got to change what we're doing to fit in with the national structure.

(employers' association official)

What they [NCVQ] didn't have in my view is the tools to enable them to do the job. They really had very few avenues other than to resort to persuasion to use with the big cats in the jungle, and if those big cats were not terribly interested then there was nothing they could do to make them play.

(DE official)

Moreover, the voluntary approach allowed the established examining and validating bodies to keep their existing awards available in the market place. The NCVQ also discovered that it had little scope to prevent them from trying to expand their markets by developing NVQs in areas where they hitherto had had no experience. The outcome of these institutional arrangements was, as Dearing (1996) implicitly acknowledged, the development of an even more complicated and confusing system of vocational qualifications than had existed before the launch of NVQ policy (c.f. Jones, 1995). Belatedly, during the 1990s, as part of their endeavour to embed the NVQ framework, policy-makers tried to instil a greater degree of 'order' into the vocational qualifications system. BTEC, for example, was compelled to cooperate with the NCVQ;[7] funding for government training programmes became increasingly linked to the attainment of NVQs and SVQs; and the publication of the 'Common Accord' in 1993 represented an attempt to establish a greater degree of coherence and consistency between the policies and practices of the various awarding bodies. These developments notwithstanding, ministers were anxious that market principles should not be violated too expressly. The formal position of the government was that the attainment of N/SVQs, and GNVQs, would be so desirable that other awards would be driven out of the market. This assumption lasted until 1995, by which time it was clear that non-NVQs and non-GNVQs, still the majority of vocational qualifications, remained in continuing heavy demand. Attention then turned to ways in which the existing awards could be slotted into a single, comprehensive framework, something that became one of the principal tasks of the QCA when it was founded in October 1997.

The principle of voluntarism also extended to the lead bodies, organizations charged with developing the occupational standards of competence to underpin N/SVQs. The official position was that voluntary collaboration, whereby it was for employers to come together on their own accord, was desirable (DE, 1988). Such an approach disadvantaged the implementation of NVQ policy in three ways. First, it encouraged a sense that the proposed reform somehow lacked importance; that if it failed then it did not matter very much because employers were not interested. An MSC official recalled that:

> [the] government had this kind of notion: well at the end of the road industry's going to pay for these things actually, so they're either going to produce something which industry buys – good luck – or they're not going to produce something, in which case it doesn't matter. The market has spoken. I'm caricaturing slightly, but not too much.

Second, the dependence on the activity of employers further encouraged the development of narrow, task-based NVQs, largely because an over-reliance on their commitment in a more market-based vocational education and training system invariably encourages 'short-term decision making rather than long-term strategic planning', and reduces the propensity for anything other than firm specific arrangements (Coffield, 1992, p. 22; c.f. Streeck, 1989). Third, the profusion of lead bodies that came into being not only meant that the NCVQ had considerable trouble in maintaining coherence and consistency in the system, but it also reinforced the trend towards job-specific and narrow NVQs.[8]

The establishment of a large number of lead bodies was in part an expression of the heterogeneity of employment in the UK. This was a significant obstacle to the furtherance of NVQ policy, given that the imperative was to establish a single, comprehensive system founded upon a standardized competence-based approach to apply universally. As a prominent employers' representative pointed out, 'you've got companies who were wanting people who were fairly narrowly focused and then you've got companies who were wanting jacks of all trades; and how on earth can you decide on a qualification that caters for both? You can't.'[9] The technical enthusiasm of some DE and NCVQ officials and the consultants, however, outweighed their sense of what might be practicable on the ground. Senior DE officials were not in the main mesmerized by the technical elegance of functional analysis; rather, they were keen to have in place a simple, understandable and above all neat system that satisfied their sense of bureaucratic rationality (c.f. Aberbach et al., 1981). According to another employers' representative, the principle of the N/SVQ system was 'a very good civil service approach which didn't take into account at all . . . human nature; and it didn't take into account the fact that the plumbers won't speak to the builders as a trade association . . . So therefore that's why they [DE officials] weren't able to control, because what on paper appears to be perfectly logical doesn't actually happen in real life.'

This was a factor that constrained the development of NVQs at higher levels in particular because of the care taken by professional bodies to guard their historic privileges and their interests. CISC, an organization that was in the vanguard of producing higher-level N/SVQs, had over 60 member bodies, making the production of a consensus problematic. In accountancy, moreover, there were six senior bodies in the UK and Ireland in addition to the Association of Accounting Technicians (AAT) that had been developing NVQs at levels two, three and four. The DE began by funding four different standards development projects simply because these bodies were reluctant to cooperate. Later on the Department managed to persuade them to collaborate in a 'Common Issues Group', but progress was protracted. It is also important to bear in mind that professional bodies themselves are heterogeneous organizations in which the presence of differing viewpoints and even factionalism are commonplace. The views of the Engineering Council, for example, appear to have fluctuated depending upon the attitude of its leadership at any one time towards N/SVQs. The representative of a body that actually made considerable progress in developing occupational standards and N/SVQs at the higher levels noted that,

> one of the things within the institutions particularly, is that you get a diversity within the individual institutions as well. You get those who are completely pro and those who are completely anti; and so you get this political infighting within the institution. This is one of the greatest difficulties because they have their own very long, complicated decision making processes . . . [and it] depends who is on which committee as to whether they are for or against it.

This case study of the reform of vocational qualifications, then, has highlighted the tension that existed between the desire of policy-makers for a simple, comprehensive and rational framework of awards and the rather more messy, complex and heterogeneous world of industry and the professions.[10] The employer community, therefore, often found the NVQ system to be an unattractive proposition. This perception was reinforced by the problem of securing the adequate representation of employers on the NCVQ, its committees and the lead bodies; not least because they found it difficult to commit sufficient time. As a result, the direction of policy was shaped and guided more by officials and, sometimes, educationalists. A lead body representative noted that:

> The most common absentees on steering groups are the employers. So that's where the cynicism begins to creep in. The people who end up able to turn up regularly are NCVQ, awarding bodies, providers; and you have to be very careful that you're not listening to that skew.

Hence, the assertions that have been made about the NVQ system not really being employer-led at all (Field, 1995), and about the way in which the GNVQ has become shaped by educational imperatives (Wolf, 1997).[11] The quest to secure adequate employer input was made difficult in two other respects. First, the sectoral infrastructure for training was insufficiently robust to support the proper development of occupational standards of competence. Not only did the ITOs have 'little leverage with their sectors' (Marquand, 1989, p. 190, c.f. Edgar, 1991; Keep, 1993), but the lead body system, which was put in place from 1987 onwards, often evolved separately. The diversity of arrangements this generated simply added to the fragmentation already inherent in the sectoral training infrastructure and thus weakened the capacity of industry to shape important initiatives such as vocational qualifications policy.[12] An employers' representative considered that:

> in many cases the ITO framework wasn't strong enough. I mean there are some very good exceptions; there are some very good ITOs. But many of them were not strong enough to have the influence in getting the Department to do it right.

Second, it might be assumed that the CBI would have been able to play a key role in coordinating the responses of employers and thus enhancing their capacity to influence the formulation and implementation of vocational qualifications policy. The organization's effectiveness as an interest group will be considered later in this chapter. At this point it is important to note that the CBI gave the reforms of vocational qualifications its strong backing from the outset (see CBI, 1987). However, those responsible for trying to promote the NVQ system discovered that while they might have the support of the CBI, there was a concern about the extent to which it represented employers.

> All of these developments have had the solid support of the CBI throughout. What I think has always been unclear to me is the extent to which the CBI really does speak for employers.
>
> (NCVQ council member)

> The CBI were supportive throughout . . . The problem was, and still is, that the CBI don't talk to employers. They talk to a group of employers who are only influential in CBI, and they're useful from that point of view. But then you go out and talk to the real people, the men [sic] who actually run industry and you get an entirely different picture.
>
> (NCVQ official)

A considerable amount of literature now exists on the shortcomings of employers' representative arrangements in the UK. Grant has argued that 'Britain has a business sector in which there is an increasing concentration of economic power, but that business remains politically weak' (1993, p. 18); Fulcher (1991) has explored the 'institutional inadequacy' of British industry in a comparative and historical perspective; and both Leys (1985) and Middlemas (1991) have noted that the heterogeneity of British capital has often divided the CBI. Vocational qualifications policy, while it was supposed to have been driven by the demands of employers, was therefore constrained by the absence of a clear, coherent and consistent employer viewpoint, and by the difficulty the CBI has in trying to sustain one.[13]

The Locus of Power

The renewed ethos of voluntarism notwithstanding, it would be a mistake to suggest that the development and implementation of the reforms to vocational qualifications were somehow characterized by a lack of intervention. GNVQs, for example, were partly created to supersede existing awards delivered through schools and colleges, the offerings of BTEC in particular. Whereas the more traditional awards were often designed with respect to local circumstances and requirements, the scope, structure and criteria of GNVQs were largely determined by a London-based quango – the NCVQ. The occupational standards programme was also heavily influenced from the centre. Not only did the DE put up the money for standards development in most cases, although lead bodies were required to contribute an equivalent amount 'in kind', and insisted that the functional analysis approach be applied, but there were instances when it also established the lead body itself, particularly in cross-sectoral occupations – the ABCTG for example. Although the importance of getting employers to take the lead in the development of occupational standards and vocational qualifications was trumpeted within the policy rhetoric (see DE, 1988), in reality departmental officials enjoyed considerably more influence in the system. As an employers' representative perceptively observed, the locus of control rested with the DE in part because of the inability of employers to articulate common, coherent and constructive views of their own. Thus there was a vacuum that needed to be filled.

> So why were they [DE officials] so heavy handed? It's partly that if you're sitting on the outside and you don't really know what employers want then you listen to the cacophony, think they're all a bit stupid and try and decide for them. The second reason . . . and with which I have much sympathy, was that they wanted the new qualifications system to be simple; because they wanted it to be admired and used.[14]

Clearly, then, while the implementation of vocational qualifications reform was guided at one level by the primacy of voluntarism and the operation of market forces, at the same time a considerable degree of state intervention can be discerned. Studies of other aspects of recent educational reform, particularly the provisions of the 1988 Education Reform Act (ERA), have highlighted the extent to which both centralizing tendencies and the operation of market mechanisms can coexist, and indeed complement one another, within a single policy initiative. The 1988 ERA, for example, allowed for the devolution of financial and managerial responsibilities from local education authorities to individual schools – Local Management of Schools (LMS). Moreover, this Act and subsequent legislation gave schools the scope to compete with one another for pupils in a more market-oriented institutional framework (see Woods et al., 1997). Yet the 1988 ERA also introduced a National Curriculum for schools, to be followed by students up to the age of 16, the provisions of which were exceedingly prescriptive (see Jenkins, 1995; Johnson and Riley, 1995; Whitty, 1989).

The apparent paradox of the coexistence of a market-led ethos with greater state intervention and centralization will be the subject of further discussion in the conclusion of this book. At this point, though, it is worth offering an interesting example of how increased voluntarism and greater steerage by central state institutions are by no means mutually exclusive developments. By the end of the 1980s the EITB was one of the few remaining statutory training boards, and it received most of its funds from a levy imposed on firms in the sector. It was able to use this money to promote and develop training arrangements in the engineering sector as it saw fit, albeit within certain broad parameters. In 1991 the statutory powers of the EITB were removed. The most immediate effect of this change was to bring about a rapid drop in its funds; the replacement non-statutory body – ENTRA – could not enforce a levy. It became more dependent upon contract funding from the DE for such initiatives as the development of occupational standards and thus less able to formulate an independent position, given the tight specifications attached to the contracts; for example the obligation to use functional analysis (see Senker, 1996).

It has been argued that an increase in the number and powers of quangos has furthered the tendency towards centralization in the British polity during the 1980s and 1990s, and that the resulting growth in influence of the central state has militated against democratic accountability (Burton and Duncan, 1996; Weir, 1995). This trend appears to have been especially pronounced in education, where the operation of the National Curriculum, the supply of teaching staff, school inspections and the funding arrangements for grant maintained schools have all been subject to increasing regulation by such bodies (see Avis et al., 1996; Johnson and Riley, 1995; Mahony and Hextall, 1997; Morris, 1996).[15] Ironically, concern about the growth of government by quango originated on the political right during the 1970s (Holland and Fallon, 1978), the rapid growth in the extent and complexity of government in the post-World War II period having impelled governments to innovate in approaches to policy formulation and delivery (Hirst, 1995).

The incoming Conservative government established a review of quangos in 1979 under Sir Leo Pliatzky. Distinguishing between three kinds of these organizations – executive bodies, advisory bodies and tribunals – Pliatzky's review emphasized that the term 'non-governmental' was something of a misnomer because they consituted the 'concealed growth of government' (Pliatzky, 1980). Pliatzky opted to use the term 'Non-Departmental Public Body' (NDPB) instead (Pliatzky, 1992). Weir and Hall (1994) preferred 'Extra Governmental Organisation' (EGO) as a descriptive tool for two reasons. First, they considered the term 'quango' to be too 'loose'; and second, they included NHS (National Health Service) bodies and 'non-recognised executive bodies', TECs for example, in their 'quango count'. By their reckoning in 1992–93 there were over 7,000 EGOs operating in the UK, responsible for over £45 billion worth of public expenditure (c.f. Wilson, 1995).

What can a case study of the NCVQ, an NDPB, tell us about the nature of government by 'quango'? Most importantly, the notion that the NCVQ was part of the 'concealed growth of government' identified by Pliatzky can be upheld in two respects. First, one of the more prominent themes to have emerged from this study of vocational qualifications policy is the extent to which the NCVQ became over time almost an appendage of the MSC and then the DE. From the time of the inception of NVQ policy in 1987, the NCVQ was substantially dependent upon the progress of the occupational standards programme. But from 1990 onwards the DE took a considerably more active role in determining the NCVQ's priorities and activities, with the Secretary of State's remit letter being perhaps the most obvious mani-festation of this:

> I would see the remit letter that was going [from] ministers to NCVQ . . . I would not have wanted to be on the receiving end of a letter like that if I was the Chairman of NCVQ or the Chief Executive or any of the executive officers.
>
> (NCVQ council member)

On a day-to-day basis, moreover, the DE maintained a close interest in how vocational qualifications policy was implemented. In the case of publicity, for example:

> it wasn't as if NCVQ was told, it's up to you to decide what percentage of your budget you want to spend on communications and marketing. It was, we [the DE] will decide how much you spend and we will decide the ways in which you spend it, right down to the last 't' and the last 'i'.
>
> (NCVQ official)

Nevertheless, the nature of the grant-in-aid funding regime meant that the NCVQ had some scope for independent activity. This source of income dried up in 1994, however, causing the NCVQ to become increasingly reliant on contract funding from the DE, and subsequently the DfEE, in addition to the revenue it accrued from the NVQ levy. As time went on, then, the autonomy of the NCVQ was severely constrained, or indeed barely evident at all, and it appears to have become little more than an outpost of the Department.[16]

Second, the role of the NCVQ council in overseeing the progress of the NVQ and GNVQ policies appears to have been rather circumscribed. In addition to a part-time Chairman, the NCVQ council generally comprised 13 other members, each of whom was appointed on the basis of their individual experience and expertise, be it in education, industry, the trade union movement or local government, and not as representatives of particular interest groups. The effectiveness and influence of the NCVQ's council was limited from the very beginning. According to one individual who was present at the first meeting of the council in late 1986, 'nobody had got any idea as to what we were doing.' A number of senior MSC officials recalled that in the first year of its existence the council found it difficult to get a grip on what was required of the NCVQ:

> certainly the new council of NCVQ during its first year of operation really had very little idea of what was going on. That was quite clear. You had one or two people there who knew what they were doing, but the council as a whole was very much at sea.

> The council of NCVQ in my view didn't exercise sufficient supervision. Why? Because most of them couldn't understand what was going on [and] all its implications.

One of the then council members confirmed that it took a while before the nature and scope of the NCVQ's proposed activities sank in:

> my recollections of the first few meetings of the council, and indeed the various committees that I was on, were that a lot of ground had to be rehearsed a few times before people understood the agenda; and therefore it was quite slow to get going.

The council very quickly settled into a overly reactive role; it rarely initiated anything, but responded to proposals put to it by NCVQ officials. The principal outcome of this state of affairs was that the priorities of officials came to dominate the organization's agenda; and their major concern was often to do with the technical aspects of the qualifications. The NCVQ quickly acquired an introverted character and a reputation for technocratism.[17] This bare representation of a weak NCVQ council needs to be qualified or, rather, amended in three respects, however. First, until 1995 the council formally decided whether or not submissions should be accepted and accredited as NVQs; although much of this responsibility was devolved to a sub-committee. One might assume, therefore, that this gave council members a considerable degree of authority. However, in practice they possessed insufficient expertise to be able to make a proper judgment. A council member recalled that they:

> would get a couple of days before a meeting a wodge of documents. I remember it was like a red box. It was a hideous thing . . . with the latest range of applications for accreditation. And, well, there was no way the individual council members could get through those in detail without any knowledge of the thing or [the] industry . . . generally and make any sensible pronouncement.

Thus the expectation that it would be sufficient for members of the council to rely on their own knowledge and experience as individuals in overseeing developments was a clear shortcoming of the NCVQ (c.f. DfEE, 1996c). By way of contrast, according to Holland (1995), one of the major strengths of the MSC had been the way in which individual commissioners made use of the expertise and research capacities of their respective organizations, the TUC and the CBI for example. It would be a mistake, however, and this is the second point, to characterize the NCVQ council as being uniformly feeble. Throughout the history of the organization certain individual council members were able to exert a degree of authority, particularly if they chaired one of the two main sub-committees on NVQs or GNVQs respectively. Finally, it is important to note that the extent of the influence of the NCVQ's council appears to have declined over time. Although we have shown that the council started off with considerable difficulties, the very fact that the policy was in its developmental phase meant that it had decisions to take, even if the agenda was largely determined by its officials. As time went on, however, the DE exerted greater control over the NCVQ's activities, for example by means of the remit letter, and the initiation of policy developments appears to have been almost entirely restricted to discussions between officials of the two organizations. Commenting on the role of the council an NCVQ official noted that latterly 'they've really had no impact at all because they haven't really been given anything to decide.' The passive character of the council was recognized by an official review of the NCVQ in 1995–96, in which it was observed that:

> beyond carrying out their financial stewardship responsibilities, the role Council has been able to play seems to have been more constrained than one might have hoped . . . there was a lack of opportunity for the Council to take a collective interest in strategy and corporate planning or to make sure that, as a body, it contributed to Government thinking about what NCVQ should be asked to do.
>
> (DfEE, 1996c, p. 38)

Given the extent to which the NCVQ was dependent on the DE, then, and the largely passive part played by the council, what does this imply about the nature of accountability within government? Arguably, sufficient accountability can be maintained in two ways. First, the former Conservative minister William Waldegrave has reportedly claimed that responsiveness to customers is a key measure of accountability (Weir, 1995). In respect of vocational qualifications policy, however, it is difficult to make the case that customers exerted a significant influence, not least because of the frustration felt by many in the employer community at the way in which it was implemented. Second, the lack of independence from government experienced by the NCVQ can be seen as a desirable state of affairs if the accountability of ministers to Parliament is considered a key aspect of the UK's democratic system. Therefore it was only right that government departments should have had a powerful role in shaping the direction and components of vocational qualifications policy. Weir and Hall, though, have suggested not only that NDPBs are 'to all intents and purposes government bodies' and that the ostensible arms-length relationship between them and their sponsoring departments is 'more fiction than fact' (1994, p. 13; c.f. Pierson, 1996), things which this case study of the NCVQ confirms, but also that 'ministerial responsibility is a most fragile instrument of accountability' (p. 14), given the way in which the House of Commons is frequently dominated by a single political party (p. 41). Power consequently becomes increasingly concentrated in the hands of ministers (c.f. Foster and Plowden, 1996).

In this case there are two problems with such an interpretation. Ministers reflected on how difficult it was for them to intervene in the implementation of vocational qualifications policy, even when they had reservations about it:

> Ministers may be accountable, but their ability to influence these things is quite small . . . NVQ policy was up and running and underway; and you know one's job as a minister was basically to sort of help keep the show on the road, rather than move it in different directions.

> Ministers have a whole vast range of responsibilities. It's impossible to spend a great deal of time on each one. There is also the overall philosophical approach of the role of the minister, which in the ideal world is [that] the minister sets the policy and the civil servants implement it. There is a tremendous tendency on a minister to want to get involved on the implementation and management of the system . . . and you know the more you find civil servants interpreting things in a way that you hadn't really intended, the more the inclination is to get in there yourself. The trouble is that once you do that you become subsumed in the whole system and you can't sort of get out and make the strategic decisions that you ought to be making.

A thing I often talk about, privately at least . . . is the difficulty of government with quangos. By the nature of the case, if something goes radically wrong or pressure builds up, you're the one who gets the bundle on your desk; but you've actually got no day to day control.

A senior NCVQ official remarked that 'the fiction is that ministers make policy. I mean the reality is that they can't. I mean they can make very broad policies, but at the level of detail at which we're operating there is no way that they could.' This absence of ministerial direction was exacerbated by the high degree of ministerial turnover. It has been commonly argued that the high degree of ministerial turnover has militated against effective policy formulation and implementation, because new ministers are keen to develop initiatives of their own and attach less importance to those of their predecessors (see Finegold, 1996; Holland, 1995; Plowden, 1994). Alderman (1995), however, has pointed to some of the advantages that can accrue from short ministerial tenure. Among other things ministers can, for example, exhibit a degree of 'detachment' from their respective departments and thus view policy developments more objectively than their officials; a high turnover rate can increase the overall effectiveness of the government by reducing the attachment of ministers to particular posts; and change may be politically advantageous insofar as it gives the impression of a dynamic administration. These arguments notwithstanding, the transience of ministers meant that it was difficult for them to amass sufficient expertise and knowledge about vocational qualifications to be able to make an effective contribution. We are not suggesting that ministerial intervention was consistently ineffectual. On the contrary, at certain times it had a considerable impact, the scepticism of Michael Portillo in 1994–95 in particular. Yet even he did not stay at the DE long enough to be able to alter NVQ policy too greatly.

For the most part, officials, particularly those in the NCVQ and the DE, were largely responsible for dictating the way in which the reform of vocational qualifications progressed. One of the most widely acknowledged features of the British civil service has been the extent to which it has been staffed largely by generalist administrators (Drewry and Butcher, 1988; Kellner and Crowther-Hunt, 1980; Plowden, 1994). Yet an interesting facet of the way in which vocational qualifications policy was advanced was the large degree of enthusiasm for reform, going above and beyond normal considerations, exhibited by DE officials. Now the extent to which officials are active in actually making policy has long been recognized (see Aberbach et al., 1981). Yet the commitment of some DE officials to the reform of vocational qualifications was striking nonetheless; indeed it bore all the hallmarks of a crusade. Their general aim was to improve vocational education and training and thus not only improve skill levels in the economy, but also diminish the superiority of the more ostensibly elitist, academic provision. This can be interpreted as a residual effect of the former MSC and the element of strategic thinking that characterized that organization; it is interesting to note that the commitment to vocationalism within the department arguably diminished on the merger of the DE with the DfE in 1995. Moreover, given the extent of the criticism that the new vocational qualifications attracted and the ambivalence towards them regularly exhibited by ministers, it becomes clear that the resilience of NVQ policy can be substantially explained by the strong support given to it by officials in the DE.[18]

Certainly this is a far more plausible factor than the support of interest groups outside government. The study of the impact of pressure groups and other non-governmental bodies on policy outcomes has intensified in recent years as writers and researchers have increasingly looked to explain their activities with reference to concepts like policy 'communities' and 'networks' (see Jordan and Richardson, 1979; Marsh and Rhodes, 1992; Smith, 1993). Briefly, government departments are shown to amass around them bodies with which negotiation and interaction assist in the formulation, development and implementation of policy. In the advancement of vocational qualifications policy, the activity of several external interest groups has been identified: employers' associations; vocational awarding bodies; further education interests and other educational concerns; sectoral training bodies; quangos other than the NCVQ; Scottish interests; and professional bodies among others. The influence of these groups on the implementation of NVQ and GNVQ policy has been considerable at times, for example the way in which Scotland was able to resist the imposition of NVQs. For the most part, however, the influence of external bodies was limited to occasions when their interests were challenged by reform. Their activities, then, were largely reactive in character because the direction of vocational qualifications policy has largely been determined by officials, the occasional political interventions notwithstanding.

The policy network approach, then, while it is a significant improvement on the basic pluralist position, is not an entirely satisfactory way of analysing the course of vocational qualifications policy. In examining a related area, that of the progress of youth employment measures during the 1970s and 1980s, Marsh (1992) argues not only that there existed no stable policy network, but also that the very concept underestimates the significance of power relations. Our case study has shown that the direction of policy was determined by the government, and sometimes the NCVQ, with officials being predominant; external bodies responded and became involved in policy debates generally only when their interests were challenged. Thus there were few constant, established groups involved in dealing with the government on vocational qualifications policy. Indeed, those that did have a longstanding engagement were either dependent upon the DE, the sectoral ITOs for example, or reactive, the awarding bodies in particular.

It might be argued that the CBI could be cited as an exception to the general picture of ineffectual and transient interest groups. The employers' confederation gave strong support to the reform of vocational qualifications from the outset (see CBI, 1987; CBI, 1989; CBI, 1994). Moreover, when the direction of NVQ policy was in jeopardy during 1994–95, government officials presented the backing of the CBI as evidence of the support of employers. For the most part, though, the significance of the CBI's support was minimal, not least because government ministers – even those sympathetic to the NVQ and GNVQ reforms – did not accept that it represented the legitimate views of employers. Given that the locus of power is seen to rest largely within government departments, and among officials in particular, the second point made by Marsh (1992), concerning the unsatisfactory nature of the pluralist assumption that underpins the policy network approach and the way in which the existence of power relations is underplayed (c.f. Grant, 1995), is upheld by this study of vocational qualifications policy. We can suggest, then, that it is perhaps more appropriate to set this account of the reform of vocational qualifications within an analytical framework in which institutional factors and political interventions are emphasized (c.f. Pierson, 1996), rather than one in which policy is interpreted as the outcome of interactions between different groups both in and out of government.

Institutional Coherence in Government

One of the more striking institutional factors to have affected the direction of vocational qualifications policy was the presence of distinctive departmental cultures and ideologies within government. Although the approach of the DE was characterized by a particular kind of refoming zeal, the commitment to its vision of vocationalism was not shared elsewhere. We have already examined the somewhat tepid reaction of the Scottish Office to the proposal that the NVQ system should be extended to Scotland. Perhaps the most significant inter-departmental tension, however, was that which existed between the DES (DfE) and DE until their merger in July 1995. To begin with, it is important to bear in mind that there were important structural differences between the two departments. The DE was a much larger department; it had a considerable presence on the ground, particularly because of its responsibilities for the Employment Service; it had built up considerable experience of dealing with employers; and its status as an 'economic' department, as well as the residual ethos of the MSC, meant that it had a strong reputation for active policy innovation. The DES, however, had a more administrative character. It had a very small central core of officials, and most of its functions had traditionally been delegated to local authorities and universities (Pile, 1979). A minister who had had some experience within both departments characterized them in the following way:

> I always said, probably unfairly, that the Department of Employment was a can-do department, and the Department of Education was a

can-analyse department; and there is quite a lot of truth in that. The weakness of the Employment [Department] was that it used to go up and do things without thinking it through properly, and the weakness of the Department of Education was that it analysed it and then never did anything.

Their shared sponsorship of the RVQ in 1985–86 and the NCVQ notwithstanding, the DES was, according to one senior government figure, 'on the whole a bit hesitant' about NVQ policy. For an MSC official this was because they:

> had their own agenda . . . [it] was very much that of attempting to maintain the pristine quality of A levels and GCSEs and so on, and to keep totally clear of the vocational education system, No that's not true – to keep their presence in the vocational education system, but not to allow any sullying of the pure waters of particular school qualifications.

The whole area of vocational education, training and qualifications was, according to one of its officials, a 'backwater' in the DES. Indeed it was this that had in part allowed MSC such considerable scope to innovate in this area during the early and mid-1980s. An education minister noted that people in the DES:

> had never come across it [vocational education]. They did not expect their children to come across it . . . So there was a complete cultural problem with the status of vocational education, further education and so on. Quite extraordinary. Understandable, but a bit of a shock.

From 1991 onwards, however, with the development and introduction of the GNVQ the DES exhibited a greater regard for vocational provision. Although there was a greater appreciation of the importance of non-academic education among some ministers and senior officials within the department, particularly given the cross-fertilization of personnel with the DE that had been initiated, this interest in vocational qualifications policy was pursued only insofar as it applied to the curriculum for 16- to 19-year-olds. The DES was, therefore, largely concerned with establishing 'parity of esteem' with A levels and with the provision of progression routes into higher education. Because the agenda of the DE was shaped by the imperative of providing the skills necessary for employment and thus to help people into work, 'turf disputes' were an inevitable outcome (see Unwin and Wellington, 1995), such as the ones that arose over the purpose and structure of the GNVQ. Although the 1995 merger clearly diminished the scope for such territorial conflict, it also appears to have brought about a lessening of the enthusiasm for vocationalism that had up until then characterized the DE.

The absence of a clear commitment to the reform of vocational qualifications across government was evident in one other important respect. From the time the NVQ policy was initiated the Treasury supplied funds for the NCVQ on condition that it worked towards becoming self-financing. To begin with, NCVQ officials supported such an approach on account of the independence that self-sufficiency would presumably give the NCVQ. The main problem, however, was that the throughput of accredited NVQs did not come through anything like as quickly as policy-makers had originally anticipated. In 1990 the Treasury had to be persuaded to release additional grant-in-aid for NCVQ, and when this expired in 1994, further funding difficulties ensued. The Treasury, in fact, questioned the need to support the reform of vocational qualifications at all because it was seen to be something for which industry should pay. An employment minister recalled that:

> the Treasury's role [was] to say, yes, we support this strategy because you know we can see that it is connected to the achievement of competitiveness, but on the other hand, you know, why doesn't industry pay for it? We have a voluntary system.

Not only was the Treasury reluctant to provide funds for measures that would improve skills and vocational training, unless they were to designed to help manage the effects of high unemployment (an attitude that persisted until 1993 and the announcement of the Modern Apprenticeship programme), but it was also, more generally, looking to reassert its 'traditional values' of thrift, economy and tight control over public expenditure (Thain and Wright, 1995; c.f. Jenkins, 1995). While the reluctance of the DES to engage with, and contribute to, the evolution of NVQ policy was in part responsible for the limited educational content of the new qualifications, both it and the attitude of the Treasury gave the impression that the government as a whole was insufficiently serious about the reforms.

One of the main ways in which the Treasury has recently sought to keep public expenditure under control in general has been by increasingly making funds available for policy programmes on condition that certain pre-ordained outputs are delivered (Thain and Wright, 1995). Not only has this approach been seen to offer a more effective and efficient way of controlling public expenditure, but, insofar as the desired policy objectives are defined more specifically, it is also held to reinforce the authority of central government (Henkel, 1991). The large amount of money committed to the delivery of the YTS in the 1980s, added to the widely articulated concerns about the poor quality of many of its component programmes, meant that there was considerable pressure to make sure that it was being deployed effectively. An MSC official pointed out that they:

needed to have outcomes specified for the programmes – which were major national programmes with a lot of money going into them – that were clearly measurable and defined in terms of people doing things well in the workplace.

By 1990, moreover, according to another official, the Treasury was 'steadily tightening the screw on measurable outputs' when it came to funding government training programmes; there was, then, an even greater imperative for a universally accepted measure of attainment within them. However, the combination of the competence-based N/SVQs and outcome-related funding resulted in a number of difficulties. First, training providers have come under pressure to pass trainees as competent, even if they are not, in order to release the outcome-related element. In the further education sector, Steedman and Hawkins (1994) discovered that the 'linking of NVQ certification to YT funding creates pressures on lecturers to certify students as competent to NVQ level 2 and thereby collect a financial bonus for the college' (p. 98; c.f. Stanton, 1996). Second, both training providers and TECs, which similarly have to meet performance targets, are encouraged to restrict opportunities to individuals considered more likely to complete courses successfully and quickly (Felstead, 1994; House of Commons Employment Committee, 1996b; Noon and Ogbanna, 1998). Third, there is a danger that training provision will become increasingly concentrated in occupations where labour turnover, and thus vacancy generation, is relatively high, because they constitute a larger cohort of potential trainees. These occupations, however, are largely those where the demand for skills is relatively low, for example retailing (Felstead, 1994; House of Commons Employment Committee, 1996b). Finally, successive National Audit Office (NAO) reports, while they have welcomed improvements in the way in which the DE and DfEE have exerted financial control over TECs, have also pointed to the risk of overpayments to training providers. Attention has been drawn, for example, to the potential for claims to be made on the basis of forged certificates and trainees who either do not meet the required standard for the qualification or do not exist at all, matters that have been investigated by both the DfEE and the police (NAO, 1995; NAO, 1996; NAO, 1998).[19]

Thus the accent on quantification as the measure of effective and efficient public policy, something that was inspired largely by the efforts of the Treasury to restrict public expenditure, can have a perverse impact on its quality. Such a trend can be identified in other recent public policy initiatives. The Child Support Agency (CSA), for example, was given ambitious targets to meet in terms of raising revenue from absent parents when it was set up in 1993. This led it to concentrate its efforts on squeezing more money out of parents who were already paying some maintenance. They were easily contactable. The more difficult and time-consuming cases involving absentee parents who were making no contributions were largely pushed to one side (Jenkins, 1995; c.f. James, 1997). Furthermore, the Crown Prosecution Service (CPS) has, following Treasury pressure, placed a heavy emphasis on the attainment of perfomance targets. Attempts to produce greater efficiency, however, have frequently led the CPS either to drop charges where a conviction is uncertain, or to reduce their severity so that they can be processed more cheaply (Rose, 1996). These other examples, then, further show the extent to which the largely Treasury-inspired emphasis on targets and quantification as measures of the success of programmes can reduce the quality of public policy outcomes.

Conclusion

The principal aim of this chapter has been to provide a more thematic and analytical underpinning to the account of the progress of vocational qualifications policy presented in earlier ones. In this respect four areas for analysis have been identified: the frequent absence of a political commitment to the furtherance of vocational education; the increased emphasis on voluntarism in labour market policy; the centralization of governmental power, particularly through the use of 'quangos'; and the divergent goals of different actors and institutions within government. In focusing on these matters, however, we have been able to account for some of the difficulties that accompanied the implementation of N/SVQs and also GNVQs that were highlighted in Chapter 1. The poor take-up of NVQs and the failure to establish a single, coherent framework of vocational qualifications can be ascribed to the way in which vocational qualifications policy was dominated by the requirements of government training programmes for the unemployed, the insufficient seriousness with which the government appeared to look upon the area, and the considerable influence of officials in both the DE and the NCVQ. Those in the former were largely concerned with having a simple structure rapidly in place for operational purposes, whereas the agenda of officials in the latter, unencumbered by intervention from the passive NCVQ Council, tended to be dominated by the technical challenges presented by establishing an innovative system of competence-based vocational qualifications. Neither of these imperatives particularly commended themselves, either to employers, who operated in more complex and variegated environments, or to some providers of existing vocational awards and, given the insistence of the government that market forces be allowed to operate, unsurprisingly many other qualifications retained a strong foothold. The dominance of government training programmes for the unemployed and the technocratic approach favoured by the NCVQ and some departmental officials also contributed to the much-criticized narrowness of NVQs.

This was accentuated, moreover, by two other factors. The reluctance of the DES to involve itself in NVQs meant that the opportunity to include broader, educational elements into the qualifications was lost; and the emphasis given to getting employers together voluntarily to develop occupational standards gave rise to a large and diverse set of lead bodies and products that were largely sector specific and narrow. Finally, although the GNVQ has proved to be a very popular initiative, the ambivalence about its key purpose – whether it be progression in education or entry into employment – reflects the different ideologies of the erstwhile education and employment departments. Added to which the complexity of the early GNVQs was a reflection of these different imperatives.

All these matters notwithstanding, we have also identified two crucial factors contributing to the resilience of the reforms. The first was the enthusiasm for the provision of better vocational education exhibited by DE officials, something that was a residue of the former MSC's concern in this area; not only because it was held to improve skill levels and thus economic performance, but also because it would further the opportunities for those young people unsuited to more academic approaches. Second, in a devolved, ostensibly employer-led system of vocational education and training, and with the Treasury increasingly looking to base funding on the successful completion of government programmes, some form of standard measure of outputs became necessary. NVQs were suitable in this respect as currency (see Keep and Mayhew, 1994). In summary, then, the existence of important political and institutional imperatives appears to have shaped and guided the direction of vocational qualifications policy during the 1980s and 1990s.

Notes

1 Although without the youth training issue it is doubtful whether any significant reform would have been attempted.

2 The launch of the Modern Apprenticeship programme in 1994, and its subsequent implementation, has been a notable recent exception to this tendency, insofar as its aim has been to promote and enhance skills training to level three of the national framework. See Gospel (1998) for further details.

3 Before becoming an MP, Paice had gained experience of the YTS as a managing agent.

4 This discussion highlights the importance of treating Conservative ideology, not as a coherent, consistent philosophy, but as a rather heterogeneous collection of beliefs. Ball (1990), for example, distinguishes between the 'industrial modernisers' and the 'cultural restorationists'.

5 After the 1987 general election the MSC had its employment functions removed and it became known, briefly, as the Training Commission. In September 1988 the TUC refused to support the proposed Employment Training (ET) programme and the government used this as a pretext for winding up the Commission. Most of its functions were absorbed into the TA and subsequently the DE.

6 It is also important to note that the NVQ policy appears to have slipped down the political agenda between 1987 and 1989.

7 Although BTEC then kept its other awards in the market place.

8 As we noted above, attempts were made to rationalize the lead body network by the DE in the 1990s. This was largely from a desire to institute more effective management.

9 For example, the CBI (1994) found that 'some companies report a tension between job or company specific standards and generic standards. Some find the standards and NVQs too narrow but others find them too broad' (p. 21). Hence its support for the 'core and options' approach to the design of qualifications.

10 Eraut et al. (1996) noted that it 'is impossible to have a national system of qualifications based on current competence at work; because we do not have a national system of working practices' (p. 67).

11 Although some influential employers' representatives did have considerable influence in the initial design of NVQ policy (see Chapter 4).

12 An umbrella body for ITOs was founded in 1988 – the National Council for Industry Training Organisations (NCITO) – although its influence was limited.

13 More specifically, in the case of training policy, Keep (1986) has argued that the existence of various different, and often contradictory, imperatives, as well as time and resource constraints, prevented the CBI from contributing properly to discussions over the implementation of the YTS.

14 In this respect it is instructive to compare the reform of vocational qualifications with the development of the TEC network. Bennett et al. (1994) questioned the extent to which the TECs were employer led in the first few years of their existence, and noted that the then DE exercised a considerable amount of control over them.

15 The Teacher Training Agency (TTA), the Funding Agency for Schools (FAS), the Office for Standards in Education (OFSTED) and the School Curriculum and Assessment Authority (SCAA) among others.

16 The Quinquennial Review of the NCVQ in 1995–96 is worth quoting at length on this:

> NCVQ would clearly like to be treated by the Department as a strategically-minded organisation, responsible on behalf of the Department for vocational qualifications policy. This would involve regulating the system, monitoring its successful implementation through others, reporting back to Government and proposing and agreeing with Government the forward development agenda. What we observe happening in practice is the Department determining much of the strategy and policy which NCVQ might be expected to develop for itself within the Government's overall strategy for vocational qualifications. The Department is also more involved in the day to day management of Government funded work than would seem to be the case elsewhere. Discussions with NCVQ staff have underlined a sense within the organisation that they are expected to operate as a general factotum for the Department.
>
> (DfEE, 1996c, p. 4)

17 According to a DE official:

> I think at key stages of the development it got far too technical; [it] got almost to be a religion with core beliefs and things like that . . . I think that NCVQ weren't always well-served by the council. They should have been more challenging; they should have been bringing back more of their experience.

18 The competence-based approach that underpinned N/SVQs was also strongly supported by officials in both the DE and the NCVQ. One commentator noted that, 'contrary to the usual conception of neutral and cynical civil servants, many of them have become enthusiastic true believers, seeing themselves as shock-troops or change agents in the cause of better training and education' (Wolf, 1995, p. 127).

19 It should be pointed out that there was support expressed for outcome-related funding. According to an employment minister there was nothing intrinsically wrong with it. The problems were caused because the NVQ system was 'not robust enough'.

Conclusion: Government, Markets and Vocational Qualifications

The purpose of this concluding discussion is three-fold. In the first place we will offer a summary of the key developments in the reform of vocational qualifications in the UK between the early 1980s and 1997. Second, we shall endeavour to situate these changes within an overall analytical framework, one in which the importance of institutional factors and political interventions are given considerable prominence. Finally, we will examine the relationship between the operation of market forces and government intervention evident in the progress of the reforms of the vocational qualifications system.

In this book we have provided an account of how the reforms to vocational qualifications originated, developed and were implemented in the UK during the 1980s and 1990s. The MSC's New Training Initiative of 1981 recommended that vocational education and training should be increasingly founded on the basis of competence, although at that stage the concept itself was rather nebulous. Subsequently, some headway was made on a sectoral basis. However, the main developmental work was progressed largely in the context of the YTS. Moreover, pressure to improve the quality of YTS programmes, by ensuring that trainees had the opportunity to access relevant qualifications in particular, provided the immediate context for a substantial examination of the UK's system of vocational awards. The principal recommendation of the 1985–86 *Review of Vocational Qualifications in England and Wales* was the establishment of a new national framework of NVQs, to encompass existing awards once they had been modified to become more competence-based, which was to be overseen by a new National Council. However, given the degree of ambiguity inherent in the *Review*'s proposals, NCVQ officials, with the support of influential employers' representatives, pressed on with more fundamental reform than policy-makers had hitherto anticipated, and encouraged the development of an entirely new system of vocational qualifications in addition to existing awards.

The subsequent slow progress of NVQ policy meant that in 1990 the government had to intervene to sustain it; the NCVQ was given additional funds and was charged with ensuring that the NVQ framework covered 80 per cent of the employed workforce at levels one to four by the end of 1992. A number of developments assisted the NCVQ in this respect; 'agreements' with BTEC over the inclusion of their awards in the framework and with SCOTVEC over the mutual recognition of NVQs and the relatively new SVQs, in particular. Moreover, the reform process was accelerated by the development of GNVQs from 1991 onwards. Although the NCVQ reached the 80 per cent target by the specified deadline, there was an increasing recognition among policy-makers that, in the rush to ensure that NVQs were available, insufficient attention had been given to their quality. Further, it was becoming apparent that the penetration rate of the new qualifications was rather slow – too slow to please ministers, at any rate – and that the demand for other vocational qualifications continued to be robust. Between 1994 and 1997, then, the criteria for N/SVQs and GNVQs were made somewhat less prescriptive, and attention was increasingly directed at how a broad framework of vocational qualifications could be established, one that could encompass awards – still the majority in fact – that were not N/SVQs or GNVQs.

We have emphasized the extent to which the progress of vocational qualifications policy was influenced by important political and institutional factors. In political terms the reform of vocational qualifications was seen as desirable insofar as it was a way of coping with the changing labour market for young people; thus NVQs retained a close connection with the YTS and YT, and GNVQs were pioneered largely as a way of catering for the increasing proportion of 16-year-olds staying on in full-time education in a climate where the reform of A levels was unrealizable. Indeed, the long-standing commitment to academic education among some leading ministers occasionally gave rise to considerable tensions, given the purportedly 'anti-elitist' character of the new vocational qualifications. In this respect the progress of the reforms was not helped by the differing ideologies and priorities of the employment and education departments before they were merged in 1995. There was little interest in vocational education within the DES until the early 1990s. When it had promoted innovation, in the establishment of the CPVE for example, it was largely to prevent the MSC from further encroaching on its territory. For the most part, however, during the 1980s the furtherance of vocational education in general, and vocational qualifications policy in particular, was the province of the MSC and DE. From 1990 onwards, however, the DES (DfE) did exhibit some greater commitment to vocational education, the establishment of GNVQ policy being evidence of this. While it was stimulated by some genuine ministerial interest and the influx of senior personnel from the DE, the principal aim was nonetheless to enhance educational provision for 16- to 19-year-olds.

In advancing the reform of vocational qualifications based on standards of competence, the main aim of DE officials was economic – that is, to improve the supply of skills to the labour market. One of the strongest themes to have emerged in our account is the commitment of officials to the reform process, and we have ascribed this to the residual ethos of the MSC and the attempts it made during the 1980s to intervene in, and radically alter, the culture of work and employment in the UK (Ainley, 1988; Finn, 1987). The dominant way in which DE officials, and NCVQ officials also to a certain extent, shaped and guided the reform of vocational qualifications had a deleterious effect on the implementation of the supposedly employer-led policy. The DE and NCVQ officials who were responsible, with the help of technical consultants, for developing a competence-based approach that was founded upon the functional analysis of occupations, paid too little attention to the complex, messy and heterogeneous pattern of employment situations and structures characteristic of the UK. Although senior departmental officials did not evince such technical enthusiasm, they were nonetheless attracted to a model that could supposedly be adopted on a universal basis and thus provide the foundation for a neat, overarching framework of vocational qualifications. This satisfied their sense of bureaucratic rationality, or what Weber termed the 'belief in the "legality" of patterns of normative rules and the right of those elevated to authority under such rules to issue commands' (1964, p. 328). Although the reform of vocational qualifications was supposedly to be led by employers (DE, 1988), its implementation was largely dominated by officials. The influence of intermediary institutions, employers' organizations and the awarding bodies, for example, was somewhat limited, although support for the principle of reform, albeit not necessarily the details, from bodies such as the CBI and City and Guilds, was often important insofar as it helped to legitimize the change process.[1]

The disjuncture between the rigid and highly technical model advanced by officials and the rather more flexible approach desired by employers impeded the progress of N/SVQs, particularly their take-up. Yet the resilience of the new vocational qualifications, the heavy internal and external criticism that they have attracted notwithstanding, can be attributed to the strong support for the reforms evident within the former DE. Along with a recent in-depth study of the establishment and experience of TECs (Bennett et al., 1994), our account has shown the large extent to which the locus of power in shaping policy developments in vocational education and training has resided with departmental officials, despite the supposedly employer-led ethos of the reforms. We have also noted, moreover, the increasing extent to which, over time, the NCVQ, the body that was primarily responsible for overseeing the progress of the NVQ and GNVQ policies, became little more than an arm of the DE. During the 1980s and 1990s commentators often remarked on the extent to which successive Conservative governments had 'politicized' the civil service (e.g. Foster and Plowden, 1996). However, this is not the only study of recent policy initiatives to have highlighted the important, independent role exercised by senior civil servants over the way in which they are developed (e.g. see Butler et al., 1994). Thus it is important to recognize the part played by state officials in their own right in the policy process.

Clearly, the importance of governmental intervention, particularly by officials, in influencing the direction and shape of vocational qualifications policy must be acknowledged. Indeed it can be located within the more general recent trend towards the centralization of control over the delivery of education (see Avis et al., 1996). It also means that, in order to conceptualize the reform of vocational qualifications properly, we must employ an analytical framework within which the importance of institutional factors, the activity of state officials in particular, and political interventions are sufficiently recognized. The role of the state as an actor in its own right tends to be somewhat downplayed in classic pluralist and Marxist approaches to the study of the policy process (Hill, 1997). For the pluralists the state is often held up as simply one pressure group among others. The general Marxist view of the state as an instrument used by the capitalist class to maintain its dominant position is also unsatisfactory, given the emphasis we have placed on the central, leading role played by state officials in their own right in advancing the reform of vocational qualifications.

In conceptualizing the reform of vocational qualifications, then, we have therefore employed a modified version of the radical 'institutional' approach to the understanding of the policy process, which has been elaborated by Peter Hall in his 1986 book *Governing The Economy*, a comparative study of economic policy-making in France and the UK. Hall pointed to the way in which certain structural conditions – the organization of the state, capital and labour, the structure of a country's political system, and its position in the global economy – accounted for the direction of economic policy. His approach 'emphasizes the institutional relationships, both formal and conventional, that bind the components of the state together and structure its relations with society. While these relationships are subject to incremental change, and more radical change at critical conjunctures, they provide the context in which most normal politics is conducted.' The demands of interest groups, moreover, are 'mediated by an organizational dynamic that imprints its own image on the outcome' (Hall, 1986, p. 19).

In the case of vocational qualifications policy, it is clear that the forceful part the MSC played in intervening to reshape the UK's vocational education and training system in the 1970s and 1980s, and the way in which its influence continued to shape the DE's approach to policy formulation in this area until its merger with the DfE in 1995, was a crucially important 'organizational dynamic'. We must acknowledge, though, that Hall defends his analytical framework from the charge that it is functionalist. He recognizes that individual policy-makers can influence the direction and shape of public policy, but that they are nonetheless 'affected by the institutional structures within which they operate' (Hall, 1986, pp. 260–61).

On three occasions during the 1980s and 1990s individual politicians made substantial interventions in the development and implementation of vocational qualifications policy. In 1985 Lord Young gave his backing to the need for a review in the first place; Tim Eggar provided the crucial political support for the establishment of GNVQ policy in 1990–91; and in 1994–95 Michael Portillo questioned the basic assumptions that underpinned NVQ policy. Yet in each case ministerial intervention was influenced by broader political and institutional factors. In the case of the decision by Lord Young to launch reform, it is apparent that, while he had considerable personal interest in this area (Young, 1990), without the reputation for delivery that the MSC had built up, for example in the establishment of the YOP, the YTS and the Technical and Vocational Education Initiative, such an initiative would not have been possible; or if it had, it would have been another tentative and flaccid DES attempt. The actions of Eggar and Portillo cannot be isolated from the longstanding attachment of both the DES and a large, influential fraction of the Conservative Party to the notion that educational achievement is analogous to the attainment of academic qualifications. Thus the attraction of the 'institutional' approach to conceptualizing the policy process elaborated by Hall (1986), and used in a modified form here, is not only that the significance of the state, its agencies and its officials as actors in their own right can be properly acknowledged, but also that the way in which they interact with political interventions to shape and guide the direction of policy is recognized.

Actors involved in the policy process are influenced by the beliefs, expectations and historic responsibilities of the institutions of which they are a part. This affects the direction of policy favoured by participants. An analysis of the contrasting approaches to the reform of vocational qualifications policy taken by the three government departments most directly concerned with this area – the MSC/DE, the DES/DfE and the Treasury – highlights this dimension. Their core purposes differed significantly. As a largely 'economic' department, the DE was predominantly concerned with developing policies that would ostensibly help employers, principally the elaboration of greater vocational education and training provision. The DES, however, was a more 'social' department. Its core purpose was to sustain and enhance academic standards and, historically, provide for the personal development of young people. In order to do this it increasingly sought to control the school curriculum, an outcome it achieved with the adoption of the National Curriculum. Vocational education remained a backwater within the DES. It eventually found common cause with the DE over the introduction of the GNVQ, although here there were distinctive differences in the purpose which the two parties ascribed to the awards. The Treasury's core purpose was to contain and preferably reduce public expenditure. It favoured a reduction in the services provided by the state. Training was always regarded as the responsibility of industry and individuals. The Treasury required the NCVQ quickly to become self-sufficient – thus forcing it to adopt the much derided policy of 'conditional accreditation' – and was only persuaded, with considerable reluctance, to provide further funding in 1990 and 1994. Further, in the interest of greater efficiency, the Treasury was influential in introducing the outcome-related funding element to publicly supported training schemes.

Only once, when Modern Apprenticeships were directly and persuasively linked to the government's Competitiveness initiative, did the Treasury make an unequivocal and seemingly ungrudging funding commitment to skills formation.

Yet how is our sustained emphasis on the *dirigiste* character of the reforms to vocational qualifications consonant with another important 'organizational dynamic': the large extent to which Conservative governments of the 1980s and 1990s emphasized voluntarism and the propagation of 'market forces' as the 'best means of determining the types and amounts of training' in the economy (Keep and Rainbird, 1995, p. 518)?[2] We have already shown – in Chapter 8 – that greater centralization of state power is by no means incommensurate with the play of market forces; indeed the two can complement each other. Yet the relationship, or perhaps the tension, between government intervention and the operation of market mechanisms in the progress of vocational qualifications policy was an interesting one and needs to be traced at greater length.

Before 1987 the UK's system of vocational qualifications had, like vocational education and training in general, developed in a fragmented, incoherent manner, the tentative reforms of the 1960s notwithstanding. According to Ellis and Lee (1995), there 'was a free market in qualifications with no central coordination' (p. 7; c.f. DfEE, 1995; Jessup, 1991). Providers of vocational awards – largely private, commercial operators whose income depended on certification revenue – purportedly offered products for which the market (employers, training providers and colleges) had expressed a demand. As Steedman (1993) has pointed out, though, the 'strategies of some of these bodies consisted very largely of offering a number of new products in the fastest growing market – that of no or low skills' (p. 290). Within the MSC in the early 1980s it was felt that not only had the awards offered by the examining and validating bodies become too closely entwined with the needs of further education colleges, and therefore too divorced from what was required by employers, but also that the system of vocational qualifications as a whole needed to be made more coherent and transparent. Thus there was an imperative to establish a national framework within which awards could be posted, once they had been modified so that they better reflected the competences demanded by employers.

The NCVQ was set in place to facilitate this, although it had no statutory powers to compel providers of vocational qualifications to work with it in the reform process. The voluntary ethos which underpinned the NCVQ's work might not have mattered so much were it not for the more ambitious programme of reform upon which the organization embarked. Examining and validating bodies either withdrew their cooperation, or, more commonly, added the new competence-based NVQs to their existing roster of awards. Moreover, not only did some lead bodies set themselves up as NVQ awarding bodies, and thus release a potential stream of funding from certification fees, but some existing providers looked to expand their respective markets by developing NVQs in areas where they had hitherto had no presence. Between 1987 and 1990, then, the NVQ policy was introduced into a largely unchanged market-based institutional environment, in which competition between providers of qualifications was endemic. Furthermore, the ethos of voluntarism also extended to the lead body network; eventually over 160 of these organizations emerged to design occupational standards of competence for their respective sectors. The original aims of policy-makers notwithstanding, then, no inclusive framework of vocational qualifications was established. Indeed, if anything, confusion increased.

The period 1990 to 1993 was characterized by the increasing attention policy-makers gave to ways of managing competition so that the reform of vocational qualifications could be progressed in a coherent manner. Lead bodies were not only encouraged to cooperate with each other more expressly, but the possibility of their being merged into more generic Occupational Standards Councils (OSCs) was also raised. The prospect of forced rationalization, however, provoked considerable opposition from some employers' representatives (see Marshall, 1994), and although some lead bodies combined in OSCs voluntarily, the issue was put to one side for a while. In respect of the awarding bodies, the government ordered BTEC, which was then still a quango under the auspices of the DES, to reach an agreement with the NCVQ over the inclusion of its awards in the NVQ framework. Of course it could not be quite so autocratic with the private sector awarding bodies, and ministers were keen to ensure that competition between them should be sustained anyway. Thus progress was limited to the publication and implementation of consistent assessment and verification specifications – the 'Common Accord' (NCVQ, 1993a).

Finally, the greater degree of governmental intervention characteristic of this period is evident in two other respects: the development and implementation of the GNVQs, and the elaboration of increasingly prescriptive criteria governing the form and structure of NVQs by the DE and the NCVQ. Although ministers were always conscious that the principle of market forces should be upheld, the way in which the government appeared to be skewing the market for vocational qualifications – through the use of funding mechanisms for publicly supported training programmes and the provision of tax relief among other things – so that N/SVQs were privileged at the expense of other awards came in for criticism from right-wing advocates of competition (e.g. Marks, 1996). According to one commentator, in general 'the Government quite rightly argues the case for the minimum amount of regulation necessary in a market without putting too many burdens on participants in that market. Why is this logic not also extended to the market for qualifications?' (Robinson, 1996b, p. 2). From 1994–95 onwards, however, the government recognized that, no matter how many additional advantages they were given, N/SVQs were not going to drive other qualifications out of the market place. The attention of officials increasingly focused, then, on how a national framework of vocational qualifications could be developed that would include N/SVQs, GNVQs and other awards.

Yet it is important to bear in mind that the greater appreciation given to the operation of market forces should not be interpreted as implying a diminution in the interventionary role of the state, rather the opposite. The QCA, which succeeded the NCVQ in October 1997, was established with a remit to set the criteria that qualifications – all awards, not just NVQs and GNVQs – should meet if they were to be included in the new-style national framework. Moreover, in order to persuade the providers of vocational qualifications to reform their products, it was given statutory powers under the 1997 Education Act to advise the Secretary of State for Education and Employment on whether or not particular awards should be supported in publicly funded training programmes. According to Nick Tate, the first Chief Executive of the QCA, one of its 'key responsibilities will be to develop a national framework of vocational qualifications. No qualifications will be available in publicly funded provision . . . unless approved by QCA and offered by one of QCA's accredited awarding bodies' (quoted in *City and Guilds Broadsheet*, February 1998, p. 4). Furthermore, during 1996 and 1997 the government took steps to simplify the institutional environment within which NVQs and SVQs are designed and delivered, bringing the various lead bodies and OSCs into a new network of National Training Organisations (NTOs) and encouraging vocational and academic awarding bodies to merge. Although both bodies were initially charged with instituting a national framework of vocational qualifications it would be a mistake to equate the remit of the QCA with that given to the NCVQ over ten years earlier. The QCA enjoys potentially far more extensive powers to shape and develop the UK's vocational qualifications system than were ever held by the NCVQ.

Thus the direction of vocational qualifications policy has been characterized by the greater effort of the state to regulate the content and structure of awards and the infrastructure within which they are formulated and offered. The trend towards such centralization of state power has been identified in education generally (Avis et al., 1996), and indeed in the wider application of public policy (Jenkins, 1995; Pierson, 1996). In the case of the reforms of vocational qualifications, although the importance of allowing market forces to operate was taken as a given, regulation, which according to Pierson (1996), 'may be taken to describe all those ways in which the state intervenes administratively or legislatively to control the behaviour of market actors' (p. 106), increased dramatically. As our account has shown, however, the trend towards greater regulation was not an expression of the strategic grand design of policy-makers. For the most part it was disjointed, incremental, and reflected both the tension that existed between the interventionist tendencies of officials and the flexibility preferred by employers and awarding bodies, and the differing goals of discrete government departments. Indeed, only from 1994–95 onwards did the government begin to explore how a coherent and inclusive framework of vocational qualifications could be built, and the ways in which an accrediting body, such as the NCVQ or the QCA, would act to regulate it. Nevertheless, the most significant change to the UK's system of vocational qualifications during the 1980s and 1990s has been the gradual replacement of a largely unregulated market for vocational qualifications with one that is much more heavily regulated by the state. Although Conservative governments of the 1980s and 1990s frequently claimed to have drastically reduced the size of the state, through privatization initiatives among other things, in some areas, such as in education and training for example, its central powers have grown dramatically.

Notes

1 We have recognized, though, that in the first few months of the NCVQ's existence influential employers' representatives encouraged it to work towards the development of new awards. However, the extent to which such a 'clean sheet' approach reflected the wishes of the majority of employers, or even the CBI, is questionable; and some NCVQ officials themselves were prominent in pushing for more fundamental reform than policy-makers had originally anticipated. The changes to the NVQ criteria of 1995, particularly the formal acceptance of the 'core and options' structure, were perhaps a response to pressure from employers (see CBI, 1994). Yet it is doubtful whether such alterations would have been made had there not been ministerial pressure on officials to improve the take-up of qualifications.
2 It is interesting to note that NVQs and SVQs, insofar as they represent a standard measure of achievement in a decentralized, market-based training structure (Keep and Mayhew, 1994), can be identified as a key aspect of the government's concern with improving the supply of skills to the labour market. Increasingly, however, researchers have argued that the under-performance of the UK in vocational education and training is rather a reflection of deficient demand for skills (Finegold and Soskice, 1988; Glynn and Gospel, 1993; Keep and Mayhew, 1996). Thus one of the problems with the new qualifications has been that they reflect the existing pattern of skills and do not promote upskilling.

Methodological Appendix

The research on which this book is based started in December 1995 and was initially supported by the Open University. We began by exploring the origins and initial implementation of the reforms to vocational qualifications. From April 1997 to September 1998 the project was funded by the Economic and Social Research Council (grant no. 000237007). This additional money enabled us to extend our work to cover the implementation of vocational qualifications policy to the formation of the QCA in 1997. In addition to the secondary sources listed in the bibliography, two sources of original data were drawn upon:

1 A wide range of documentary evidence was analysed. This comprised: published official sources, including Parliamentary papers; minutes of the meetings of the NCVQ council (1986–1997); copies of unpublished papers; various NCVQ and BTEC annual reports; and the following newspapers and journals:

BTEC Briefing
CBI Education and Training Bulletin
CISC News
City and Guilds Broadsheet
Educa
Education
Financial Times
Guardian
NVQ Datanews
NVQ Update
Personnel/People Management
The Times Educational Supplement
The Times Higher Education Supplement
Transition
Update

2 Interviews with 95 key informants involved in developing, influencing and implementing the reform of vocational qualifications. These interviews were usually conducted at the home or office of the informant, although some were undertaken in cafés, bars or at the Open University; they took between half an hour and most of one day! Nearly all of the interviews were recorded and the subsequent tapes transcribed. Interviews took place with former and serving:

- officials from the MSC, TA, DE, DES and DfEE (27 interviews);
- government ministers (6 interviews);
- NCVQ and SCOTVEC officials and council members (21 interviews);
- representatives of employers, trade unions and professional bodies (12 interviews);
- representatives of awarding bodies and the education sector (10 interviews);
- technical consultants (4 interviews);
- representatives of lead bodies (15 interviews).

There is a further important point to be made about the programme of interviews. Our informants – ministers, civil servants and NCVQ officials in particular – were, or had been, involved in policy formulation and delivery at senior levels; we were fortunate that they proved so willing to help our work.

References

Aberbach, J., Putnam, R., and Rockman, B. (1981) *Bureaucrats and Politicians in Western Democracies*, Cambridge MA: Harvard University Press.

Ainley, P. (1988) *From School to YTS: Education and Training in England and Wales 1944–1987*, Milton Keynes: Open University Press.

Ainley, P., and Corney, M. (1990) *Training for the Future: The Rise and Fall of the Manpower Services Commission*, London: Cassell.

Ainley, P., and Vickerstaff, S. (1993) 'Transitions from corporatism: the privatisation of policy failure', *Contemporary Record*, **7**, 3, pp. 541–56.

Alderman, R. (1995) 'A defence of frequent ministerial turnover', *Public Administration*, **73**, 497–512.

Anderson, M., and Fairley, J. (1983) 'The politics of industrial training in the United Kingdom', *Journal of Public Policy*, **3**, 2, pp. 191–207.

Ashton, D., and Green, F. (1996) *Education, Training and the Global Economy*, Cheltenham: Edward Elgar.

Avis, J., Bloomer, M., Esland, G., Gleeson, D., and Hodkinson, P. (1996) *Knowledge and Nationhood: Education, Politics and Work*, London: Cassell.

Ball, S. (1990) *Politics and Policy Making in Education: Explorations in Policy Sociology*, London: Routledge.

Barnett, C. (1986) *An Audit of War: The Illusion and the Reality of Britain as a Great Nation*, London: Macmillan.

Bates, I. (1995) 'The competence movement: conceptualising recent research', *Studies in Science Education*, **25**, pp. 39–68.

Beaumont, G. (1996) *Review of 100 NVQs and SVQs*, London: DfEE.

Bell, D. (1973) *The Coming of Post-industrial Society*, New York: Basic Books.

Bennett, R., Wicks, P., and McCoshan, A. (1994) *Local Empowerment and Business Services: Britain's Experiment with Training and Enterprise Councils*, London: UCL Press.

Burton, P., and Duncan, S. (1996) 'Democracy and accountability in public bodies: new agendas in British governance', *Policy and Politics*, **24**, 1, pp. 5–16.

Bush, C. (1993) *From Voluntarism to Regulation: Awarding Bodies in English Education and Training: A Case Study of City and Guilds*, Occasional Paper 10, London: University of London Institute of Education.

Business and Technology Education Council (BTEC) (1994) *BTEC: The First Decade*, London: BTEC.

Butler, D., Adonis, A., and Travers, T. (1994) *Failure in British Government: The Politics of the Poll Tax*, Oxford: OUP.

Callender, C. (1992) *Will NVQs Work? Evidence from the Construction Industry*, Institute of Manpower Studies Report 228, Brighton: Institute of Manpower Studies.

Capey, J. (1995) *GNVQ Assessment Review*, London: NCVQ.

Caves, R. (1980) 'Productivity differences among industries', in Caves, R., and Krauso, L. (eds) *Britain's Economic Performance*, Washington, D.C.: The Brookings Institute, pp. 135–92.

Central Policy Review Staff (CPRS) (1980) *Education, Training and Industrial Performance*, London: CPRS.

Chapman, P. (1994) 'Investing in skills: Training policy in the UK', in Buxton, T., Chapman, P., and Temple, P. (eds) *Britain's Economic Performance*, London: Routledge, pp. 160–75.

Coates, D. (1994) *The Question of UK Decline*, London: Harvester-Wheatsheaf.

Coffield, F. (1992) 'Training and Enterprise Councils: The last throw of voluntarism?', *Policy Studies*, **23**, 4, pp. 11–32.

Committee of Vice-Chancellors and Principals (CVCP) (1994) *Strategy Paper on Vocational Higher Education*, unpublished draft, London: CVCP.

Committee of Vice-Chancellors and Principals (CVCP) (1995) *Vocational Higher Education: A Strategy Paper*, London: CVCP.

Confederation of British Industry (CBI) (1987) *National Vocational Qualifications: An Information Guide*, London: CBI.

Confederation of British Industry (CBI) (1989) *Towards a Skills Revolution*, London: CBI.

Confederation of British Industry (CBI) (1993) *Lead Bodies: An Agenda for the Future*, London: CBI.

Confederation of British Industry (CBI) (1994) *Quality Assessed: The CBI Review of NVQs and SVQs*, London: CBI.

Constable, J., and McCormick, R. (1987) *The Making of British Managers*, London: British Institute of Managers.

Coopers and Lybrand Associates (1985) *A Challenge to Complacency: Changing Attitudes Towards Training*, Sheffield: MSC.

Cox, C., and Dyson, A. (1971) *The Crisis in Education: Black Paper Two*, London: The Critical Society Quarterly.

Crompton, R., and Jones, G. (1984) *White Collar Proletariat: Deskilling and Gender in Clerical Work*, Basingstoke: Macmillan.

Cross, M. (1991) 'The role of the National Council for Vocational Qualifications', in Chitty, C. (ed.) *Post-16 Education: Studies in Access and Achievement*, London: Kogan Page, pp. 167–76.

Crouch, C. (1998) 'Skills-based full employment: The latest philosopher's stone', *British Journal of Industrial Relations*, **35**, 3, pp. 367–91.

Cutler, T. (1992) 'Vocational training and British economic performance: A further instalment of the "British Labour Problem"?', *Work, Employment and Society*, **6**, 2, pp. 161–83.

Deakin, B. (1996) *The Youth Labour Market in Britain*, Cambridge: CUP.

Dearing, R. (1994) *The National Curriculum and its Assessment*, London: SCAA.

Dearing, R. (1996) *Review of Qualifications for 16–19 Year Olds*, London: SCAA.

Department for Education (DfE) (1994) *List of Vocational Qualifications in addition to National Vocational Qualifications and General National Vocational Qualifications Approved by the Secretary of State under Section 3(1) and Schedule 2(A) of the Further and Higher Education Act 1992,* London: DfE.

Department for Education and Employment (DfEE) (1995) *NCVQ 1995 Quinquennial Review Stage One Report,* London: DfEE.

Department for Education and Employment (DfEE) (1996a) *Building the Framework,* London: DfEE.

Department for Education and Employment (DfEE) (1996b) *Higher Level Vocational Qualifications: A Government Position Paper,* London: DfEE.

Department for Education and Employment (DfEE) (1996c) *NCVQ 1995 Quinquennial Review Stage Two Report,* London: DfEE.

Department for Education and Employment (DfEE) (1997a) *Guaranteeing Standards,* London: DfEE.

Department for Education and Employment (DfEE) (1997b) *Qualifying for Success,* London: DfEE.

Department for Education and Employment (DfEE) (1998a) *Education and Training Statistics for the United Kingdom,* London: Stationery Office.

Department for Education and Employment (DfEE) (1998b) 'Blackstone announces A level improvements', *DfEE Press Release,* 3 April, London: DfEE.

Department of Education and Science (DES) (1977) *Education in Schools: A Consultative Document,* London: HMSO.

Department of Education and Science (DES) (1989) *Post-16 Education and Training: Core Skills,* London: DES.

Department of Education and Science/Department of Employment (DES/DE) (1991) *Education and Training for the 21st Century,* London: HMSO.

Department of Employment (DE) (1981) *A New Training Initiative: A Programme for Action,* London: HMSO.

Department of Employment (DE) (1984) *Training for Jobs,* London: HMSO.

Department of Employment (DE) (1988) *Employment for the 1990s,* London: HMSO.

Department of Employment (DE) (1991) *Lead Bodies for the 1990s,* Sheffield: DE.

Department of Employment (DE) (1992) *People, Jobs and Opportunity,* London: HMSO.

Department of Employment (DE) (1995) *A Vision for Higher Level Qualifications,* London: DE.

Department of Employment/Department of Education and Science (DE/DES) (1985) *Education and Training for Young People,* London: HMSO.

Department of Employment/Department of Education and Science (DE/DES) (1986) *Working Together: Education and Training,* London: HMSO.

Department of Trade and Industry (DTI) (1994) *Competitiveness: Helping Business to Win,* London: HMSO.

Department of Trade and Industry (DTI) (1995) *Competitiveness: Forging Ahead,* London: HMSO.

Drewry, G., and Butcher, T. (1988) *The Civil Service Today,* Oxford: Blackwell.

Edgar, J. (1991) 'ITOs – again under review', *Transition,* March, pp. 10–11.

Ellis, P. (1993) 'The awarding bodies common accord', *Competence and Assessment,* **23,** pp. 3–4.

Ellis, P., and Lee, D. (1995) 'The review of 100 most used NVQs and SVQs', paper presented to a *Further Education Research Association Special Conference*, University of Warwick, 19 May.

Engineering Council (1995) *Competence and Commitment*, London: Engineering Council.

Eraut, M., and Cole, G. (1993) *Assessing Competence in the Professions*, Research and Development Series Report, 14, Sheffield: DE.

Eraut, M., Steadman, S., Trill, J., and Parker, J. (1996) *The Assessment of NVQs*, Research Report 4, Brighton: University of Sussex Institute of Education.

Evans, B. (1992) *The Politics of the Training Market*, London: Routledge.

Farley, M. (1985) 'Trends and structural changes in English vocational education', in Dale, R. (ed.) *Education, Training and Employment: Towards a New Vocationalism?*, Oxford: Pergamon, pp. 73–94.

Felstead, A. (1994) 'Funding government training schemes: Mechanisms and consequences', *British Journal of Education and Work*, **7**, 3, pp. 21–42.

Felstead, A., Goodwin, J., and Green, F. (1995) *Measuring up to the National Targets: Women's Attainment of Vocational Qualifications*, Leicester: University of Leicester Centre for Labour Market Studies.

Field, J. (1995) 'Reality testing in the workplace: Are NVQs "employment-led"?', in Hodkinson, P., and Issitt, M. (eds) *The Challenge of Competence*, London: Cassell, pp. 28–43.

Finegold, D. (1996) 'Market failure and government investment in skills', in Booth, A., and Snower, D. (eds) *Acquiring Skills: Market Failures, their Symptoms and Policy Responses*, Cambridge: CUP, pp. 235–53.

Finegold, D., and Soskice, D. (1988) 'The failure of training in Britain: analysis and prescription', *Oxford Review of Economic Policy*, **4**, 3, pp. 21–53.

Finegold, D., Keep, E., Miliband, E., Raffe, D., Spours, D., and Young, M. (1990) *A British 'Baccalaureate': Ending the Division between Education and Training*, London: Institute of Public Policy Research.

Finn, D. (1984) 'The Manpower Services Commission and the Youth Training Scheme: a permanent bridge to work?', *Compare*, **14**, 2, pp. 145–56.

Finn, D. (1986) 'YTS: the jewel in the MSC's crown?', in Benn, C., and Fairley, J. (eds) *Challenging the MSC*, London: Pluto Press, pp. 52–75.

Finn, D. (1987) *Training Without Jobs*, London: Macmillan.

Foster, C., and Plowden, F. (1996) *The State Under Stress*, Buckingham: Open University Press.

Freire, P. (1972) *Pedagogy of the Oppressed*, London: Sheed and Wood.

Fulcher, J. (1991) *Labour Movements, Employers and the State*, Cambridge: CUP.

Further Education Funding Council (FEFC) (1995) *General National Vocational Qualifications in the Further Education Sector in England*, Coventry: FEFC.

Further Education Unit (FEU) (1979) *A Basis for Choice*, London: FEU.

Further Education Unit (FEU) (1983) *Supporting YTS*, London: FEU.

Glynn, S., and Gospel, H. (1993) 'Britain's low skill equilibrium: A problem of demand?', *Industrial Relations Journal*, **24**, 2, pp. 112–25.

Gokulsing, K., Ainley, P., and Tysome, T. (1996) *Beyond Competence: The National Council for Vocational Qualifications Framework and the Challenge to Higher Education in the New Millennium*, Aldershot: Avebury.

Gokulsing, K., DaCosta, C., and Jessup, G. (1997) *A Selected Bibliography of Competence-based Education and Training (CBET)*, Lampeter: The Edwin Mellen Press.

Goldstein, N. (1984) The New Training Initiative: A great leap backward', *Capital and Class*, **23**, pp. 83–106.

Gospel, H. (1995) 'The decline of apprenticeship training in Britain', *Industrial Relations Journal*, **26**, 1, pp. 32–44.

Gospel, H. (1998) 'The revival of apprenticeship training in Britain?', *British Journal of Industrial Relations*, **36**, 3, pp. 435–57.

Grant, W. (1993) *Business and Politics in Britain*, Basingstoke: Macmillan.

Grant, W. (1995) *Pressure Groups, Politics and Democracy in Britain*, Hemel Hempstead: Harvester-Wheatsheaf.

Green, A. (1990) *Education and State Formation: The Rise of Education Systems in England, France and the USA*, London: Macmillan.

Guildford Education Services (GES) (1986) *Policies and Practices of Major Validating and Examining Bodies: Report to the Review of Vocational Qualifications*, Guildford: GES.

Guildford Education Services (GES) (1990) *Qualifications and VET: EDUCA Guides to Vocational Education and Training*, 4, Guildford: GES.

Guy, R. (1991) 'Serving the needs of industry?', in Raggatt, P., and Unwin, L. (eds) *Change and Intervention: Vocational Education and Training*, London: Falmer Press, pp. 47–60.

Hall, P. (1986) *Governing the Economy*, Cambridge: Polity.

Handy, C. (1987) *The Making of Managers: A Report on Management Education, Training and Development in the United States, West Germany, France, Japan and the UK*, London: NEDO.

Hayes, C., Fonda, N., and Anderson, A. (1983) *Training for Skills Ownership: Learning to Take it With You*, Brighton: IMS.

Hayes, C., Fonda, N., and Anderson, A. (1984) *Competence and Competition: Training and Education in the Federal Republic of Germany, the US and Japan*, London: NEDC/MSC.

Henkel, M. (1991) 'The new evaluative state', *Public Administration*, **69**, pp. 121–36.

Higginson, G. (1988) *Advancing A Levels*, London: HMSO.

Hill, M. (1997) *The Policy Process in the Modern State*, London: Harvester-Wheatsheaf.

Hirst, P. (1995) 'Quangos and democratic government', in Ridley, F., and Wilson, D. (eds) *The Quango Debate*, Oxford: OUP, pp. 163–81.

Hogg, S., and Hill, J. (1995) *Too Close to Call: Power and Politics: John Major in Number Ten*, London: Little, Brown.

Holland, G. (1995) 'Alas! Sir Humphrey. I knew him well', *RSA Journal*, **5464**, pp. 39–51.

Holland, P., and Fallon, M. (1978) *The Quango Explosion*, London: Conservative Political Centre.

House of Commons Employment Committee (1991) *Training and Enterprise Councils and Vocational Training: Volume One*, report and proceedings of the committee, session 1990–91, London: HMSO.

House of Commons Employment Committee (1995) *The Work of the Employment Department*, minutes of evidence, session 1994–95, London: HMSO.

House of Commons Employment Committee (1996a) *The Work of TECs*, minutes of evidence, session 1995–96, London: HMSO.

House of Commons Employment Committee (1996b) *The Work of TECs*, London: HMSO.

House of Lords (1990) *Vocational Training and Re-training*, Select Committee on the European Communities, 21st report, session 1989–90, London: HMSO.

Hyland, T. (1994) *Competence, Education and NVQs: Dissenting Perspectives*, London: Cassell.

Illich, I. (1971) *Deschooling Society*, London: Calder and Boyars.

Jackson, T. (1995) 'Piloting GNVQ', in Burke, J. (ed.) *Outcomes, Learning and the Curriculum: Implications for NVQs, GNVQs and other Qualifications*, London: Falmer Press, pp. 130–41.

James, S. (ed.) (1997) *British Government: A Reader in Policy Making*, London: Routledge.

Jenkins, S. (1995) *Accountable to None: The Tory Nationalisation of Britain*, London: Hamish Hamilton.

Jessup, G. (1991) *Outcomes: NVQs and the Emerging Model of Education and Training*, London: Falmer Press.

Johnson, H., and Riley, K. (1995) 'The impact of quangos and new government agencies on education', *Parliamentary Affairs*, **48**, 2, pp. 284–96.

Jones, H. (1995) 'Too many awarding bodies', *City and Guilds Broadsheet*, **133**, pp. 10–11.

Jordan, G., and Richardson, J. (1979) *Governing Under Pressure: The Policy Process in a Post-parliamentary Democracy*, Oxford: Martin Robertson.

Keep, E. (1986) 'Designing the stable door: A study of how YTS was planned', *Warwick Papers in Industrial Relations*, 8, Warwick: University of Warwick.

Keep, E. (1993) 'Missing, presumed skilled: Training policy in the UK', in Edwards, R., Sieminski, S., and Zeldin, D. (eds) *Adult Learners, Education and Training*, London: Routledge, pp. 91–111.

Keep, E., and Mayhew, K. (1988) 'The assessment: education, training and economic performance', *Oxford Review of Economic Policy*, **4**, 3, pp. i–xv.

Keep, E., and Mayhew, K. (1994) 'The changing structure of training provision', in Buxton, T., Chapman, P., and Temple, P. (eds) *Britain's Economic Performance*, London: Routledge, pp. 308–41.

Keep, E., and Mayhew, K. (1996) 'Evaluating the assumptions that underline training policy', in Booth, A., and Snower, D. (eds) *Acquiring Skills: Market Failures, their Symptoms and Policy Responses*, Cambridge: CUP, pp. 305–35.

Keep, E., and Rainbird, H. (1995) 'Training', in Edwards, P. (ed.) *Industrial Relations: Theory and Practice in Britain*, Oxford: Blackwell, pp. 515–42.

Kellner, P., and Lord Crowther-Hunt (1980) *The Civil Servants: An Inquiry into Britain's Ruling Class*, London: Macdonald General Books.

King, D. (1993) 'The Conservatives and training policy 1979–1992: From a tripartite to a neo-liberal regime', *Political Studies*, **16**, 2, pp. 214–35.

Kumar, K. (1986) *Prophecy and Progress: The Sociology of Industrial and Post-industrial Societies*, Harmondsworth: Penguin.

Labour Party (1991) *Today's Education and Training*, London: Labour Party.

Laffin, M., and Young, K. (1990) *Professionalism in Local Government*, London: Longman.

Lee, D. (1989) 'The transformation of training and the transformation of work in Britain', in Wood, S. (ed.) *The Transformation of Work*, London: Unwin Hyman, pp. 156–70.

Lee, D., Marsden, D., Rickman, P., and Duncombe, J. (1990) *Scheming for Youth: A Study of the YTS in the Enterprise Culture*, Buckingham: Open University Press.

Levy, M. (1987) *The Core Skills Project and Work-based Learning*, Sheffield: MSC/FESC.

Levy, M. (1995) 'Work-based learning and outcomes', in Burke, J. (ed.) (1995) *Outcomes, Learning and the Curriculum: Implications for NVQs and GNVQs and other Qualifications*, London: Falmer Press, pp. 228–43.

Leys, C. (1985) 'Thatcherism and British manufacturing: A question of hegemony', *New Left Review*, 151, pp. 5–25.

MacInnes, J. (1987) *Thatcherism at Work*, Milton Keynes: Open University Press.

Mahony, P., and Hextall, I. (1997) 'Problems of accountability in reinvented government: a case study of the Teacher Training Agency', *Journal of Education Policy*, **12**, 4, pp. 267–83.

Manpower Services Commission (MSC) (1975) *Vocational Preparation for Young People: A Discussion Paper*, Sheffield: MSC.

Manpower Services Commission (MSC) (1976) *Towards a Comprehensive Manpower Policy*, Sheffield: MSC.

Manpower Services Commission (MSC) (1977a) *Training for Skills*, Sheffield: MSC.

Manpower Services Commission (MSC) (1977b) *Young People and Work*, Sheffield: MSC.

Manpower Services Commission (MSC) (1980) *Outlook on Training: A Review of the 1973 Employment and Training Act*, Sheffield: MSC.

Manpower Services Commission (MSC) (1981a) *A New Training Initiative: A Consultative Document*, Sheffield: MSC.

Manpower Services Commission (MSC) (1981b) *A New Training Initiative: An Agenda for Action*, Sheffield: MSC.

Manpower Services Commission (MSC) (1984) *The Modernisation of Occupational Training*, Sheffield: MSC.

Manpower Services Commission (MSC) (1985) *Report of the Working Group on Contents and Standards for YTS*, Sheffield: MSC.

Manpower Services Commission (MSC) (1988a) *The CATERBASE Project: Workplace Assessment and Accreditation for the Hotel and Catering Industry*, Sheffield: MSC.

Manpower Services Commission (MSC) (1988b) *Development of Assessable Standards for National Certification: A Code of Practice and a Development Model*, Technical Advisory Group Guidance Note 1, Sheffield: MSC.

Manpower Services Commission/Department of Education and Science (MSC/DES) (1985) *Review of Vocational Qualifications in England and Wales: Interim Report*, Sheffield: MSC.

Manpower Services Commission/Department of Education and Science (MSC/DES) (1986) *Review of Vocational Qualifications in England and Wales*, London: HMSO.

Mansfield, B. (1991) 'Deriving standards of competence', in Fennell, E. (ed.) *Development of Assessable Standards for National Certification*, London: HMSO, pp. 12–24.

Mansfield, B. (1993) 'Competence-based qualifications: A response', *Journal of European Industrial Training*, **17**, 3, pp. 19–22.

Mansfield, B., and Mathews, D. (1985) *Job Competence: A Description for use in Vocational Education and Training*, Bristol: FESC.

Mansfield, B., and Mitchell, L. (1996) *Towards a Competent Workforce*, Aldershot: Gower.

Marks, J. (1996) *Vocational Education, Training and Qualifications in Britain*, London: Institute of Economic Affairs.

Marquand, J. (1989) *Autonomy and Change: The Sources of Economic Growth*, Hemel Hempstead: Harvester-Wheatsheaf.

Marsh, D. (1992) 'Youth employment policy 1970–1990: Towards the exclusion of the trade unions', in Marsh, D., and Rhodes, R. (eds) *Policy Networks in British Government*, Oxford: Clarendon, pp. 167–99.

Marsh, D., and Rhodes, R. (eds) (1992) *Policy Networks in British Government*, Oxford: Clarendon.

Marshall, V. (1994) 'Employers beware: don't lose your control of NVQs', *Personnel Management*, March, pp. 30–33.

Massey, A. (1988) 'Producing Engineers', *British Journal of Education and Work*, **2**, 3, pp. 49–69.

Mathews, D. (1991) 'The purpose of standards', in Fennell, E. (ed.) *Development of Assessable Standards for National Certification*, London: HMSO, pp. 3–11.

Melling, G. (1978) *Report of a Visit to Canada to Investigate Research into Generic Skills*, London (mimeo).

Methven, J. (1976) 'What industry wants', *Times Educational Supplement*, 29 October.

Middlemas, K. (1979) *Politics in Industrial Society*, London: Andre Deutsch.

Middlemas, K. (1991) *Power, Competition and the State* (vol. 3): *The End of the Post-War Era, Britain since 1974*, Basingstoke: Macmillan.

Mitchell, L. (1989) *The Relationship Between Knowledge and Standards*, Sheffield: TA (mimeo).

Mitchell, L., and Bartram, D. (1994) 'The place of knowledge and understanding in the development of NVQs and SVQs', *Competence and Assessment Briefing Series*, 10, Sheffield: DE.

More, C. (1980) *Skill and the English Working Class, 1870–1914*, London: Croom Helm.

Morley, P. (1988) 'Retail industry scores a first', *Transition*, November, pp. 14–16.

Morris, R. (1996) 'New magistracies and commissariats', in Ahier, J., Cosin, B., and Hales, M. (eds) *Diversity and Change: Education Policy and Selection*, London: Routledge, pp. 265–72.

National Audit Office (NAO) (1995) *Department of Employment: Financial Controls in Training and Enterprise Councils in England*, Report by the Comptroller and Auditor General, HC 361.

National Audit Office (NAO) (1996) *Financial Control of Payments Made under the Training for Work and Youth Training Programmes in England*, Report by the Comptroller and Auditor General, HC 402.

National Audit Office (NAO) (1998) *Appropriation Accounts 1996–97: Class IX, Vote 1: Department for Education and Employment: Programmes and Central Services*, HC 251 – IX.

National Council for Vocational Qualifications (NCVQ) (1987a) *The National Council for Vocational Qualifications: Its Purposes and Aims*, London: NCVQ.

National Council for Vocational Qualifications (NCVQ) (1987b) *Professional Bodies, their Qualifications and the National Council for Vocational Qualifications*, London: NCVQ.

National Council for Vocational Qualifications (NCVQ) (1988) *NVQ Criteria and Guidance*, London: NCVQ.

National Council for Vocational Qualifications (NCVQ) (1989) *Extension of the NVQ Framework above Level IV: A Consultative Document*, London: NCVQ.

National Council for Vocational Qualifications (NCVQ) (1990) *Common Learning Outcomes: Core Skills in A/AS Levels and NVQs*, London: NCVQ.

National Council for Vocational Qualifications (NCVQ) (1991a) *General National Vocational Qualifications: Proposals for the New Qualifications, a Consultation Paper*, London: NCVQ.

National Council for Vocational Qualifications (NCVQ) (1991b) *Guide to National Vocational Qualifications*, London: NCVQ.

National Council for Vocational Qualifications (NCVQ) (1991c) *NVQ Update*, September, London: NCVQ.

National Council for Vocational Qualifications (NCVQ) (1992) *Response to the Consultation on General National Vocational Qualifications*, London: NCVQ.

National Council for Vocational Qualifications (NCVQ) (1993a) *Awarding Bodies Common Accord*, London: NCVQ.

National Council for Vocational Qualifications (NCVQ) (1993b) 'Intellectual battle for NVQs won says Sir Bryan Nicholson', *NCVQ Press Release*, 29 September, London: NCVQ.

National Council for Vocational Qualifications (NCVQ) (1994) 'TV programme damagingly inaccurate', *NCVQ Press Release*, 7 January, London: NCVQ.

National Council for Vocational Qualifications (NCVQ) (1995a) *GNVQs at Higher Levels: A Consultation Paper*, London: NCVQ.

National Council for Vocational Qualifications (NCVQ) (1995b) *NVQ Criteria and Guidance*, London: NCVQ.

National Council for Vocational Qualifications (NCVQ) (1997a) *Data News*, Spring, London: NCVQ.

National Council for Vocational Qualifications (NCVQ) (1997b) *Data News Annual NVQ Statistics Supplement*, London: NCVQ.

National Council for Vocational Qualifications (NCVQ) (1997c) *Higher Level Vocational Qualifications: Case Studies*, London: NCVQ.

National Council for Vocational Qualifications/United Kingdom Inter-Professional Group (NCVQ/UK–IPG) (1989) *Joint Statement by NCVQ and Member Bodies of the UK Inter-Professional Group*, London: NCVQ/UK–IPG.

National Council for Vocational Qualifications/Scottish Qualifications Authority (NCVQ/SQA) (1997) *The Assessment of Occupational Competence and the Role of Independent Assessment in NVQs/SVQs*, London: NCVQ.

National Curriculum Council (NCC) (1990) *Core Skills 16–19*, York: NCC.

Nichols, T. (1986) *The British Worker Question*, London: Routledge.

Noon, M., and Ogbanna, E. (1998) 'Unequal provision? Ethnic minorities and employment training policy', *Journal of Education and Work*, **11**, 1, pp. 23–40.

Office for Standards in Education (OFSTED) (1993) *GNVQs in Schools: The Introduction of General National Vocational Qualifications 1992*, London: HMSO.

Office for Standards in Education (OFSTED) (1994) *GNVQS in Schools 1993/94: Quality and Standards of General National Vocational Qualifications*, London: HMSO.

Office for Standards in Education (OFSTED) (1996) *Assessment of General National Vocational Qualifications in Schools 1995/96*, London: HMSO.

Organisation for Economic and Cultural Development (OECD) (1975) *Educational Development Strategy in England and Wales*, Paris: OECD.

Perry, P. (1976) *The Evolution of British Manpower Policy: From the Statute of Artificers 1563 to the Industrial Training Act 1964*, London: British Association for Commercial and Industrial Education.

Pickard, J. (1996) 'Barriers ahead to a single currency', *People Management*, 21 March, pp. 22–7.

Pierson, C. (1996) *The Modern State*, London: Routledge.

Pile, W. (1979) *The Department of Education and Science*, London: Allen and Unwin.

Pliatzky, L. (1980) *Report on Non–Departmental Public Bodies*, Cmnd 7797, London: HMSO.

Pliatzky, L. (1992) 'Quangos and Agencies', *Public Administration*, **70**, pp. 555–63.

Plowden, W. (1994) *Ministers and Mandarins*, London: Institute for Public Policy Research.

Porter, M. (1990) *The Competitive Advantage of Nations*, London: Macmillan.

Prais, S. (1989) 'How Europe would see the new British initiative for standardising vocational qualifications', *National Institute Economic Review*, August, pp. 52–4.

Pratten, C. (1976) *Labour Productivity Differentials within International Companies*, Cambridge: CUP.

Qualifications and Curriculum Authority (QCA) (1997a) *Data News*, **6**, London: QCA.

Qualifications and Curriculum Authority (QCA) (1997b) *Qualifications and Curriculum Authority: An Introduction*, London: QCA.

Qualifications and Curriculum Authority (QCA) (1998) *Assessing NVQs*, London: QCA.

Raffe, D. (1988) 'Modules and the strategy of institutional versatility: The first two years of the 16 plus action plan in Scotland', in Raffe, D. (ed.) *Education and the Youth Labour Market*, Lewes: Falmer Press, pp. 162–96.

Rainbird, H., and Grant, W. (1985) 'Non Statutory Training Organisations and the privatisation of public policy', *Public Administration*, **63**, pp. 91–5.

Ranson, S. (1984) 'Towards a tertiary tripartism: New codes of social control and the 17 + ', in Raggatt, P., and Weiner, G. (eds) (1985) *Curriculum and Assessment: Some Policy Issues*, Oxford: Pergamon, pp. 75–90.

Ranson. S. (1995) 'Theorizing Education Policy', *Journal of Education Policy*, **10**, 4, pp. 427–48.

Reich, R. (1991) *The Work of Nations*, New York: Simon and Schuster.

Reimer, E. (1971) *School is Dead: An Essay on Alternatives in Education*, Harmondsworth: Penguin.

Richardson, W. (1991) *Education and Training Post-16: Options for Reform and the Public Policy Process in England and Wales*, Centre for Education and Industry: University of Warwick.

Richardson, W. (1993) 'The 16–19 education debate: "deciding factors" in the British public policy process', in Richardson, W., Woolhouse, J., and Finegold, D. (eds)

The Reform of Post-16 Education and Training in England and Wales, London: Longman, pp. 1–33.

Robinson, P. (1996a) *Rhetoric and Reality: Britain's New Vocational Qualifications*, London: Centre for Economic Performance.

Robinson, P. (1996b) 'The future role of NVQs – the economic context', paper presented to the *Gatsby Charitable Foundation Seminar on the Future Role of NVQs*, Ware, 21–22 October.

Rose, D. (1996) *In the Name of the Law: The Collapse of Criminal Justice*, London: Jonathan Cape.

Royal Commission (1968) *Report of the Royal Commission on Trade Unions and Employers' Associations*, London: HMSO.

Royal Society of Arts Examining Board (RSA) (1987) *Tomorrow's Qualifications Today*, Coventry: RSA.

Ryan, P. (1984) 'The New Training Initiative after two years', *Lloyds Bank Review*, April, pp. 31–45.

Schools Council (1968) *Young School Leavers: Report of an Enquiry carried out for the Schools Council by the Government Social Survey*, London: HMSO.

Scottish Education Department (SED) (1983) *16s to 18s in Scotland: An Action Plan*, Edinburgh: SED.

Scottish Education Department (SED) (1988) *Consultation Paper: Relationship between Scotland and the National Council for Vocational Qualifications*, Edinburgh: SED.

Senker, P. (1992) *Industrial Training in a Cold Climate*, Aldershot: Avebury.

Senker, P. (1996) 'The development and implementation of National Vocational Qualifications: An engineering case study', *New Technology, Work and Employment*, **11**, 2, pp. 83–95.

Sharp, P. (1998) 'The beginnings of GNVQs: an analysis of key determining events and factors', *Journal of Education and Work*, **11**, 3, pp. 293–311.

Sheldrake, J., and Vickerstaff, S. (1987) *A History of Industrial Training in the UK*, Aldershot: Gower.

Silver, H. (1990) *Education, Change and the Policy Process*, London: Falmer Press.

Smith, M. (1993) *Pressure, Power and Policy: State Autonomy and Policy Networks in Britain and the United States*, Hemel Hempstead: Harvester-Wheatsheaf.

Smithers, A. (1993) *All Our Futures: Britain's Education Revolution*, London: Channel Four.

Spilsbury, M., Moralee, J., and Evans, C. (1995) *Employers' Use of the NVQ System*, Institute of Employment Studies Report 293, Brighton: Institute of Employment Studies.

Stanton, G. (1996) *Output-related Funding and the Quality of Education and Training*, London: University of London Institute of Education.

Steedman, H. (1993) 'Do workforce skills matter?', *British Journal of Industrial Relations*, **31**, 2, pp. 285–92.

Steedman, H., and Hawkins, J. (1994) 'Shifting foundations: the impact of NVQs on youth training for the building trades', *National Institute Economic Review*, 149, pp. 93–102.

Stevens, P. (1993) *City and Guilds of London Institute: A Short History 1878–1992*, London: City and Guilds.

Stewart, J., and Hamlin, B. (1992) 'Competence-based qualifications: The case against change', *Journal of European Industrial Training*, **16**, 7, pp. 21–32.

Streeck, W. (1989) 'Skills and the limits of neo-liberalism: the enterprise of the future as a place of learning', *Work, Employment and Society*, **3**, 1, pp. 89–104.

Stringer, J., and Richardson, J. (1982) 'Policy stability and policy change: industrial training 1964–1982', *Public Administration Bulletin*, **39**, pp. 22–39.

Stuart, M. (1996) 'The industrial relations of training: A reconsideration of training arrangements', *Industrial Relations Journal*, **27**, 3, pp. 253–65.

Thain, C., and Wright, M. (1995) *The Treasury and Whitehall*, Oxford: Clarendon.

Tolley, G. (1986) 'Putting labels on people: The qualifications business', *Journal of the Royal Society of Arts*, **5363**, pp. 707–14.

Training Agency (TA) (1988a) *Development of Assessable Standards for National Certification: Developing Standards by Reference to Functions*, Technical Advisory Group Guidance Note 2, Sheffield: TA.

Training Agency (TA) (1988b) *Development of Assessable Standards for National Certification: The Definition of Competences and Performance Criteria*, Technical Advisory Group Guidance Note 3, Sheffield: TA.

Training Agency (TA) (1989a) *Development of Assessable Standards for National Certification: Assessment of Competence*, Technical Advisory Group Guidance Note 5, Sheffield: TA.

Training Agency (TA) (1989b) *Development of Assessable Standards for National Certification: Verification or Monitoring of Assessment Procedures*, Technical Advisory Group Guidance Note 6, Sheffield: TA.

Training Agency (TA) (1989c) *Training of Trainers*, Sheffield: TA.

Tuxworth, E. (1989) 'Competence-based education and training: Background and origin', in Burke, J. (ed.) *Competency Based Education and Training*, Lewes: Falmer Press, pp. 10–25.

Unwin, L., and Wellington, J. (1995) 'Reconstructing the work-based route: Lessons from the modern apprenticeship', *The Vocational Aspect of Education*, **47**, 4, pp. 337–51.

Weber, M. (1964) *The Theory of Social and Economic Organization*, Parsons, T. (ed.), New York: Free Press.

Weinstock, A. (1976) 'I blame the teachers', *Times Educational Supplement*, 23 January.

Weir, S. (1995) 'Quangos: questions of democratic accountability', in Ridley, F., and Wilson, D. (eds) *The Quango Debate*, Oxford: OUP, pp. 128–44.

Weir, S., and Hall, W. (1994) *EGO-Trip: Extra Governmental Organisations in the United Kingdom and their Accountability*, London: Charter 88.

Whitty, G. (1989) 'The New Right and the national curriculum: state control or market forces?', *Journal of Education Policy*, **4**, 4, pp. 329–41.

Wiener, M. (1981) *English Culture and the Decline of the Industrial Spirit, 1850–1980*, Cambridge: CUP.

Wilson, D. (1995) 'Quangos in the skeletal state', in Ridley, F., and Wilson, D. (eds) *The Quango Debate*, Oxford: OUP, pp. 3–13.

Wolf, A. (1995) *Competence and Assessment*, Buckingham: Open University Press.

Wolf, A. (1997) *The Evolution of GNVQs: Emerging Enrolment and Delivery Patterns and their Policy Implications*, London: FEDA.

Wood, R., Johnson, C., Blinkhorn, S., Anderson, S., and Hall, J. (1988) *Boning, Blanching and Backtracking: Assessing Performance in the Workplace*, Sheffield: TA.

Woods, P., Bagley, C., and Glatter, R. (1997) *School Choice and Competition: Markets in the Public Interest?*, London: Routledge.

Wray, M., Hill, S., and Coolbear, J. (1982) *Employer Involvement in Schemes of Unified Vocational Preparation*, Windsor: NFER-Nelson.

Young, D. (1990) *The Enterprise Years: A Businessman in the Cabinet*, London: Headline.

Youthaid (1981) *The Youth Training Scheme: Briefing Paper*, London: Youthaid.

Index

Lightning Source UK Ltd.
Milton Keynes UK
UKOW06f0730240216

269012UK00008B/324/P